WILLIE NELSON ON WILLIE NELSON

OTHER BOOKS IN THE MUSICIANS IN THEIR OWN WORDS SERIES

Bowie on Bowie: Interviews and Encounters with David Bowie
Cash on Cash: Interviews and Encounters with Johnny Cash
The Clash on the Clash: Interviews and Encounters
Cobain on Cobain: Interviews and Encounters
Coltrane on Coltrane: The John Coltrane Interviews
Dolly on Dolly: Interviews and Encounters with Dolly Parton
Dylan on Dylan: Interviews and Encounters
Fleetwood Mac on Fleetwood Mac: Interviews and Encounters
George Harrison on George Harrison: Interviews and Encounters
Hendrix on Hendrix: Interviews and Encounters with Jimi Hendrix
Joni on Joni: Interviews and Encounters with Joni Mitchell
Judy Garland on Judy Garland: Interviews and Encounters
Keith Richards on Keith Richards: Interviews and Encounters
Led Zeppelin on Led Zeppelin: Interviews and Encounters
Lennon on Lennon: Conversations with John Lennon
Leonard Cohen on Leonard Cohen: Interviews and Encounters
Miles on Miles: Interviews and Encounters with Miles Davis
Neil Young on Neil Young: Interviews and Encounters
Patti Smith on Patti Smith: Interviews and Encounters
Prince on Prince: Interviews and Encounters
Prine on Prine: Interviews and Encounters with John Prine
Springsteen on Springsteen: Interviews, Speeches, and Encounters
Tom Waits on Tom Waits: Interviews and Encounters
The Who on the Who: Interviews and Encounters

WILLIE NELSON ON WILLIE NELSON

INTERVIEWS AND ENCOUNTERS

EDITED BY PAUL MAHER JR.

Published by Chicago Review Press Incorporated
814 North Franklin Street
Chicago, Illinois 60610

ISBN 978-0-89733-363-4

Library of Congress Control Number: 2025941003

A list of credits and copyright notices for the individual pieces in this collection can be found on pages 247–249.

Cover design: Jonathan Hahn
Cover photograph: AJ Pics / Alamy Stock Photo
Interior layout: Nord Compo

Printed in the United States of America

CONTENTS

FROM OUTLAW TO LEGEND

The Unrivaled Legacy of Willie Nelson

I am listening to Willie Nelson's 1996 album *Spirit* on a portable boom box. The first notes capture the profound and emotional range and unique authenticity that make this work so compelling. It's all there in the cover photo of the album, a sepia-tint photograph like you'd see in a Wild West daguerreotype. Willie wears a bandanna and a distressed fedora. Unshaven. Black eyes pierce to establish a steely rapport before the listener hears even a single note. His opening flamenco-style guitar (performed on the song "Matador") evokes images of a drifter by a campfire deep in the hollows of a Texas canyon. It's like something out of a Zane Grey novel. The song's imagery aligns well with the romantic, rugged wildness of those books. I can practically smell the night-blooming cereus. Damp desert sands indelibly marred by the traveler's footprints. A campfire casts long shadows upon the canyon wall. Willie's deep resonance pours through this hollow velvet night. He evokes the pathos he wishes to convey. Somewhere deep, we as listeners tap into his heart-sourced memories. Maybe it's a bad breakup. A lament rising out of stinging loneliness. A merciless tide of ever-present longing. A secretly nurtured memory: "She is gone / But she was here / And her presence is still heavy in the air."

Contrast this with his first album, . . . *And Then I Wrote*, from 1962, in which Willie's dissatisfaction with the Nashville sound (which was in favor of extensive overdubs in lieu of a more organic "live" sound) is barely evident. It is reported that he was unhappy with the recordings.

Yet his remarkable charisma shines through. The country blues classic "Wake Me When It's Over" elevates Nelson from the previous song on . . . *And Then I Wrote*, a Hank Cochran composition titled "Touch Me." Though Willie's cover is respectable, it isn't his. That honor goes to many of the tracks. Willie's first album has perhaps the superior version of "Crazy." Though it scored a huge hit for singer Patsy Cline, Willie delivers the song with a purity of intent. In "Mr. Record Man" he sings of a "lonely song about a lonely man like me." It is said that "Mr. Record Man" was a favorite song of rodeos and state fairs. It could be heard pouring out of mounted loudspeakers under the long blue Texan skies. Or you could catch wind of it from an old pickup speeding by, Willie's singsong "Texas in my soul" voice belting out from a back-in-the-day 8-track dash player. These are words everybody can understand. They evoke as easily as they impart.

This is Willie's allure.

Though tasked with writing this introduction for this volume of interviews, I find myself challenged to condense the essence of a man like Willie Nelson into a few pages. Throughout these interviews, he shares his thoughts on life, music, and his cherished causes. He has already recounted many of his experiences through his memoirs, and many biographies have filled in the gaps with anecdotes he opted to leave out. Yet his life, indeed, is quite literally an open book because of the songs. Here, with merciful brevity, I will try to do justice to his remarkable journey.

Willie Hugh Nelson was born on April 29, 1933, in Abbott, Texas.* His character is typical of those who lived through the Great Depression: An adherence to practicality. Thriftiness. He, like many of his ilk during this time, is spiritually centered. Unlike those many others, he is also musically inclined. From inauspicious beginnings, Willie Nelson became one of the most visible and influential country music songwriters and

---

* Nelson was born just before midnight on April 29, and his birth wasn't officially registered until the next day, so sources sometimes give his birthday as April 30—including Willie himself in the first interview in this collection.

performers of the second half of the twentieth century. He has breathed the rarefied air of assuming a household name. Willie never would have guessed all of this was coming back in his early days, when he was struggling as a singer, guitar picker, radio DJ, and for-hire songwriter. It is the last that Willie ultimately banked his far-from-promising future on. His success was hard won. He faced the daunting specter of encroaching poverty and domestic instability. Through it all, Willie remained grounded by humility. It is that trait that ties all these interviews together.

With each selection, I strove to curate a book that can be opened at any point and will, in some way, inspire. One must forestall the temptation to expect all-new original content in every interview. Customarily, journalists and reporters thrive on the same talking points passed to them by a friendly publicist. In larger-format magazines, there is often a polished air that somehow eludes the intimate nature of the subject. For this reason, I have chosen mostly interviews from early country music magazines and newspapers. I relied primarily on those spanning the 1970s through the 1990s. It is in this period Willie built much of his fame through routine television appearances, a grueling touring schedule, and a singular recording output putting him oftentimes front and center on the country music charts. The brunt of these interviews are sourced from *Country Music* magazine, a particularly rich repository of the history of the genre that has long since closed its doors. They are "sweet memories." Through the pages of *Country Music* and magazines of its ilk, we enter a time portal into another dimension of America that has become nostalgia, like straw hats, taxi dancers, and flappers of the Jazz Age. In this country music world, there's no nonsensical rivalry pumped up by aggressive publicist tweets meant to inflame and/or entertain, their quest only to reach number one with a bullet through their nightmarish TikTok terrain. No, this era was when country music reigned as a dominating Pickett's Charge through American culture. It's the real deal. There's an amiable respect across the board. A diamond-point emphasis on family fare. There are country music festivals, picnics, jamborees, ads for Floyd Cramer records, appreciative letters to the editors gushing over the likes of Conway Twitty and Jerry Lee Lewis. Many of the magazines I tracked down through eBay have Willie's grinning visage, trademark locks, and a few months' worth of beard growth gracing their covers. Though some readers thrive on a cult of personality, with Willie there is a stubborn grit that can't be flicked off through a shallow assessment. These musicians are seeded too deep into the damp, fertile loam of American culture, which somehow embeds them despite itself.

I want to share Willie in his own words because I believe that through them we can reexperience an optimism and spiritual healing sadly lacking in today's digital culture. His music is a prism to the past yet a beacon for the future. We are so focused on the hall of mirrors called social media that we forget that there once was a time when a person could make it simply on the strength of their ingenuity. Reading Willie's life story, we sense that all of it was predicated on self-reliance and folk wisdom. Listening to Willie harks back to another era. The diversity and joy he insists upon through his many concerts and Fourth of July picnics is ever-present in these interviews. There is a frothy effervescence in Willie and Family's performances. It is contagious. The audience catches on; it becomes one big party. It's not that Willie whitewashes his troubles, but rather that he does not allow them to serve as his weather vane. His troubles are not his prevailing winds. Instead, he exudes a steely faith in God. Adversity becomes songwriting fodder for all of his albums.

Willie shared with television host Johnny Carson during one of his many *Tonight Show* appearances that he once thought of being a pastor, and that he and sister Bobbie Nelson were raised in the gospel theater of their local church. They sang hymns and accompanied others with guitar and piano. They raised the roof singing to the cherubs on the ceiling. Willie has turned the pages of his well-thumbed family Bible and not only came to know its verses but learned to incorporate them into daily living—the best that he could, anyway.

Willie shows a focused work ethic and an absolute fidelity to family. Through the public persona of this American treasure, we discover vestiges and hints of a bygone America rapidly vanishing from the landscape. He was once considered common stock. White trash. A dime-a-dozen Southern hillbilly redneck whose punishing adversity was his common stock and store. He came from a generation that withstood both an economic depression *and* a world war. In WWE wrestling parlance, it's like withstanding a brainbuster only to be throttled by a chokeslam. Out of this singular experience, the loser endures inscrutable as its victor. When we think of the Depression, we are often picturing Dust Bowl stories. We know of those "Okies" who were in search of the Promised Land. They had John Steinbeck to tell their tale. The rest of America has Willie. There is a drab patina to the poverty that Willie appeared from, and it must not be underestimated. There is nothing formulaic about building solid character on the basis of morality. For a child, such things exist only in embryonic intimations. Being among wholesome and positive influences in his early life helped shape Willie for the best even if only to overcome the worst. He's a lemonade-from-lemons kind of guy. A steely practitioner, whether he knows it or not, of Ralph Waldo Emerson's concept of self-reliance. Any quotation lifted from Emerson's influential transcendental essay could apply. Here's a go at it: "Insist on yourself; never imitate"; "No law can be sacred to me but that of my nature"; "To be great is to be misunderstood." The list could go on.

We listen to Willie Nelson songs because they have the ability to restore. He sings of love, heartache, and faith, and who hasn't had decent helpings of each? The words are all there hoarded in a vast cornucopia. Willie does not need the encouragement of fame to pluck them from the stockpile of his mind. Each song has its own measure of personal currency. With each, Willie can buy our hearts.

Willie has always conveyed a deep-rooted affection and respect for hardworking folks. This may explain his disdain for the business side of music and performing. He maintains these necessities (payrolls, taxes, business expenses) as a Faustian bargain. He believes that a musician must share their art for entertainment or to help with social causes. He believes that talent is God-given and must be honored. Over the years, he has busied himself doing so, including cofounding Farm Aid, where he assists farmers faced with the daunting prospect of bank foreclosure. He helps them have a chance fighting against corporate bullies and big banks. He, America's sanctioned rebel, wants American farmers to successfully fight for their rights. He even uses a biofuel sourced from farmers to fuel his tour buses. It's called BioWillie. The depth and breadth of his involvement with these and other causes reveal Willie's exemplary character—which, in turn, feeds into his songwriting skills. He's an artist who has paid his dues.

In a 1985 press release, Nelson said that he has never stopped wanting to be a singer/songwriter to earn his living. Shortly after writing "Family Bible" in 1957, he began performing his songs while on a trip to Houston. He had been working as a disc jockey in Washington State. Before recording the song—on which he also played guitar behind a somewhat hesitant vocal—Nelson was further encouraged by future confidant and singer Paul Buskirk, who told him he knew life had been rough on him lately but there was something unique in his voice. Willie had his own style, Buskirk said, and he should develop it, even though it might take time. This advice did not go unheeded.

Nelson knew that Buskirk was well respected. He also had grown up poor just like Willie. When Buskirk caught a bus, he often did so without wearing shoes. It was that kind of deep, grinding poverty that lent so much weight to his advice. It wasn't empty praise. Buskirk was an observer. He had a solid ear for musical talent. In songs like Buskirk's western swing instrumental "Panhandle," we can clearly hear his influence on Willie's singular phrasing. It wasn't easy, but Willie never stopped. His timbre resembles, to my uninitiated ears, something like Sanford Clark's "Black Jack County Chain" (of which Nelson recorded a version in 1967). The aching solitude in Willie's songs harks back to my past, where my loneliness always manifested a greater good. Songs aren't written in a vacuum. The good ones rely on a life lived authentically. Authentic experience counts, as Emerson duly reported, and Willie has it in droves. He's no poseur.

My late father would have loved to sit here with me and listen to all of these songs. He knew them well. I felt his loneliness through these songs that I took no real interest in at the time. It was the 1980s and I was in my twenties. My father was not of Willie's generation, but a baby boomer from the 1940s. My memories are of summer nights at a campground in Plaistow, New Hampshire. My father was lonely though he was among his relatives. There was an 8-track boom box playing music on an endless loop. A few of them were Willie Nelson albums: "She's gone now / She couldn't stand to be alone." Willie in happenstance becomes a soundtrack of those times I may have otherwise forgotten. Of the firelight on their faces in brooding contemplation staring into the flames, back when life seemed simpler. Most of them are gone now. Only music now can take me there.

Through the years, we have come to admire Willie's tremendous musical output. A quick count from the liner notes included in his retrospective 2008 box set gives us ninety-two record albums. A few years later in 2020, *Texas Monthly* ranked 152 studio and live albums. Then there are hundreds of unreleased songs that Willie has hinted at in various interviews. Through each, Willie expresses a multitude of musical mediums with a unique homegrown sensibility. *Texas Monthly* classified Nelson's albums as bluegrass, western swing, flamenco, gospel, small-combo jazz, full-on orchestra, solo acoustic, and hard-core country. It is hard to get a real handle on Willie.

During my work on this book, I tasked myself with listening to most of them, a feat made possible because most albums are now uploaded to streaming services. Other times, I bought them, hesitant at first because I was one of the uninitiated. I had to ask myself, Are there any bombs in Willie's output? Not really. Instead, each album has its own patina. There is an album for every mood. None are contrived moneymakers, and if some lean that way, they still aim for a different mark. Willie does not have that kind of mercenary appeal to record labels, of cashing out while the going is good. Throughout his studio solo efforts and live recorded concerts, Willie perseveres doggedly on the wayward path of his muse.

Initiated from his West Texas roots, Willie had it rough from the start. His father, Ira, was an Ozark transplant. Ira was sixteen when he married fifteen-year-old Myrle Marie Greenhaw. She was beautiful and of Cherokee heritage. But she was also a wild child possessed with wanderlust. Texans thought she was Mexican. Oklahomans rightly guessed her as Native American. Together, Ira and Myrle searched for work in north central Texas. Things got rough after Willie was born. Myrle had enough and split. She was immature and unwilling to commit herself to a life of drudgery in perpetuity. Ira, also wanting to sow his wild oats, behaved like an alley cat. He remarried and left Willie under the care of his grandparents.

Willie's grandparents spoiled Willie and his older sister, Bobbie (and their cousin Mildred). Mama and Daddy Nelson had first learned music from a correspondence course. They transferred that knowledge to young Willie. When he turned five years old, Ira bought Willie a guitar. By the time he was eight, Willie was writing songs. "In the beginning I created," he joked to reporter Judy Myers in 1969. At thirteen, he was playing lead guitar. Piano-playing Bobbie joined him in singing gospel songs at a local church. They were reared in the Holy Ghost, learning and committing to memory a vast array of spiritual songs that would become stage staples in the years to come. Then they were playing clubs, managed by Willie's brother-in-law (he married Bobbie when she was sixteen), Bud Fletcher, who dubbed them Bud Fletcher and His Texans. Fletcher joined at times with a broomstick that had a hunk of roofing shingle attached to it so that it could be beaten back and forth to provide the rhythm. Occasionally, Ira backed with a fiddle or rhythm guitar.

Then they made the local radio station, KHBR in Hillsboro, Texas. It was a Sunday-morning gig. This meant performing Saturday nights and then driving all the way to Hillsboro. A group of preachers slated to perform after Bud Fletcher and His Texans directed their proselytizing at the motley group. As Willie recalled to Judy Myers, "They thought we were wicked hillbillys."

Then came a string of unrelated gigs. Money became tight. Or became *tighter*. The specter of poverty was constantly breathing down Willie's neck. For a time, he was working Saturday nights as a relief phone operator on a central switchboard. At that point, puberty had reached him. His voice was changing. He thought that maybe he sounded like a girl over the airwaves. His first "real" job was as a tree trimmer. He'd ride a lift up to the heights to trim branches away from high-tension wires. This was not without its complications. One day his coworker needed a rope. Willie tried to bring it to him by climbing to meet him, but somehow got caught up by a finger. He was helpless; he couldn't go up or down. His only choice was to cut the rope. Willie fell through the high-tension wires and tree branches. With God on his side, Willie stood, brushed himself off, and walked off, never to return.

Other gigs followed. None were promising or a way out of the impending doom of crushing debt and an ever-flowing river of bills. Willie worked in a pawn shop. He joined the US Air Force and lasted nine months until he was medically discharged. He fell into bouncing at a Texas roadhouse where there was a fistfight every night. Willie quickly parted ways with that gig: he was a lover, not a fighter. But he knew there were brighter days ahead. Eventually, Willie was hired on as a disc jockey. He was excited to have free sway over the airwaves. The country was swept up by rock 'n' roll. Willie was excited by the new sounds it promised. He sensed the future of a new art form rapidly unfolding. Around this time, he had gone to a burger joint and was served by a fifteen-year-old carhop wearing a halter top and cutoff jeans. She took his order. He fell in love. Her name was Martha Matthews, a wild child like his mama. A member of the Cherokee nation, too. She set Willie afire. They bonded as friends before they started dating.

Martha avoided telling her folks that she was thinking of marrying Willie. They would have protested anyway. After all, she was sixteen now and Willie was nineteen. Legally they could marry as consenting adults, yes, but still Martha's folks took umbrage. They knew that Willie and Martha had a few things in common: drinking, carousing, and fighting (with each other). In defiance, they eloped in October 1952 to become newlywed drifters. Over the next ten years, the young Nelsons persisted in their reckless but legally binding union through a series of violent drinking binges. There were financial struggles aplenty, yet they still managed to birth three children into their uncertain world: Lana, Susie, and Billy. Wherever the Nelsons tried, they weren't cutting it. Discouragement was a constant bedfellow sleeping between them. Perhaps a new start would do it. They set their hopes on Nashville, the country music–making capital of the United States.

Willie was alone when he reached the city. Martha and the kids were living with her folks in Waco until he found a place to live and a job to pay for it. He opted for a trailer for twenty-five dollars a week. It wasn't his dream house, but it was all he could afford. Willie summoned Martha. The family moved in with their paltry belongings. The kids went to school. Willie plucked his guitar and continued writing songs. Martha became even more sullen and argumentative. This wasn't the life she imagined for herself. Despite this, Willie did what he could to raise his family. He sold auto parts. Returned to trimming trees. Worked in the oil fields. His pay barely covered the cost of the dreary trailer. Martha found work as a server. Cash tips plugged the holes of their sinking ship. Though Willie was grateful, he was also humiliated. Martha's employment meant time away from their children. It was not the West Texas social code in those days. Because of this, they fought. Alcohol became Willie's mistress. Booze was the go-to for many of West Texas's disenfranchised young men, many of them war vets set adrift in a wilderness of despair. Willie patronized Tootsie's Orchid Lounge, where he looked to meet local musicians. But he also drank. A lot. Booze piqued the worst of his tendencies. It made him ornery, petty, and jealous. He imagined Martha with another man. He raged and drank more. He wore her resolve down and so she resorted to beating him. That, too, went with the social code. The men worked, their women kept them and the kids in line.

Willie joined local bands as a guitar player—a picker. He wrote more songs. Singer/songwriter Johnny Bush let him sing, too. Over time, Willie gained confidence. He refined his vocal delivery. To this end, he believed it served him better to be a disc jockey and *not* a singer. Projecting his voice publicly further built his confidence. Later, it became second nature after singing at first before dozens, then hundreds, and later thousands.

But life did not improve for Willie and Martha. There were more fights. Martha threw a fork into his side. She bit his index finger down to the bone. Their love ran hot and cold. Sometimes Martha vanished with the children for a day or two. Though it angered and frustrated Willie, he admitted that had he been in her shoes, he would have done the same.

He needed to work on himself as a person. Shake off the booze. Build his skills musically. He heard that Ray Price needed a bass player. Willie never played bass guitar. He lied and told Price that he did. He bought himself a used bass and practiced until he could play it competently. He stuck out this gig for a year.

By then, Nelson had written songs like "Crazy" and "Funny How Time Slips Away," both of which had done well for other artists. Willie signed on to the Liberty Records label with Joe Allison, who produced Nelson's first album, . . . *And Then I Wrote.* The first single was "Mr. Record Man." Willie recorded two albums for Liberty. Though things began to look up, his marriage had completely fallen apart. After ten years, Willie and Martha called it quits. He returned to Fort Worth, Texas. In less than a year, he was back in love.

Willie married Shirley Collie, a singer, songwriter, guitarist, and yodeler. They both had music in their veins. Music and marriage grounded them in life. They knew it as a way out of poverty if one worked hard enough. He scored a gig with Uncle Hank Craig of KCUL and kept his big toe in the local music scene, working paying jobs by day and plying his musical trade by night. Wanderlust struck again. In 1963, Willie and Shirley moved to California, restless for betterment. Then they moved on to Tennessee and bought a farm just outside Nashville.

In 1964, Willie signed with RCA Victor.

On April 18, 2001, I attended a Willie Nelson concert in Lowell, Massachusetts. In the auditorium, men and women stood and shouted with each other for about an hour before the band appeared from behind the stage. They were unusually loud and raucous. I remember being a kid and sitting in that same auditorium with my brother and father watching wrestler Chief Jay Strongbow go on the warpath against Bruno Sammartino. It was pretty much the same atmosphere back then, too. Draft beer in red cups. Hot dogs slathered with relish and mustard. Willie and his band came out and started playing along a torrential river of music, much of it at the same tempo. A musical whirlwind. I did not know many of the songs. They took on an aural blur. Yet I was absorbed by the hypnotic sweep of it. It was the kind of music that talked to people. Evangelizing them like a spiritual healing. A river baptism in sound with ol' Willie as their John the Baptist.

There are many themes present in Willie's music. Because of this, it is difficult to analyze all of them in so constrained a space. Willie does an ample job of exploring them. He is a storyteller crooner bridging genres by spanning time. There is an ever-present struggle with authority, not of the "I fought the law, and the law won" variety, but that of a man caught up in legal circumstances. Trouble seems to find him. For example, many pot busts have cemented his reputation as a fearless marijuana indulger. A DWI or two. He and singer/songwriter Waylon Jennings are the forerunners of the "outlaw country" movement. Both aptly define the genre. The outlaw moniker originates from an article—"In Defense of the Telecaster Cowboy Outlaws," written by *Country Music* magazine regular Dave Hickey—that signaled a then-defining shift in country music. The writer describes Nelson and Jennings as avatars of this dynamic shift. The artists were not poseurs, either. They respectively secured their outlaw sobriquets from such stigmatizing factors as IRS troubles, pot busts, and a tenable opposition to the overall Big Brother–like factions of the federal government.

Willie taps the heart of the world. His songs are country manna leavened out of the common woes of all of us. Willie brings to the table what other artists lack (for me). His songs transport us through a spiritual undercurrent. It's like God is speaking through Willie, telling us that everything will be OK in the end. Just stick it out. Those bills will get paid. That lover will return. Everything is going to be all right. And it would make sense that God would use a man of utmost humility as his musical mouthpiece. Through Willie's music we can unravel the tenuous fabric of humanity: love, hope, charity, and the means to endure at all costs. We hear the voices of America, like a Walt Whitman poem, through the urgency of Willie's voice and his faithful Martin N-20 acoustic guitar Trigger. The hillbilly poet strums his junkyard lyre over the West Texas hills every bit as earnestly as Homer.

There is an advantage to entering Willie Nelson's discography as a novice. It gives me a fresh advantage in writing this book. Songs like "Crazy," "Hello Walls," and "Good-Hearted Woman" I already knew. The more I listened to the rest of them, though, the more enriched I became. His music isn't junk food for the ears. It's a balm for the soul. One feels the incessant rhythm of good street poetry breezing through his entire oeuvre. His songs take you places, whether it's a bus station, a church, or a graveyard. After a long day's work, hearing Willie on the radio on the way home restores one's dignity. There is a common bond we share. He *is* us. He elevates your spirits when they're down. You can almost feel his arm draped over your shoulder telling you that everything will be all right. Willie is a trusted comrade. A brother-in-arms through brutish life or ragged joy. He'll tell you that he has already been through all of this, and you will too, but you will emerge still standing, just like him. Just sit back and listen.

THE WILLIE NELSON STORY

Judy Myers | February 1969 | *Country Song Roundup*

The first interview opens this collection with Willie's rundown of his life up to the time of this sitting. He details his struggles trying to make his mark as a guitar picker, singer, and songwriter. Eventually, he became accomplished at all three to become an artist of singular stature. But before then, there were spells of discouragement. Though he managed to succeed through the 1960s, Nelson "retired" after the commercial/critical failure of his album *Yesterday's Wine* (1971). By the next year, Nelson unretired himself after becoming enlivened by the Austin music scene. —Ed.

When I was given the assignment to do a story on Willie Nelson, I couldn't have been more pleased. You see, I'm a big Willie Nelson fan! Not only do I appreciate his song writing, but he's one of the best song writers ever. Proof can be found in the listening to such songs as "It Should Be Easier Now" (one of my favorites), "Night Life," "Crazy," "Funny How Time Slips Away," "Hello Walls," and I could go on and on . . . I really "dig" Willie's singing. I'd just about rather hear Willie sing than anyone I can think of.

The day finally arrived and I met Willie at his office for the interview. His manner was charming and relaxed.

"Where do I start?" Willie asked . . .

"Why not start at the beginning," I said.

"In the beginning I created" . . . . he began laughing. Then he got serious and there followed a series of reminiscence that had me sitting on the edge of my chair, listening to Willie, who has a mind that works like a human tape recorder. He had almost total recall of everything. It was one of the most enchanting hours I've ever spent. Now, I want to share it with you. . . .

"I was born in Abbott, Texas on April 30, 1933. That's in West Texas. My grandparents raised us, and my daddy (Ira) was a blacksmith. My grandparents taught music that they had learned by studying a correspondence course. My father got me a guitar when I was about four or five years old, and I learned to play. I guess I started writing songs when I was about eight or a little younger. My first song was pretty bad! My mother still has it, along with a lot of others in a scrapbook, and she says one day she's going to publish it. I'd sure like to have that book, but she won't give it up."

"When I was thirteen, I started playing clubs with my sister, Bobbie. She played the piano, my brother-in-law was our manager and he played a broomstick. You know, a broomstick with a piece of shingle attached that he could beat back and forth to create a little rhythm. He later took up playing the bass, but mostly he just hit it and swung it around. My father played a little fiddle and rhythm guitar and I played lead guitar. We were called "Bud Fletcher and His Texans." Bud is my brother-in-law.

"We had a sign-on show on KHBR Radio in Hillsboro, Texas, every Sunday morning. We'd come dragging in after playing and driving all night, making us late most of the time. We were followed by preachers, and most of the time they directed their preaching right at us. You know, they thought we were wicked hillbillys."

"I was a relief telephone operator there in Abbott. We had a central switchboard and the woman who ran it liked to go out on Saturday nights so my sister or I would take over for her. My voice was changing then and I guess they thought I was a girl. They didn't know I was a boy, but I sure knew everything that was going on in the county.

"My first real job was that of a tree trimmer. We went around cutting branches away from the high tension wires. Once my buddy was about forty feet up and needed a rope, so I took it up the tree. Then, rather than climb down, I decided to go down the rope. I got about four feet down and got my finger hung up. I couldn't go up or down, and I was too far from my friend for him to help, so the only choice I had was to have him cut the rope. I fell down through those high tension wires and branches and I was able to get up and walk away, but I never went back to that job.

"Then I worked in a pawn shop, went into the Air Force, got out, worked as a bouncer in one of the roughest joints in Texas, (that didn't last long, there was a fight every night, and I don't like fights). I got married, worked as a parts man in an auto house, trimmed trees again, formed a band and started pickin' again, made saddles, worked in the oil fields in Texas, got married for the second time, and worked for a short time at a radio station in San Antonio.

"I went to work for Johnny Bush. He had a band and I played lead guitar. I asked him if I could sing, so he did let me sing some, but then he asked me to just play guitar. I don't think he liked my singing. I managed him for awhile.

"We moved to Pleasanton, Texas, where I saw an ad for a D.J. job on KBOP Radio. I had two kids by then, Lana and Susie. I'd never worked as a D.J., but I wanted that job. I went to see Dr. Ben Parker, who incidentally did more to help me than almost anyone. He asked me if I had had any experience and I told him that I had. He then asked me if I was familiar with the board there. I said, 'That's a Gates board isn't it?' Anybody could see it was a Gates board, it was written right across it. I told him I didn't know that board as I'd worked on an RCA Victor Board. I remember that's what they had at the other station. He'd have to show me how to use that one because they looked different."

"My test was to do fifteen minutes of news . . . *live* . . . the first time I'd ever been on the air as an announcer. Then he gave me a commercial to do. It was for the Pleasanton Pharmacy. It went like this . . . 'The Pleasanton Pharmacy Pharmaceutical department accurately and precisely fills your doctor's prescription,' and after I got through with that, he knew I'd never done radio work. It was the hardest commercial I've ever done. He gave me the job anyway. Then he worked with me to show me all about radio work.

"Dr. Ben Parker really helped me a lot.

"I worked at KBOP for awhile, and then got itchy feet. I went to Denton, Texas where I got a job as salesman for KDNT radio. I wasn't on the air so I didn't like that much. I went on to Ft. Worth, where I worked with Uncle Hank Cragg [Craig —Ed.] on station KCUL. I learned some more about radio work from him. From there I went to KCNC and Western Express. I was still working nights pickin'.

"Well, I got itchy feet again. I decided we should go to San Diego. The only catch was, we didn't have any money, and no car. I saw an ad in the paper where you could drive cars to different places. I went to see them and asked about taking a car to San Diego. They said that they had a car to go that way, and they would pay for the oil . . . but they had to know that I could get the car there. They said they would have to see at least $50.00. Well, I was down to my last $25.00, and that was that. However, I told them I'd go get the money as I didn't have it on me. I went out and found a friend and asked him to let me have $50.00. I didn't want to borrow it, I explained about the car, I just wanted to show it. He let me have the money and I took it to show, and they let me have the car. I gave the money back to my friend, but we still had to get to San Diego, buy gas and food, and only had $25.00 to do it on. Well, we made it, but I won't go into details about how it was done." He gave a sort of half chuckle.

"Well, when we got to San Diego, I couldn't find any work. My wife got a job, and I didn't like that much, her working and me not working. So I decided to go to my mother's in Portland, Oregon and see what I could get there. I planned to get something going and then send for my family. So I started hitchhiking with $10 and a suitcase. That was some trip. We could get a whole story just out of the details of that trip alone. I'll just tell one thing that happened along the way. I got to Orange, California. It was night time and I was tired and broke, and awfully tired of carrying that ole' suitcase. I found a country music nightclub, went in, and found I had just enough money for one beer. By buying that beer and making it last all night, I was able to stay there without getting thrown out. When the band was packing up, I asked if they knew of anybody who might give me a job, but they didn't. One old boy told me to stick around for a few minutes and he would make some phone calls for me, and maybe find something. I waited, and he did make the calls, but with no luck. Then, I had an idea. This old suitcase was getting heavier every mile, and I thought I could trust him, so I gave him my mother's address in Portland, and asked him if he would send the suitcase to me there. Well, I never did see that suitcase again!!

"I made Portland eventually. I got a job with KVAN in Vancouver, Washington, just across the river. I also had my own weekly TV show.

"I sent for my family to join me, and things were going pretty well in Portland, but . . . . I got restless. . . .

"On the move again, we headed for Springfield, Mo. On the way, we went through Denver, Colorado, and I got a job pickin' there, at a place called "Heart's Corner." The guy that ran the place rented a guitar for me, and I guess I stayed there about six weeks. Then we were on the move again. When we got to Springfield, I ran into Billy Walker. He was working the Ozark Jubilee at the time. His wife and my wife had been friends in Texas, so they invited us to stay with them for a few days. Billy even set up an interview for me with Si Simon, who was running the Jubilee. Si didn't seem to think I was too good, so I took the only job I could find, dishwashing . . . .

"I wasn't too happy as a dishwasher, so I took my family and headed south to Waco, Texas. Right after that, we moved to Ft. Worth and I quit the music business for a year. During that time, I sold just about everything, door to door. They even made me manager for Americana Encyclopedia.

"But I wanted to pick. I went back to Waco, then to Houston. I had, in the meantime, written "Family Bible" for Frankie Miller, who was recording on Starday, but Don Pierce wouldn't let him record it. When in Houston, I ran into a guy I'd known before, Paul Buskirk. I was pretty broke so I decided to sell the song, "Family Bible" . . . . Paul, Walt Breelin, and Claude Grey split it three ways and gave $25.00 for it

"Looking for work, I went to the Esquire Club where Larry Butler was the head of the band. I asked him for a job, but he said that he didn't need anyone at that time. I asked him if he would buy some of my songs then, for $10.00 each. I sang him about ten or twelve of my best ones, including "Mr. Record Man," "Crazy," "Night Life" and "What a Way to Live." He wouldn't buy my songs, not because they weren't good he said, but because they were too good, and if I needed money that bad, he would loan me some, and he did. That kept me from being completely broke.

"Paul Buskirk had a recording studio and he offered me a job teaching guitar. Well, I didn't know how to read music, but he said that was okay, he'd teach me. I got my first lesson on Wednesday, and gave my first lesson on Monday. I always managed to stay one lesson ahead of the students. They didn't know any better, since I did know how to play. I didn't know how to read music, that's all, but I learned that!

"I finally went to work for Larry Butler, pickin' in the evenings, and I worked the Sunday morning sign-on D.J. show at KRCT radio, which now has the call letters, KIKK. Leroy Gloger was the manager there, and he fired me. That hurt my ego, and I left town.

I took my family to Waco, and I headed for Nashville, and the first person I ran into there was my old buddy, Billy Walker. I sent for my family, and brought them to Nashville. Billy took me to Starday records and introduced me to Tommy Hill. I sang some of my songs for him, and he told me that he'd set up a recording and writer's contract for me, but Don Pierce turned us both down.

"One night when a bunch of us were jammin' in Tootsie's, Hank Cochran heard me and took me to Pamper music, where I signed an exclusive writer's contract. Faron Young had heard me sing "Hello Walls" at Tootsie's and told me that he wanted to record it. I was working on the road with Bobby Sykes, playing lead guitar, and Faron, who was on the show that night, asked me to sing the song again so that he could learn it. I also sang "Congratulations" that same night, and the next week, he recorded both of them, back to back.

"I moved my family into a trailer house, and I had three kids by then. I found out later that it was the very same trailer Hank Cochran and his wife and three children lived in when they first came to Nashville. It was green and ugly and the rent was $25 a week, and it was worth about $3, but they were always there to collect the rent every rent day.

"I heard that Ray Price needed a man to play bass and front his band. I didn't know how to play bass, but I told Ray I did, got the job, then went out and got a bass and learned real quick. If he ever knew I didn't know how to play, he was kind enough not to mention it. I worked for Ray for a year.

"Crazy" was doing real good then, and Billy had recorded "Funny How Time Slips Away." I wrote it for him, to follow "Thank You For Calling." Joe Allison signed me to Liberty Records, and produced an album and single for me. The album was "And Then I Wrote," and the single was "Mr. Record Man." I did two albums on Liberty.

"My marriage broke up about that time and I moved to Texas. I met and married my present wife, Shirley there. Incidentally, she was a regular on the Ozark Jubilee the time I went through Springfield, but we didn't know each other then.

"I stayed in Ft. Worth until 1963. After that I went to California to run the office for Pamper Music. I didn't like that because I wasn't pickin', just running the office. So we came back to Tennessee, and bought a farm at Ridgetop, just out of Nashville.

"I had been on Monument Records in the meantime, and had a record with them, but in 1964 I signed with RCA Victor. My first release for them was "Pretty Paper." I've had six albums on Victor, and my latest single is, "Johnny One Time," written by Dallas Frazier. I am really sold on the song, and I think we've got the most commercial sound on it of any of my other records. We're hoping that this one will make it, but if it doesn't, well, maybe next time.

"That's it, up to now. I remember some things I left out, but let's save them for next time."

That's Wille's story, and the hour I spent getting it was one of the most interesting I've had in a long time. There's nothing left for me to add, it's all been said. . . . .

WILLIE NELSON FIRST IN NASHVILLE CLUB

March 1972 | *Country Music Reporter*

This piece is less a formal interview than it is a glimpse into Willie Nelson's emergence into the Nashville club scene before defecting to Austin several years later. Nelson's reputation as a songwriter had already preceded him. He had yet to emerge as a self-billing stage performer. The Captain's Table, a Music City dancing/dining joint in Nashville's Printer's Alley, was one of the first venues to give Nelson his break as a performer in his own right. –Ed.

NASHVILLE: RCA Artist Willie Nelson scored a first in more ways than one when he appeared for two nights recently at The Captain's Table, one of the more plush night spots in Music City. This was the first time a known country artist had appeared at The Table and the results were fantastic! It was also the first time that owner Sam Cagle had to put up the rope barriers to hold back the crowd which included many from the Nashville music community which some estimated to be about 50 per cent of the audience. Those included some of the top artists, both country and pop, representatives from many of the top booking agencies and licensing agencies plus that ever-faithful following of musicians and songwriters who rarely miss an opportunity to see Nelson perform.

This was a totally new concept for Nelson . . . more of a personalized contact with his audience as a solo artist. He was accompanied, at times, by bass and drums, but basically it was just Nelson, his guitar, his songs and his tremendous talent.

Not only was it a first from Willie's point of view, it was the first time this writer could remember people standing in line in Printers' Alley only to be turned away because of a packed and most appreciative house that saw a show of great talent in the raw. No gimmicks . . . no hoopla . . . just Willie Nelson as we all know him.

AN INTERVIEW WITH WILLIE NELSON

Debbie Brimer | July 1974 | *Country Music Reporter*

Willie is known for his deep connection with his fans. He often spends time after shows signing autographs, taking pictures, and chatting with concertgoers, making each performance a personal experience. He shuns ego trips and star power: "I like to listen to other people talk. . . . I like to watch other people live. I like to observe what's going on around me, and at the same time, I observe what I'm doing myself. I usually write about myself or somebody else." –Ed.

I recently had the opportunity to sit down and talk to Willie Nelson briefly at the grand opening of the Water Hole Club in Grand Prairie, Texas. This was not a "back stage" or "private office" interview. Willie and I sat at a table near the bandstand and talked about his music. Of course, we had several interruptions, but one has to admire Willie for his loyalty to his fans.

Ten years ago, spectators would have probably found Willie decked out in a grey suit, and his hair would have been flat and slicked back on his head. The Willie Nelson of today is very different . . . appearance wise. Willie was sporting a faded pair of blue jeans, a denim shirt, and shoulder length hair. Due to his appearance, the basic rock fans look to Willie Nelson as their new rock music discovery. They don't realize that Willie is the same country song stylist that he was ten years ago.

His music has not changed Whether these rock fans know it or not . . . if they like Willie Nelson's music, they like Country Music.

DEBBIE: Willie, you seem to be trying to project a different image now than you did several years ago. Is that for any special reason?

WILLIE: Well, I think I'm doing what I want to do. I think that's the only reason.

DEBBIE: Recently the young people, the basic rock fans, have discovered Willie Nelson. They are attracted to your music and accept you as one of them. Does this please you?

WILLIE: Oh, yeah. That always makes an old man feel good!

DEBBIE: Well, I think you are one of the entertainers most instrumental in getting young people to liking Country Music.

WILLIE: Well, I refuse to ever get old. I'm just not ever going to get old.

DEBBIE: What are you doing writing-wise now, Willie? Are you just kind of doing your own thing?

WILLIE: Yeah, well, I wrote everything in my new album, "Phases and Stages." I don't know whether you've heard it or not. It's the last thing I've written. I haven't written anything lately. I may not write anything else this year. I might take off for a while.

DEBBIE: What do you think inspires you to write most of your songs?

WILLIE: It's hard to say. I like to listen to other people talk. I like to watch other people's actions. I like to watch other people live. I like to observe what's going on around me, and at the same time, I observe what I'm doing myself. I usually write about myself or somebody else.

DEBBIE: What percentage of your songs have you written about yourself?

WILLIE: About 90%.

DEBBIE: Like the song "Me and Paul," for instance?

WILLIE: Oh, yeah.

DEBBIE: You, Jerry Jeff Walker, Sammi Smith, and some more entertainers are now living and working out of Austin. Are you all trying to create a new Nashville there?

WILLIE: No, we're really not trying to create anything. We're just trying to make it.

DEBBIE: I like what you all are doing, and I think it's great that you're all friends and help each other and work together.

WILLIE: Well, I'm just glad we can do things together. I hope we can always do things together. I think everybody ought to do things together.

DEBBIE: What about Dripping Springs last year? Were you real satisfied with the way your July 4th Picnic turned out?

WILLIE: Oh, yeah. Yeah, there was about 90% young people there, and they were the best behaved group of 50,000 I've ever seen in my life.

DEBBIE: Are you going to have another July 4th Picnic at Dripping Springs this year?

WILLIE: We're going to have a Fourth of July Picnic. It's not going to be at Dripping Springs this year. It's going to be in College Station. It'll be at the Texas World Speedway six miles south of College Station. We're going to have three days this year. It'll be Thursday, Friday, and Saturday—July 4, 5, and 6. We're going to try to have everybody there that was there last year plus a lot more . . . Roger Miller, Loretta Lynn, Johnny Rodriguez, Lefty Frizzell, and others.

WILLIE NELSON: THE EMPEROR OF AUSTIN

Nick Patoski | July 18, 1974 | *Zoo World*

Music journalist, biographer, and former senior editor for *Texas Monthly* magazine Joe Nick Patoski has been covering the Austin music scene for over five decades. This interview explores Willie's emergence in the Austin music scene, not as a local musician but as an international recording artist. October 1974 would mark the first days of filming for *Austin City Limits*, a publicly funded musical showcase hosted by PBS and premiering with an appearance by Willie Nelson and Family. On the road, Willie frequently collaborated with other musicians. His tours often featured impromptu jam sessions with fellow artists, creating unique and memorable musical moments. –Ed.

"I was living in Nashville," Willie Nelson recalls. "I had just written a song called 'What Can You Do To Me Now?' and the next day my house burned down. Me and my entire group moved down to a dude ranch near Bandera while they rebuilt the house. In the meantime, I got Texas Fever . . ."

Willie wasn't your average cry-in-the-bucket Nashville musician. An intensely personal poet, he spread his autobiography over 22 albums in classics like "Night Life" and "Hello Walls," subsequently earning a niche in the Country Music Hall of Fame. An accomplished picker, he was part of the late sixties Music City vanguard—alongside Tom T. Hall, Kristofferson, and Waylon Jennings—that signaled a fresh, free-wheeling approach to the established Nashville style of music and living. But these are old stories. There's this whole new phase, now that Willie Nelson has come home.

Four years ago he packed his family and settled in the outlying Hill Country, his old fans unflinchingly welcoming back their native son. He then turned around with a newly cultivated beard and sometimes earring, and turned on hipsters at Armadillo World Headquarters to songs their mommas and daddies knew by rote. Today there's a sound around here they call progressive country with roots proudly exposed. Hank Wilson hobnobs with the Coach (UT football mentor Darrell Royal), pickup trucks sell at a premium, and Willie Nelson *owns* this town.

He draws 'em to car lot openings, symphony benefits and beerhalls, but it's the festivals that have canonized Willie for the new roper/doper crossbreed. The new buckaroos were predominant among the fifty thousand folks who assembled last Fourth of July in Dripping Springs to bake in the sun and listen to Willie and the rest of the bunch, including Kris, Waylon, Billy Joe Shaver, Leon Russell, and John Prine. Come the fall and he repeated the all-day affair with many of the 'Springs vets up in Abbott for the PTA-sponsored Homecoming.

The Pick-Nick this Fourth is the to-do of em all: Three solid days of one giant party pick at the Texas World Speedway in Bryan. Two stages, continuous music (Leon, Waylon, Bill Monroe and a cowpoke's wet dream lineup of fifty more), enough beer to drown in, and plenty of Port-A-Lets. Damn, Willie, you do it up right.

Meeting at a local radio station, the Emperor of Austin is near butt-nekkid in T-shirt, cut-offs and tennies, with nary a stitch of Western regalia. The summer sun outdoors is burning white hot as the small grinning man, a picture of comfort, emerges from the production studio after cutting some Pick-Nick spots. We seek out an empty conference room and get to talking about the Willie Way of songwriting.

"I was only writing what I was feeling, what I was thinking. Maybe some people in Nashville weren't ready for what I was doing at the time. I think now a lot of the people are listening to lyrics more and they're finding what I was saying ten, fifteen years ago wasn't all that far out. It made sense back then but there might have been some chords or phrases that weren't country, so they didn't know what to do with me exactly.

"I think my best material came out of depressive moods when I was really down and out, feeling sorry for myself," he reflects, scratching his head and leaning forward on his elbows. "I was writing all these sad songs like 'Pretty Paper' (covered by Roy Orbison), 'Healing Hands of Time' and 'Funny How Time Slips Away.'

"When you get happy you don't wanna write, you don't wanna do anything. I'm going through that kind of period. I know after enough time elapses I'll start getting guilt feelings and I'm sure something will depress me enough to write about it. It always has."

The wrinkles on the weather beaten face crease impishly as he remembers boyhood achievements in his central Texas hometown of West. Not yet into melody, Willie penciled his first poem at age six ("I don't want to get into that," he feigns. "It was pretty bad."). He turned pro as a teenager playing Bohemian polkas, waltzes, and throwyouoffs in the numerous Czech communities around West, and he's been moving down the road ever since, with an ever open eye towards home.

"I've been in Texas all my life. I go out of state every now and then and live awhile, but I always come back. I guess one of the reasons I'm so well known in Texas," he muses, "is I've worked all these joints at least once. I know practically very bartender in the state that ever pulled a cap on a bottle of beer.

"About the furthest I've been lately is Dallas and I got arrested there, DWI. I'd just worked a four hour set and got in my car. They stopped and arrested me, put the handcuffs on (Willie's driving habits are notorious). Fortunately I was clean and didn't have nothing on me . . . and you know that's unusual for me."

Were the cops nice to you?

"Probably nicer than I was."

Pshaw, Willie. You mean you lead a fast life?

"No, I'm not rushing it," he explains. "I'm taking it as it comes. I work a lot, but I enjoy what I'm doing. Oh, sometimes I get tired of traveling the highways, but that's why I play round here so much."

A week's rest at home doesn't suppress the wandering gypsy in Willie. He is all over Austin—headlining a cozy fest in the nearby hills; popping in unannounced to pick a few with both Waylon and Nashville cohort Bobby Bare; serenading Bob Hope and Tennessee Ernie Ford at a celebrity golf tournament before taking off for Houston and an arena full of urban cowboys hungry for a taste of country.

Perhaps he will join Kris and Rita for a round of "Amazing Grace," strum a few pre-game tunes to inspire the Texas Longhorns before a gridiron clash, or wail away the nite owl blues with Doug Sahm. It's been a constant four year housewarming for Willie and he can't stop playing the thank-you notes.

The return of the Good Ol' Boy has opened a new chapter in Texas country music and spawned an eager audience of youngin's to go with it. The rednecks have picked up the tempo too, Wille Nelson says. "They're becoming a lot more liberalized in their thinking. They're seeing changes. They're seeing their kids dig country music and you know, they like that."

A TRIBUTE TO BOB WILLS

Willie Nelson | August 1974 | *Country Music*

Willie Nelson was invited by *Country Music* magazine to write a tribute to ailing Bob Wills, an influential Texas musician who served as a friend and colleague. Wills died at age seventy on May 13, 1975, in Fort Worth, Texas. –Ed.

At the time we go to press Bob Wills is in a Texas nursing home, totally incapacitated by a stroke which happened during the early morning of December 4th, 1973. The "Father of Western Swing" had been directing the last reunion of his Texas Playboys in a Dallas recording studio on December 3rd. Already weakened and confined to a wheelchair by a series of progressively more serious strokes, he had stopped working quite a while before those last sessions, appearing in public only for benefit concerts made necessary by his lack of wealth and high medical bills. It is a tragic irony—all too common in the music business—that one of the stylistic giants of American popular music, a man who in his prime was revered and respected as a figure larger than life, finds himself in those circumstances late in life.

Bob Wills is very much a Texan. He was born and raised there, learning his first music from Black jazz and blues musicians, and it was in the dancehalls of Texas that he created Western Swing music. Today, although Western Swing has all but disappeared from the national music scene, it continues in Texas; not only through the old-timers who still play the dancehalls, but through a new generation which is becoming increasingly aware of its musical heritage. And one pivotal figure in that "revival" is Willie Nelson. When Willie—who bases himself in Austin, Texas, and is slowly developing that town into a Mecca for pickers, singers and writers—gets up on a Texas stage and lights into "Bubbles In My Beer," that Western Swing feeling comes all the way back and the kids take notice.

Willie Nelson is an ardent Bob Wills fan and a Texan who, like Wills, is happy to stay in Texas and make a special kind of music you don't find anywhere else. He has a unique perspective on Wills. Having grown up under his musical influence—to which he readily admits—Willie has since spent close to 25 years in country music as a highly respected song-writer and a performer whose brilliance is just now being realized by the lucky people who get to hear him play. Like Merle Haggard, he is concerned to preserve and revitalize the roots of modern country music—and, for that matter, blues and jazz—and to keep the musical innovations of the past alive today by whatever means are available to him. It was no surprise, therefore, that when we asked him to write a story on Bob Wills and Western Swing, he agreed immediately.

Willie did not actually sit down at a typewriter and produce this story, but the words are his—recorded on tape, transcribed and edited by the editor of COUNTRY MUSIC, and approved by Willie. What follows is Willie Nelson's own tribute to a man whose music he deeply respects.

The first time I met Bob Wills was in Whitney, Texas, when I was about thirteen or fourteen. My brother-in-law and I booked him into Whitney—even back then I was into the promotion business. We had a band, and my brother-in-law was the band leader. He'd go around and book all the jobs and everything, and in order to make a little extra money now and then, we'd do a little promoting and rent a hall and put somebody in there. We did that with Bob. It was after Tommy Duncan had left the Texas Playboys, and Jack Lloyd was with them. He did "I Don't See Me In Your Eyes Anymore"—the Charlie Rich song that's out now—and a whole bunch of others. This was in '47, '48, something like that. I got up there and sang a song with Bob, a Bob Wills song.

By then, Bob Wills was already a legend, and there's no way to describe what a Bob Wills show or dance was like unless you were there.

That man had the magnetism, or whatever a man has which has every eye in the house glued on him all night long. He just controlled the whole situation all the time. He had good bands and he had mediocre bands, but it didn't seem to make any difference. The people who were there listening weren't really hearing the music that was being played on the bandstand: They were hearing the records, and they already knew them. They knew what Bob Wills was going to sound like before they got there, so it really didn't matter whether he was having a good night or a bad night. The people were such Bob Wills addicts and fans that every night was a good night. It was just indescribable.

The Whitney date was in an outside dance pavilion, a patio-type thing out close to Lake Whitney in the country outside town. There were probably about 1200 to 1500 people—just about the same kind of people you see at the Texas Opry House here in Austin, only their grandmothers and grandaddies; a lot of beer drinkers who like to dance. It really hasn't changed that much. It's amazing to have seen it then and to see it now, to see the same music getting all these people stirred up and enjoying themselves the same way they were 25 or 30 years ago. The same songs, even.

The next time I saw Bob Wills perform, he was on the show the first time Charley Pride came to Texas—I brought him into Dallas, Fort Worth, Shreveport, San Antonio—and *then* he was only working as a single. He only had one man with him. This was just a few years ago. He had disbanded his band. Then the last time I saw him was when we worked a date together in Pomona, California. He was in good health then. The years, naturally, were visible, but he still had the spark, the same spirit or magnetism that he always had.

About the time I first met Bob there were several road bands in Texas playing Western Swing. In fact, Western Swing was just about the only kind of music you could hear in the state of Texas. Until Hank Williams came along, it was just Bob Wills. He was *it*. All through my growing-up period, Bob Wills' and Timmy Duncan's music was what everybody listened to down in this part of the country—"Take Me Back To Tulsa," "San Antonio Rose," "Sun Bonnet Sue," all of those.

If you cut up what they call "Western Swing" music, you'll find that there's some jazz and some blues, and maybe that's it. It came from the Black jazz players and blues singers in Louisiana and Texas, and it's definitely a sound that originated in the Southwest. What happened was that men like Milton Brown were using jazz and blues musicians to play the songs that they had written, and it came out Western Swing. The big people back then, before Bob really became popular, were Jack Teagarden, Lightnin' Hopkins, Duke Ellington, people like that. A lot of white people used to go hear Black blues in those days—a lot more than they do now, I guess. It used to be that the white people were the only ones that could afford to go see the Black blues singers unless they happened to be singing in the corner bar or someplace like that. It seemed to me that the blues and jazz were here, and then came Western Swing right in the middle, using musicians out of both blues and jazz.

There were very few, if any, full-time country music stations in those days, so you listened to a station that had country music maybe an hour a day, and the rest of the time it would be playing popular music—"Stardust," "Harbor Lights," "Coming In On A Wing And A Prayer," the pop music of the war years. I knew all of those, plus my mother and my sister were music teachers, so they had all the songbooks with the lyrics to these songs. I used to learn them on guitar from the chord sheets. I was raised up on all kinds of music. Country was the one that was more easy for me to play, and I enjoyed playing it more.

Everyone listened to the Grand Ole Opry on Saturday nights, but the Nashville music never was as popular as Western Swing in Texas. Hank Williams was big, and Lefty Frizzell, but Lefty was from Texas and Hank was from Alabama. For a while, Johnny Horton was real popular after "North To Alaska," but he was from Louisiana—the Louisiana Hayride, which was *another* world. We were all doing *our* thing over here in Texas.

Originally, Bob Wills was a member of Milton Brown's band, the Brownies, until he left and branched out on his own. He was on Blue Bonnet Records back then, a Texas label, and he was the first Western Swing artist to really get national prominence. Milton Brown was killed in an automobile accident just when he was getting ready to do a lot of things. He had a song called "My Mary" and two or three more that were big hits in Texas, but when he got killed, Bob Wills continued on with that same style, improved on it, added more musicians—and the musicians became better, too, as time went on. Tommy Duncan came to sing with him, and he and Tommy turned out to be a very good combination. They started doing "Still Water Runs Deepest" and "The Kind of Girl I Can't Forget," and all those Bob Wills classics like "Faded Lover."

In the early days there were only a few road bands. Of course, there weren't any amplifiers or public address systems, so it wasn't until they came along that there were a lot of traveling bands around Texas.

Competitive wouldn't be a good word for the scene among the various bands at that time. The geography had a lot to do with it: Travelling from one place to another was such a hassle. It was hard enough to get one group into one place on a given night, much less several. I don't think it was necessary, either. I think that one group back then, if it was the right group, could draw as many people and fill a house to capacity as two or three "names" can now. Every band played Bob Wills songs, and there were probably a couple of dozen bands across the state playing Western swing music. There was Adolf Hoffner, Easy Adams, Texas Tophand, Dewey Groom, Hoyle Nicks, Spade Cooley—he was California Western Swing—and from Spade Cooley there was Tex Williams, who branched out on his own. There was Olie Rasmussen from Nebraska and the Nebraska Corn Huskers. Teddy Wiles was the featured vocalist with his group, and they were practically an exact copy of Bob Wills.

All of these guys were bandleaders, and it was the same structure as Bob Wills and the Texas Playboys. Usually they'd try to get the exact number of whatever Bob was carrying. If he had two fiddles, everybody else got two fiddles. If he had three, they'd go hire another fiddle player. They wanted to do it like Bob was doing it.

Bob loved it onstage. He had to have loved it, to have stuck with it as long as he did, even until he had his most recent stroke, which totally incapacitated him. But he worked as long as he could, right up to that last recording session in Dallas.

He never took an intermission in his shows. He'd start at eight and play straight through until midnight without a break, and the people would be dancing all the time. He sometimes carried a girl singer with him—Ramona Reed was with him for a while, and Laura Lee McBride—both of them would sing up-tempo songs, not ballads, and yodel. He hired himself female yodelers. As far as I know, they were the only extra people he carried with him, except for Tommy Duncan or whoever happened to be his featured vocalist at the time.

Every musician's eye was on him, for the whole four hours of his shows, because at any given time he'd point the fiddle bow at you, and you'd better be ready to know where it was at and jump in and do *something*, whatever. Even though he had his arrangements, which came on in certain places in a song, Bob allowed his musicians to *play*. He'd give them individual breaks and let them do their stuff, play their licks. Other bands weren't doing that at the time. That was Bob Wills' technique. He made individual stars out of everybody on the bandstand, or at least he tried to. On records, he'd mention their names—like "Take it away, Leon," which made Leon McAuliffe famous forever. Bob didn't have to say, "Take it away, Leon." He didn't have to say anything. It's the same way with Ernest Tubb and his musicians. He'd introduce them on record. I thought that was really good.

Bob didn't do many of the lead vocals—a few, but not many. He was a band leader: He *directed* the band, and he was respected probably more than any other band leader. He was not an easy man to work for—I never worked for him, but I've talked to a lot of the people who did—he was very disciplinary. He had certain things that had to be done, and if you didn't do them that way, then you didn't work for Bob Wills. He was a fair man, though. He'd stand around and smoke a cigar—he always had a cigar and a big white hat. That was his trademark.

The musicians came from a lot of different places. Everybody wanted to work with Bob Wills. His was the band to work with, and there was usually quite a bit of turnover in his band. Quite a few musicians came through there. Then they'd move off into one of the other bands when they stopped working with Bob.

One guy would say, "*This* band was the best," and another would say, "No, he was better in '45," but it's all a matter of opinion. *I* liked his early recordings when he had Eldon Shamblin playing guitar. Tiny Moore, a mandolin player, used to work with him, and they did some really good three- and four-part arrangements on some of the songs. It used to be that when you learned a Bob Wills song, you also learned the exact arrangement, because the arrangement was so good. They were head arrangements of jazz riffs which the musicians would put together and add three- and four-part harmonies. "Still Water Runs Deep" was one of the best. Now, that was *really* unusual to hear in a Western band. These guys were really good back when they were doing those arrangements. After that one band, it seemed that each group of musicians that worked with Bob would still play the same arrangements that were done when the songs were originally recorded. The arrangements didn't change: They were right off the original records.

The arrangements were a group thing. I don't think Bob had as much to do with it as maybe Eldon or Tiny or Johnny Gimble. The better musicians of the group would usually work out all these intricate arrangements. Bob was not the best musician on the bandstand, by any means, but he just happened to be the best *bandleader* on the bandstand.

I have my favorite Bob Wills songs. I've got maybe 25 that I could name off fairly easily, and then somebody else could say, "Well, what about *this* one?" and I'd have to agree. I just like the style, and it really didn't matter too much what he was playing. It was just a good *sound*. I'm sure I have taken a lot of influence from Bob Wills. I was greatly influenced by a lot of the musicians who went through the Bob Wills organization over the years—the guitar players and fiddle players especially. I tried to steal all the hot licks I could from all of those good musicians. In fact, I still do "Bubbles In My Beer" and "Stay All Night, Stay a Little Longer," and I'm planning on doing some more of his tunes. I'm not planning to do a whole album of them: I'll just put one in every now and then, and I'd like to continue doing that forever. There are enough Bob Wills songs that every year I could come out with one or two that the young people haven't heard.

There are still a lot of old guys doing his tunes: they're just too old to change, they've been doing it so long. In fact, there are a lot of places in Texas where Western Swing is still the main kind of music. There are two or three big ballrooms in Dallas that still stick to Western Swing. Dewey Groom's Longhorn Club in Dallas has had the same group of musicians for about 25 years. Then there's the new groups—especially Asleep at the Wheel. Those guys do the Bob Wills songs *exactly*. It's like going back in time thirty years to hear their stuff. I think the young people here in Austin know about him. They know about him through their parents—*everybody* has heard a Bob Wills record if they've lived in Texas any length of time at all—but if you were to ask them, "name me five Bob Wills songs," they probably couldn't do it. But once they hear one on the bandstand, they'll say, "Oh yeah, I know *that* one. I heard my daddy playin' that."

Everyone I knew when I was a kid was a Bob Wills fan. I didn't know anybody who didn't like Bob Wills' music. With his fans, there was a communication. You really had to be there to see how he communicated, and the magnetism, how those people *love* him. And *he* loves *them*, too.

Western Swing really started to get popular in the late 1930s, maybe even the mid-1930s. Bob went into the Army at the peak of his career—he was drafted—and when he came back from the Army, I guess he never really did regain the popularity that he had before he went in. He kind of lost the momentum. He spent too much time in there, and I don't think he liked it too well.

He very rarely worked anyplace but Texas, Oklahoma, and California. He stayed within those few states and didn't try to cover too much territory, which I think was a good idea. Of course, it kept him from being known in some of the other fields of music. If he'd done national tours and international tours—all the *right* things—then a lot of other people would have been aware of how good he was, but he's known well enough in the country Western Swing area as being a bandleader's bandleader that it doesn't matter if the rest of the people knew about him or not. He was still that great. I don't know how many national hits or international hits or awards he had, but I'm sure it would surprise everyone to know how much his records are selling even today.

I think that whether modern country artists know about Bob Wills or not depends on where they're from. If they're from Texas, it would be impossible for them not to be slightly familiar with Bob Wills. If they came from other parts of the country, it's quite possible that they've never heard of him in all their lives. I would think probably, more country artists don't know about him than do. There's a whole group of people in the country music business that have never listened to a Bob Wills record. Anywhere east of here, his records were never really promoted because they were into a different kind of music altogether in Nashville. It was more bluegrass in Nashville: Rather than coming from jazz bands or blues bands, the musicians came from bluegrass bands.

When Bob went to the Grand Ole Opry for the first time, first of all they didn't want him to use his drums, so he refused to appear. They finally conceded that he could use his drums. Then he went out on the stage, and he had his cigar in his mouth. So then they wanted him to not smoke his cigar on the stage. And he refused again. Consequently, that was the first and only time Bob Wills ever played the Grand Ole Opry, so far as I know. He had to have his drums and his cigar.

I've never heard of Bob Wills refusing help to anyone. I don't think he ever took over the responsibility of managing one talent, taking them by the arm and into the studio, because he was into something else altogether and he really didn't have time for that. When you have an eight or ten or twelve-piece group, it means that you have that many families of three or four or five people each, and you're responsible for their livelihood. Plus there's all the people *they're* taking care of, so one bandleader could come up with a whole group of people to support. If he worked, they ate. If he didn't work, they didn't eat.

As a businessman, I guess he would rate somewhere next to me. He had several managers and agents and bookers, the normal number of thieves who hang around. Bob was too good-hearted to ever accumulate anything: There was always someone there who needed the money at the moment. He wasn't what people would call a good businessman. He had more important things to think about, and consequently he's sick and broke today. Still, I think he would rather have it this way.

WILLIE NELSON TALKS

Nelson Allen | May 1975 | *Picking Up the Tempo*

This is the first of three interviews reprinted herein by Nelson Allen Jr., a veteran country music scene journalist who was one of the first to interview Willie Nelson at length. It is easy to perceive Nelson's comfort. Sitting down with Allen for the country music newspaper *Picking Up the Tempo* (*PUTT*), Nelson discerned the interviewer's congeniality and professionalism and became more inclined to open up about his personal and professional life. This would set a precedent for Willie's exceptional candidness toward the public, through the media and in his performances. –Ed.

The interview took place a day early because Willie wanted to play golf. So that's were we started.

PUTT: You're going to play gold with Johnny Rodriguez tomorrow, is that right?

WILLIE: No, I'm going to play golf with Darrel Royal in the morning and then we are all going to have lunch, go over to a place called the Back Door here in Austin. It's over on 6th Street, over in Chicano-town. It's men only. No women allowed.

PUTT: The place behind Cisco's?

WILLIE: Yeah, yeah . . . I like the food over there and the atmosphere, and they've got a place next door to pitch washers at Bully's. You ever been over there?

PUTT: No, I've been to the Back Door.

WILLIE: Bully's is a place right across from the Back Door and they've got places where you pitch washers back behind the bar, like pitching horseshoes, those kinds of games you know.

PUTT: Oh yeah . . . I found a bar in south San Antonio where they had a string hanging from the ceiling with a ring on it and a post with a hook and the game was to throw the ring onto the hook. The old boys in there were great at it, they did figure eights and never missed. I stayed there 6 hours trying to master that.

WILLIE: Horseshoes is an oldtime game. I used to play it when I was a kid and I used to pitch washers too. I guess in different parts of the country people have games they make up like that to do when there is nothing else to do.

PUTT: How good a golfer are you?

WILLIE: I'm a little below average I guess.

PUTT: Are you good enough to beat Darrel?

WILLIE: I can't beat Darrel. No way.

PUTT: Well, you are going to do the 4th again?

WILLIE: Yeah, in Liberty Hill, Texas. Liberty Hill . . . is . . . you go out Hwy. 183 North until you get to 29W and Liberty Hill is on 29W about 5 miles out. It's actually about 30 miles from Austin.

PUTT: Who are you going to have this time besides yourself?

WILLIE: So far the only three that are confirmed to me are Charlie Daniels and the Pointer Sisters. I want Ray Wylie Hubbard and I am talking to several people. I hate to start mentioning names because I want to wait until I talk to people first.

PUTT: Is Waylon going to appear this time?

WILLIE: He's going to be at Bull Creek. I don't know whether he will come back the 4th. I'm going to invite him to come down. I don't know if he is going to be billed on the show or not, but I would like to try to get some people on the show who have never been on the show before. George Jones or Merle Haggard or Johnny Rodriguez or some other people that are Texas people who haven't been on the show yet.

PUTT: George Jones is playing Gilley's on the 10th I think.

WILLIE: Is he? I talked to some people in his office today, but I haven't had a chance to talk to him yet, so really all of these names I'm throwing out, none of them are definite, they're just people I would like to have on the show.

PUTT: Last year a lot of good things happened, but a lot of things happened that some people didn't like and I guess somethings that you didn't like also. What are you going to do different this year?

WILLIE: I'm going to run it myself. I'm not going to have a lot of partners or any partners really. Geno is going to handle the promotion on it and I'm just going to kind of run it myself. [Likely refers to Dallas event promoter Geno McCoslin. —Ed.] It's only going to be one day and it's not going to be expensive. I think we are going to charge $5.50 for the day for advance tickets. It's going to be something that everybody can afford and it's probably going to last 10 to 12 hours. We'll have to stay within the 12 hour limit in order to stay within the law.

PUTT: What have you learned from the other picnics over these three or four years? I know it isn't an easy thing to put together. A lot of people blame you for the bad stuff and a lot of people give you credit for the good stuff.

WILLIE: Well, I think they are all right. Not any of them are wrong. I don't mind riding the heat for the bad shit and I don't mind taking credit for the good shit. There were a lot of things that happened that I wish hadn't happened, but since it's the Willie Nelson Picnic, I will [be] glad to ride the heat for whatever happened to anybody. I think there has been more good than bad come out of them. I still do and that's the reason that we are having one this year. I think that every time we have one, we learn a little bit more. It's a good showcase for new talent, plus it's a good showcase for established people who want to work in front of a new audience. That's the reason I am talking about people like Johnny Rodriguez.

PUTT: Yeah, I would like to see that.

WILLIE: And George Jones. I think George Jones could sell out to this crowd, without any problem. All he has got to do is start singing.

PUTT: George Jones and Ernest Tubb.

WILLIE: I think the people would love them, and they do love them, and are just waiting to let them know they do.

PUTT: How come we can't get Tompall here? Because he has been associated with you and Waylon for a long time, but he doesn't go on tour or he doesn't want to go on tour, or what?

WILLIE: Oh, he don't like to work much. He's kind of like the rest of us, he lays back and works places he wants to work, but there's really nothing wrong as far as I know, it's just that he's . . . are you talking about Tom T.?

PUTT: No, I meant Tompall Glaser, but what about Tom T. Hall?

WILLIE: I really don't know. I know that Tom T. and several of those people from Nashville are being pressured by a lot of different people not to have anything to do with us.

PUTT: Yeah?

WILLIE: Well, you know they would be.

PUTT: So they're not completely ignoring us out there?

WILLIE: They're not ignoring us whenever we come up. I think we have been designated as anti-Nashville. That's the image that has come down, which is not really true, but whenever our names come up, we are considered anti-Nashville to begin with so there is really no need in bringing us up, because we are out of it, we've left and we have gone back to Texas and they had just as soon forget about us as quick as they can. But the people in Nashville still bring a lot of pressure on each other to sell their own ideas and get their own particular trip.

PUTT: Who are the big kingpins now? Is it Billy Sherrill or who is it that is really running Nashville?

WILLIE: The last big Kingpin was Billy Sherrill, I don't know whether he still is or not. I'm not sure.

PUTT: Is he anti-Texas also in that kind of way?

WILLIE: I don't know. Billy Sherrill and I never had anything but kind words to say to each other. There is a lot of people that like to pitch me and Billy Sherrill against each other, but I am not going to go for it because I like Billy Sherrill. I think, hell, he is like the rest of us, trying to make it and he came across an idea that would sell records and he got some writers together and he put together a little package that included himself along with it and I don't blame him. But I don't think he is anti-anything. I think Billy Sherrill is just like we are. He's just trying to make it.

PUTT: But there is pressure in Nashville to keep away from us?

WILLIE: Yeah, there is pressure not to have anything to do with the long-hairs and the hippies and anything that is going to bring a bad name to country music.

PUTT: They don't want them on the Grand Ol' Opry.

WILLIE: No. They don't want them on the Grand Ol' Opry, because they don't believe in that type of thing and whatever they are into over there, I haven't been there in so long, but whatever they are into they are still into it and it's still the same thing that was there when I was there.

PUTT: I guess I'll probably ask you some things that you've been asked before.

WILLIE: Okay, I'll probably answer them different.

PUTT: That'll be good. The questions are always the same.

WILLIE: The answers are always different.

PUTT: One question I know you've been asked a lot and I might as well get it out of the way . . . why did you leave Nashville and come back to Austin?

WILLIE: Really, the reason is my house burned in Tennessee and while the insurance company was rebuilding my house I moved to Texas, down to Bandera, and while I was down here I got Texas fever again. You know I'm from here and I had been away for ten years and living down here again I decided I didn't want to go back to anywhere, I wanted to stay in Texas. And I also realized that most of the people that were interest in listening to what I was doing were in Texas at the time. I've been working down here all my life and knew a lot of people already so Texas is just a natural spot for me to settle. Austin is a more natural spot because of the young people here and their interest in country music. It was just a matter of . . . this is where the best audience was at the time for me. It was around Austin and Texas in general.

PUTT: What do you think about people who hadn't particularly been interested in country music before, becoming your fans? Did you have a sense of that when you first came here? Did you know that there was a possibility for a newer kind of audience?

WILLIE: Working around, over not only Texas, but around the country, I found a lot of interest in country music by young people and I also knew that they didn't have any place to go and listen to country music, for one reason or another, their hair was too long to get in some of these places without getting in trouble, at least they thought it was and there are times when I'm sure it was. There are a lot of places maybe it still is, but that situation has pretty well taken care of itself. Anyway I knew there was an audience there, so I went to Armadillo World Headquarters and told them I would like to play to their audience and see if what I was thinking was right and it turned out that it was. There is an audience and there has been for awhile and it's getting bigger and bigger.

PUTT: Yeah, it's spreading everywhere. I think the first time I saw you was at Bevo's a long time back. You got up unannounced one night and half the people there had never heard of you.

WILLIE: Yeah, remember Kenneth Threadgill was there. I remember that.

PUTT: "Family Bible" was the first song you sold?

WILLIE: Yeah, the second one was "Night Life." I got it back.

PUTT: What about "Family Bible"? Do you get royalties from it?

WILLIE: No, I get my name on it every now and then. When I found out somebody's recorded it, I call them up and tell them I wrote it.

PUTT: So you got $50 for "Family Bible" and that was it?

WILLIE: Yeah.

PUTT: Did Ray Price do "Night Life" before Patsy Cline did "Crazy"?

WILLIE: Patsy Cline did "Crazy" after "Night Life."

PUTT: Was that the first hit you had that someone else recorded?

WILLIE: No, the first one, other than "Family Bible," was "Hello Walls."

PUTT: By Faron Young?

WILLIE: Yeah, that was the first really big one in '61, it sold a lot of records.

PUTT: When did Patsy do "Crazy"?

WILLIE: It was a few months after "Hello Walls," but in the same year . . . '61, I believe.

PUTT: When did Roy Orbison do "Pretty Papers"?

WILLIE: That was in '64. I wrote it in '63.

PUTT: Hadn't you worked before that as a disc jockey in Houston and Ft. Worth? Where did you start working in radio?

WILLIE: I was a disc jockey for 7 years. I started out in Vancouver, Washington, for KVAN.

PUTT: How did you happen to get a job way up there from way down here?

WILLIE: Well, my mother, she still lives in the state of Washington, and I hitchhiked up there to see her one time and stayed for awhile. She was living right out of Portland, Oregon, which is right across the Columbia River from Vancouver. They had a little country radio station there and I just went over and applied for a job. That wasn't the first radio station job I had had. The first one was down in Pleasanton, Texas, down below San Antonio on KBOB. Dr. Ben Parker is the owner of that station down there and he hired me to open up in the mornings and sign on. That was actually the first job that I had in radio.

PUTT: Then you went to Ft. Worth and Houston?

WILLIE: Yeah, Houston, then to Nashville.

PUTT: You were a disc jockey in Nashville too?

WILLIE: No, not there, I did sell some books while I was in Nashville.

PUTT: Bibles?

WILLIE: Some encyclopedias.

PUTT: I heard someone told you that you looked like a preacher on the cover of the "Live at Panther Hall" album and you answered that you almost were back then.

WILLIE: Yeah, I really never was in any danger of becoming a preacher, but I was a Sunday school teacher there until they found out I was working in those beer joints during the week and then they suggested that I do one or the other.

PUTT: You played bass for Ray Price. Was that the first name band you were in?

WILLIE: Yeah, I fronted his band, played bass. Donny Young, or Johnny Paycheck as he is known now, he had the job and quit and Ray was left without a bass player so I applied for the job.

PUTT: Did you know how to play the bass?

WILLIE: No, I didn't know anything about it. I had never even held one in my hands.

PUTT: But you told them you could do it?

WILLIE: Oh yeah, well, I knew the top 4 strings on the guitar were the same as the bass and I could play the guitar, so I knew I could figure it out.

PUTT: I've always wondered how you got that hole in your guitar? Is that just from wear?

WILLIE: Yeah, it wore through with my fingers and the pick. You're really not supposed to use a pick on those classical guitars, but I do and there's no pick guard on it, so that's what happens over the years to a guitar if you don't have a pick guard on it.

PUTT: On some of the older albums you're pictured with a solid-body electric, a Fender. How come you're using an amplified acoustic guitar now?

WILLIE: Well, mainly because of the tone that I get out of it, plus you can use an acoustical guitar in a motel room partying, you can sit around and play anywhere. If you have an electric guitar, you have to hook up an amp and all that bullshit, and I wanted a guitar I could play with or without electricity. I started out with a Baldwin which I liked, but I busted the Baldwin so I took the pickup that was in the Baldwin, it was a fantastic pickup. All the guitar players ask me where do you get that sound on your guitar, but it comes out of that Baldwin pickup. I don't have anything to do with that. I don't think they make them anymore but it can only be used in a Baldwin amp so I kind of have a bastard setup, with a Martin guitar and a Baldwin pickup and amp.

PUTT: You use a Martin thick-necked classical guitar. Why don't you use the thinner Western style neck?

WILLIE: Well, I got used to playing the Baldwin, which has a wide neck and once you get used to playing one size neck, when you change, I don't know, you play a different way. I play a different way on an electric guitar, a Fender. I play a lot of different licks, I hear different things. I just like what I hear better off the wide string and it keeps me from trying to get too funny and too clever because with the strings that far apart and the neck that wide I have to keep it pretty basic or I'll make too many mistakes.

PUTT: I guess it's easiest to fake on a Fender?

WILLIE: Yeah, you just hit any kind of note and it sounds good.

PUTT: What is the story about you shooting Ray Price's chicken?

WILLIE: Ray has, let me put it this way, Ray used to have some fighting roosters back early in his career. I don't know if he still has them or not. I imagine he still does. He lived in Henderson, Tennessee, and I lived in Ridgetop. I had a farm there and he wanted a place to walk some of his roosters, to exercise them, and he asked me if he could put one of his roosters on my farm. I said sure. I said but I've got some hens out there, he won't bother those hens will he? No he won't bother them he said. So I said ok. Shirley, the girl I was married to at the time had those hens named. I only had 8 hens and they were all pets. So he brought his rooster out and left him and I woke up about 2 days later and went out there and there was one of the hens lying dead, the rooster had killed one of Shirley's laying hens, so I called Ray and I said Ray you had better come get this rooster because he's killed one of Shirley's hens. Okay, he said, I'll come get it and you tell her I'll bring her another hen out there. I said no we don't want no more hens, I just want you to come get the rooster. Okay hoss, I'll be right out. And about 3 weeks later he still hadn't shown up to get his rooster and I got up one morning and there was another hen dead, so Shirley is really pissed off and she went to get the shotgun to shoot the rooster and I knew that if she got out there with a shotgun she was liable to kill the horses and cows, chickens and everything else, as mad as she was, so I got the gun and I shot the rooster and gave it to the lady that was keeping house for us. I guess she took it home and ate it. And then I called Ray.

PUTT: That was an expensive dinner. About a $300.00 chicken dinner there.

WILLIE: Only Ray said it was more than that, he said you just killed a $1000.00 rooster. I told him there wasn't no fighting rooster in the world worth a good laying hen. Of course I was just bullshitting, I knew it was worth a lot of money, but he had a chance to come and get it and he didn't. He wouldn't speak to me for years.

PUTT: Just because of that?

WILLIE: Yeah, he got hot about it. He said that killing that rooster would cost me thousands of dollars because he never would record one of my songs again. We're still friends, he just has never recorded one of my songs since then.

PUTT: Ray Price has changed a lot since those days. The last I saw him he had 3 or 4 violins, I mean violins instead of fiddles, and tuxedos and all that.

WILLIE: Well Ray left the sound that he really originated in the country music field, the Ray Price Sound, he left that and went to another sound. One time there he was carrying 20 and 30 pieces with him on the road and I like that sound too, shit if he likes it, which is the main thing. A lot of other people didn't like it, but it wasn't none of their business really.

PUTT: I know you've got some horses because everytime I stop at the feed store they tell me that Willie Nelson's been in.

WILLIE: I've got some horses out there, some plow horses, and some peacocks and some laying hens, but a varmint either a ringtail or a weasel got them, and I had 12 hens.

PUTT: They got every one of them?

WILLIE: Yeah, it finally got down to two, and me and Bea set some traps out there and tried to get it but nothing happened. We couldn't get it and I only had two hens left I didn't do it, but I started to just poison the two hens that were left and kill him that way . . . when he ate the poison chicken he'd die. Then I figured that the dirty son-of-a-bitch would probably go down and crawl in my well to die and get me back and I'd have to drink water off of him for a year, so I decided that I would just leave him alone or give him the other two chickens and move. I'm glad he didn't eat horses. Some people tell me there ain't no weasels around here. Do you know?

PUTT: I don't know, I've never seen one.

WILLIE: Do you know what a ringtail is?

PUTT: No, a raccoon?

WILLIE: They look a lot like weasels, in that family, but they're long and have a long bushy tail like a squirrel and it's got a ring around it. And they're small like a weasel and they get in and out of chicken houses pretty good.

PUTT: I remember talking to Billy Joe Shaver one time and he was telling me that when you first went to Nashville there were people around who didn't think you could play guitar because you were laying down licks they hadn't heard yet. Since you play lead guitar and you're known as a guitar player besides being a songwriter and singer . . . who are the guitar players that you really respect?

WILLIE: There are a lot of guitar players that I have liked. Do you remember Hank Sugarfoot Garland, the "Sugarfoot Rag"? He was in an auto wreck and he can't play any more, but he was a fantastic player. Also, George Barnes the jazz guitar player. Eldon Shamblin who used to play with Bob Wills. Chet Atkins is a fantastic guitar player. Django Rinehart is the daddy of them all really. I guess I am probably more of a Django Rinehart fan than anybody's as far as guitar playing goes. Bucky Meadows is a good guitar player. He was playing piano on that tape we were just listening to. He's one of the good young guitar players around. Well, he's as old as I am.

PUTT: What do you think of the war that is going on in Nashville now? The thing with Bill Anderson and George Jones and Porter Wagoner and all of those people on one side and the established CMA bunch on the other?

WILLIE: I think it's interesting. I'm enjoying it.

PUTT: They seem to ignore you and Waylon Jennings. Where do you fit into the war?

WILLIE: We don't fit in anywhere. We're not in that war at all. I thought what was funny is Ray Stevens going around with a petition, this is just all rumor, I don't know if any of it is true, but he was going around with a petition because the Grand Ole Opry has about 80 bus loads of tourists that come by the stars' houses every week and they take pictures and all of that and about 90 people fall out of a bus with Brownies and Kodaks and he lives across the street from Webb Pierce and they come by there to look at the guitar swimming pool. Busloads of them. Of course, Webb is out there selling them binoculars and his kids have set up lemonade stands and Ray Stevens didn't dig it so he was out with a petition trying to get it stopped. And they asked Webb what he thought about it and he said well shit Stevens shouldn't have moved across the street from a star. So they are having a lot of fun in Nashville. I really hate to be missing out on that.

PUTT: When did you first start playing music. When you were growing up in Abbot?

WILLIE: My grandparents were music teachers and when I was 6 years old they bought me a guitar and my granddad taught me a couple of chords and gave me a chord book and then he died and I was on my own. My grandmother couldn't play a guitar, she played the piano and she taught my sister to play. My sister reads and does everything great. She's a great musician. I learned to read music a little bit after I was grown just enough to know what key I was playing in. If I looked at a piece of sheet music I could tell what key it was in and if it was waltz time or fox trot and it takes a long time but I can read a lead sheet, but I'm really not that good at it. I just learned to play a few chords on a guitar and started listening to the radio a lot. I listened to the Grand Ole Opry on radio and listened to Bob Wills and Ernest Tubb. I was raised with that kind of music.

PUTT: Have you ever written any songs about that period in your life?

WILLIE: "The Family Bible." And probably some more, but that's the first one that comes to mind.

PUTT: When you first had your guitar and knew a couple of chords and would hear that stuff on the radio, did you think that that was something you could do?

WILLIE: Yeah, I would do it. I would learn licks from guitar players and the Billy Bird licks on Ernest Tubb when Billy Bird was with Ernest Tubb. Da Da Da Dee . . . Those simple things that were his trademark. I picked those up and learned them and I found out I could do them and really got into it.

PUTT: Was there ever a time when you thought you would do anything else?

WILLIE: No. But I thought I was going to be a lawyer if I didn't make it as a musician.

PUTT: It might not hurt to be both at once.

WILLIE: Yeah, since then I found out I should have studied more law and less music.

PUTT: Who influenced you the most back on those days, who did you listen to the most, that you got the most from?

WILLIE: After I got up to the age where I was influenced by people, Floyd Tillman, Leon Payne, of course Bob Wills and Tommy Duncan and Wade Ray, those were basically my heroes when I was growing up. Tommy Duncan was lead vocalist with Bob Wills for so many years and Floyd Tillman wrote songs like "Slipping Around" and "I Love You So Much It Hurts," "It Makes No Difference Now."

PUTT: A lot of people, my people in East Texas who still play music and always did, they all got into Texas swing and from there into jazz but they never got out of it or took it anywhere. That seemed to happen to a lot of people back then.

WILLIE: Well I think it was because of Bob Wills' influence. He was so strong and powerful, plus blues or jazz or whatever you associate with Bob Wills' music, other than country, you have got to add some jazz and some blues in there to cover Bob Wills. The same musicians that worked for Bob Wills were Django Rinehart fans too. You can see it in their playing. Also Steffen Graffetti the fiddle player. All the good musicians back then that were associated with country music at all were trying to play the same licks that Bob Wills' musicians were playing, which were not the same but similar to the type of music that Django was doing back in '33 or '23 whenever he was doing it.

PUTT: I guess it was the new ground to cover, jazz.

WILLIE: It was. The only problem was unless you were good at it it sounded like shit. And what they were doing in Nashville at the time was, I think the Bluegrass scene started along about then, and Bill Monroe and the Nashville sound. People started making records up there and of course Hank Williams went there from Shreveport and started making that type of sound. The simple open chord country music with seldom a drum. Mostly no drums. If you had any drums at all it was brushes. You used brushes instead of sticks.

PUTT: Hank Williams used a bass string for that didn't he?

WILLIE: Yeah, I think probably, I don't ever remember hearing a drum on any of his early records. I don't think he used them. But he had a fiddle, he had a steel guitar, and a lead guitar and a bass and a rhythm guitar and that was really about all he ever used and it was really simple. Then he got the Hank Williams sound and that type of sound really started and so people started thinking Nashville was where to go to make a hit record. To make a lot of money you had to go to Nashville. And all the new studios and everything started. There were some good studios. There were some studios in Dallas that used to cut some good records on Lefty Frizzell when he just started out. He cut some of his first hits in Dallas and for some reason we let it slip out of Texas and go to Tennessee.

PUTT: Do you think it will come back to Texas? Do you think Austin will get some recording studios?

WILLIE: Yeah, eventually, I don't see anyway it can keep from happening. Eventually it will happen. It costs a lot of money to put in a studio and do it right and hire the right personnel. In order to compete with studios in the rest of the world which we have to do. If we are going to put something in, it has got to be as good as they have in New York or Nashville and you have got to have good people, so you are talking about half a million dollars for a studio. Whenever someone gets ready to talk about spending that kind of money, then we'll have a good studio.

PUTT: Since you had a lot to do with what has happened in Austin, do you think it's coming along in a good way?

WILLIE: I was going to say that I would take the blame for some of it, but not all of it. It is coming along in a good way. I don't see how it could be anything but good, because you are getting a lot of people to think in one direction and a lot of Texas pride enters into it too. A lot of Austin pride and Texas pride. A lot of people in Texas think that Austin is getting too much credit and they're showing it too, they are showing up at shows and they want to prove that they like country music as well as Austin does. That's only good for business. It can't be anything but good.

PUTT: In Dallas now, they reopened Panther Hall and the Longhorn, and the Long Neck in San Antonio and it's in Houston now because of

Gilley's club. I was amazed at Gilley's because I used to live in Pasadena and it was hard-core redneck then. When I lived there I had long hair but it was a long time ago and nobody paid any attention to it then.

WILLIE: It was before they knew what to call you.

PUTT: Right. But I like redneck scenes. I'm comfortable there.

WILLIE: Redneck scenes don't bother me at all. I guess I feel at home there. I'm not afraid they're going to hurt me.

PUTT: In fact, if rednecks had ever realized in the '60s how afraid hippies were of them, they'd have had a lot more fun.

WILLIE: They really would have had a big time on Saturday night. There would have been pickup loads going around different places and finding and running down hippies. Fortunately they got over it before they found about it. Do you like mescaline?

PUTT: Well, I'm afraid I'm already too drunk to do this right . . . but I don't like to deal with psychedelics anymore, it was getting too weird. I was thinking I was going to have to go out into the mountains and face down the devil, it'd be him or me and I finally figured out that I don't need to worry about that shit.

WILLIE: You found out who it was, it wasn't him, it was you.

PUTT: Well, I'll leave him up there, wherever he is.

WILLIE: Yeah, leave him in the mountains as long as he ain't down here bothering us.

PUTT: When did you run into Paul [English, Nelson's drummer —Ed.]?

WILLIE: Paul, I met in Fort Worth in 1954. I was a disc jockey up there and I had a little radio program during the day time where I would pick and sing for about 30 minutes. Me and a little band. Oliver, Paul's brother, was playing guitar in the band and the drummer didn't show up one day and Paul happened to come up one day and Paul happened to come down with Oliver to the radio show. Paul had never played drums in his life, he'd been playing trumpet for the Salvation Army.

PUTT: Was he a true believer or was he just doing it for practice?

WILLIE: I never did ask him, but anyway we got him to sit down on drums and he played drums that day and that's the first time he had ever played drums in his life. On that radio show. We just told him what to do. We told him when to hit and got the beat going for him and kept it going, of course he obviously had some natural talent so he picked it up pretty quick.

PUTT: In the song, "Me and Paul," what happened at the airport, what happened on the border? What was that all about?

WILLIE: On the border, I left some weed in the motel room and it was found by some friends who saved us from getting busted over it, that was what that was, and in the airport in Milwaukee, Paul was trying to get them to hold the plane because he had left his brief case in the taxi and I had run back after his brief case and so he mentioned to them, could you do something, is there anyway that you can sabotage one of those motors for a few minutes till Willie gets here, and the next thing he knew there were 18 policemen surrounding him and then I came back running with the brief case and I run right into all of those policemen and everybody is gathered around Paul and they weren't going to let us go on the airplane so this guy standing there with his 25 year pin decided it was time that he played big security chief and he was going to keep us from getting on the airplane, but then they saw that we were really (all we were trying to do was get out of town) trying to leave the godammed place so they let us go.

PUTT: None of them knew who you were particularly?

WILLIE: No.

PUTT: I know a guy who has gotten out of at least two speeding tickets by giving the cop Willie Nelson albums.

WILLIE: Well I've done that before. I used to carry them in the back of my trunk. I was going through Odessa one night, me and Herman Lawyers were over there getting drunk and I was going back to the motel and I must have really been going fast, but the next thing I know, I was pulled over and there are 4 squad cars around and I give them all albums and it turned out that they all know me and they all know

Herman Lawyers so everything is cool in Odessa. They should have taken me to jail because I was really drunk. But in Dallas there was one down there that never heard oof Willie Nelson and didn't want to know the son-of-a-bitch. He took me to jail.

PUTT: I was stopped in Houston one time. I was speeding and I was probably drunk, but this guy passed me doing 140 mph, and right then is when the cops stopped me. I asked them if they saw the guy pass me and the cop said yeah they had but that they'd been sittin' there waitin' on me all night.

WILLIE: It was easier for them to get you than it was him. They had to run him down.

PUTT: You were about to lose your license for a while?

WILLIE: I was about to lose it for a while, then I lost it, and then I got it back and then I lost it again and I got it back again. I have an occupational license now which allows me to drive between the hours of 4:00 P.M. to 2:00 A.M. or something like that.

PUTT: Apparently you don't watch that too closely.

WILLIE: Well, I don't pull over at 2:00 in the morning, like they require me to do.

PUTT: You have to be home by 2:00 A.M., huh?

WILLIE: Yeah. 4:00 P.M. to 2:00 A.M. each day.

PUTT: Let me write that in here . . . Willie has to be home and in bed by 2:00 A.M.

WILLIE: I have to be pulled over and stopped by 2:00 A.M., so if they find me on the side of the road stopped, well that's the reason. I'm waiting 'till 4:00 P.M. so that I can get out again.

PUTT: When did you run into Waylon?

WILLIE: He was in Phoenix, Arizona, living there, had a house band, was making good money. He built up in Arizona and New Mexico about the same way that I worked Texas, so he came to me and said he had a chance to go to Nashville and record and he was thinking about moving up there and he asked me what I thought about it. I told him to stay where the fuck he was. Don't move nowhere, stay. Because I was out on the road when I met him. I was coming through Phoenix on about a 30 day tour.

PUTT: Kind of bummed out with Nashville?

WILLIE: Well not really Nashville, but the thing about it . . . he had a good deal where he was and why quit something that is doing good and go to something that you're not sure of? But it turned out that he made the right decision, that he probably couldn't have stayed in Phoenix and do what he has done. He had to go through the Nashville scene in order to get where he is at now, because Nashville . . . It's like when I left Texas and went to Nashville, the reason I did that was because Nashville was where things were happening. That's where the action was, that's where the business was and if you wanted to stay in the business it made sense to go to Nashville, then once you were there, if you established yourself then you could leave and live anywhere.

PUTT: I have heard people, old-time people and clubowners say that Nashville artists always talked about Texas and Oklahoma audiences . . . as the places to play on the road.

WILLIE: It's really not necessary to live in Tennessee, if you are working Texas on the weekends. That's why I came back. I was driving a 1,000 miles to Texas and a 1,000 miles back—2,000 miles every week to work and it just made sense to live here, especially since I liked it here anyway.

PUTT: You had some trouble after you were in Nashville with RCA didn't you? With Chet Atkins? I got that from reading the Red Neck Rock Book. Are there things in that book that are wrong or that you don't like?

WILLIE: No, I like everything that's in there. There may be some things in there that aren't exactly accurate, but I love everything that's in there. I think Jan was saying exactly what he thought and writing it exactly the way he felt it. He has that right and he ain't that far off. He had it figured pretty close.

PUTT: Then you did have some trouble with RCA and Nashville.

WILLIE: Trouble to the extent that I didn't have any promotion. I was an artist on RCA, but there was no money being spent promotion-wise on Willie Nelson and it seemed like I was only cutting my albums there like dub sessions. They would release them and see if anybody wanted to record them. I just didn't feel like the promotional department of RCA was behind me and in fact I knew they weren't and they admit that they weren't. It was just lack of communication between me and Nashville and New York. I felt like I was working for a giant computer in New York and everytime something came up we would have to check with New York and everything had to be cleared through New York, so I could see . . . well, I knew once the computer gets it, it is going to say Willie Who? I was with RCA for 8 years. When I went with them I felt it was the greatest record company in the world and I still believe that. With that name RCA they should be able to do anything they want to do with an artist. If an artist has got any talent at all they have enough money and promotional work and experience to at least get that artist's material out somewhere and get it exposed and they can do that if they want to. They are big enough to do anything they want to do. To get behind any artist as they have proven with Elvis and different people. But unless there is someone in high places that has some definite, direct interest in an artist, he's not any better off on RCA than he is on any other label.

PUTT: You have a new album coming out.

WILLIE: "The Red Headed Stranger" on Columbia.

PUTT: It's a kind of departure. It all fits together in a real concept way with a lot of ballad type songs in it.

WILLIE: Yeah, it's a ballad album. There is a certain mood that we try to keep all through the album and we didn't . . . right in the middle of a mood, we didn't throw an up tempo, a "Shotgun Willie," in on them. I just have a theory about albums. I think they should follow a theme. If you're sitting in a living room and you're listening to an album and you have a certain mood going, you don't want that trip broken. You want to keep it all the way through. That's what I tried to do with "Red Headed Stranger."

PUTT: Where did you record it?

WILLIE: In Garland outside of Dallas. Mickey Raphield [Raphael] found the studio. Phil York was the engineer and I produced it.

PUTT: You used your own band this time?

WILLIE: Yes, plus Bucky Meadows and Billy English.

PUTT: Was Columbia ready for this kind of an album?

WILLIE: Well, they expected a "Shotgun Willie," a more up tempo album but I went up and explained what I was doing and they're happy with it now.

PUTT: The same circular pattern from "Phases and Stages" seems to be re-emerging with this album. Why do you see things in circles?

WILLIE: I was just tired of albums with 12 separate moods and 12 separate ideas and with nothing to connect them, no thought following through the album. It's not original with me, concept albums are nothing now . . . I was just interested in making an album that followed a story.

PUTT: Aside from a way of collecting songs, it's a circular way of relating experience . . . do you think life follows a circular pattern or patterns?

WILLIE: Yes, I think so. Mine does.

PUTT: Someone said the other night that what a lot of people don't understand about Willie is that he's spooky . . . that he's actually very mystical. What do you think of that description?

WILLIE: Well, no. At least not to myself. I don't seem that way to me.

PUTT: There are a lot of old songs on the album. "Red Headed Stranger" is an old song.

WILLIE: Yeah, I just tied them together. Connie and I were driving back from Steamboat Springs in Colorado and we decided it would be a good thing to do "Red Headed Stranger" sometime. So I started thinking about it and when it came time to do the album I just sat down one day and wrote it. Then when we got to the studio I found out I didn't have enough so I spent another day writing.

PUTT: Is that the way you do most of your songwriting . . . right before it's time to do an album?

WILLIE: Yeah, usually.

PUTT: Is songwriting hard, or has it become easy for you?

WILLIE: At first it was something I felt I had to do but now it's a little more like going to work. It takes a lot of self-starting.

PUTT: How many songs have you written?

WILLIE: About 500.

PUTT: What else do you think is different about this album from things you've done in the past?

WILLIE: Nothing.

PUTT: Just doing some more songs?

WILLIE: That's all.

PUTT: Well someone told me you said that you were writing different songs now. That you're not writing real sad country songs now because things are going good for you. Is that true?

WILLIE: To a certain point, it is. Yeah, I don't write the real sad tear-jerking songs that I used to write because I'm not real sad anymore. Sometimes I will write something, well the latest thing that I have written is a song called "Sound in Your Mind." It's still not an unhappy song either . . . is it Lana? It's not a sad song. I don't write sad songs. I can write about other people's experiences which are sad, like the Red Headed Stranger's experiences were sad there for awhile, but it picked up in the end.

PUTT: I guess "I Still Can't Believe You're Gone" is a song like that.

WILLIE: Right. That was written about a specific incident and a person that I knew and loved and I really felt that way when I wrote the song. But even if you don't know the inside story on the song, the song still stands on its own, I think.

PUTT: We've talked a lot about Texas and one thing that has always interested me about Texas and New Mexico and other parts of the

Southwest . . . is the way a 100 years ago is all mixed up with the present. If you can imagine yourself living 100 years ago . . . do you think you'd be doing the same thing, making music and writing songs?

WILLIE: Well . . . I'd like to think I'd be doing the same thing but I probably wasn't.

PUTT: Why is there so much music and so many different kinds of music that come out of Texas?

WILLIE: I don't know. I've always thought it was strange when you start looking at it . . . just looking at the country music . . . it seems like at least 75–80% of all country artists have either come from Tennessee or Texas. I don't know why or if not from Texas, from Texas-Louisiana, Mississippi, Alabama. I don't know why that is, but between Texas and Louisiana and the South, there is a lot of music. It seems like more than any other geographical point in the country, in the world really, there is more music. It comes out of this area. And there is a lot of it in Texas. Not only country, but there is Bobby Blue Bland . . . But I think regardless, looking at it from an individual standpoint, regardless of where you were born you would be doing what you are doing today. You would be a writer because that's what you like to do. The question is why were so many of us born down in this part of the country? I don't know. I really don't know the answer to that. But a lot of us were and we scattered and it looks like some of us are drifting back in now from just getting tired of running around other places I guess.

PUTT: I think it would be great to live in Hawaii for awhile, but sooner or later, I would want to come back to Texas. I don't even know why.

WILLIE: I think if I had another spot, if I were going to move or had to move today, I would move to Hawaii.

PUTT: Maybe Montana during the summer.

WILLIE: Yeah. What we always do is move around. If they say move, we will move one place for a little while and then go somewhere else. As long as it's good in Hawaii we'll stay there and come back to Montana and then to Denver and then to Florida.

PUTT: And sooner or later back to Texas.

WILLIE: You come back here to rest, I guess. I don't know.

PUTT: Well, you aren't planning on leaving any time soon are you?

WILLIE: Leave Texas? No, I don't have any plans of leaving Texas permanently.

PUTT: Someone told me that your place was up for sale.

WILLIE: I have moved into town and my place out in the country is up for sale. But, I don't really care if I sell it or not. I would like to keep it really. But, I have it up for sale, because it costs a lot of money every month to keep it. But, if it don't sell, I won't be disappointed.

PUTT: Well, something is killing all of your hens.

WILLIE: I wanted to move away from the goddammed weasel out there.

PUTT: How was Las Vegas this last time around?

WILLIE: It was good. We worked at the Golden Nugget, the only place I have really worked in Las Vegas. A lot of our people are coming in there, because of a 2 drink minimum and no cover charge or you can sit over and play black jack if you want to and get a dollar and listen to the music. They have got speakers all over the joint. There's a new owner of the Golden Nugget, Steve Wynn is his name. He's a good man and knows what he is doing, a good promoter, and he likes our audience and he likes for a lot of young people to come in there and encourages them to come in there. It's one of the few places in Las Vegas that does that.

PUTT: You took a lot of Texas people out there with you. Some of them left a little money behind too.

WILLIE: Yeah that's true, I'm sure they did. If they went through Las Vegas at all they left something somewhere.

PUTT: Do you gamble when you're out in Vegas?

WILLIE: I don't really do that much gambling. I like to play nickel slot machines and a little black jack, not anything heavy.

PUTT: You brought back a band with you too, Honeybuns McCoy.

WILLIE: Right. They have gone back to Las Vegas now. They're a good group, but they didn't come down here with their band. They came down with just 2 of them and they tried to put a band behind them and it didn't work out so they have gone back to Las Vegas to work with their band.

PUTT: I heard them the other night.

WILLIE: They didn't impress a lot of people down here.

PUTT: No they didn't.

WILLIE: I heard them when I was working Las Vegas. I went out to this club and I heard them with their band and they were a lot better group with their own band than they were with a pickup band behind them.

PUTT: Well that's a pretty hard transition I guess.

WILLIE: It really is. They left and came on down without their band, it was a mistake but they did it and now they are back up there It's one of those trips that you go through and you realize your mistake once you get into it, but it's too late and you just go ahead and make the trip. Now they are back up there trying to get their shit together and get it worked out right.

PUTT: How is Austin music affecting the rest of the country? Is it growing beyond Texas?

WILLIE: Of course, it may be with just the people I run across and the people that I see in the rest of the parts of the country, but everyone is asking what's going on in Texas. That's all I hear . . . tell me what's going on in Texas. All I hear is Texas . . . now tell me what's going on down there. We're just playing and picking and singing is all. Just doing what we always did.

PUTT: Do you think Nashville is scared of Austin?

WILLIE: They don't have any reason to be. They really don't have any reason to be at all.

PUTT: They were pretty excited about trying to break into the pop markets for awhile.

WILLIE: Well you know there was the whole Nashville sound that went from one thing to another. It went from a country sound to a pop sound, into a slick pop sound.

PUTT: From Eddie Arnold country to Eddie Arnold pop.

WILLIE: Right. And the slick pop sound, the Nashville sound, was very commercial, it sold for a while very well. I think now they are going to have to come around to what is happening today. They are going to have to deal with these people out of here, if they want to sell records.

PUTT: I read somewhere that Chet Atkins said he was sorry he did all that slick sound stuff and he wished now he had never done it. He decided it had been bad for country music.

WILLIE: He said he was sorry? I didn't know he said that. They have got to have a meeting of the minds somewhere along the way and I enjoy seeing them working it out up there.

PUTT: Yeah, you're just watching it all. Well I was just watching John Denver in TV a few weeks ago, and I ain't got nothing against John Denver, but I hardly think he's the top country and western singer in the world. I think a better choice would've been Guy Lombardo. I read about Barbi Benton . . . and I just think Texas represents something a lot more real than that. There's still plenty of good music coming out of Nashville, though.

WILLIE: It's slowing down a lot from what the pace is in Nashville. They say the pace is . . . well in Los Angeles the pace is a 100 miles an hour and people who go from Los Angeles back to Nashville think they're going into the back woods country because the pace is slowed down considerably in Nashville from Los Angeles or New York, they're all going faster that we are, I feel, they're all moving faster than I want to move and they are doing a lot more in a day's time than I want to do. They're trying to crowd too much into a 24 hour period to suit me. Now, it may suit them fine, but I don't like to work that hard. I don't like to think business 24 hours a day. I don't want to have to constantly think about how much money I am going to make before I do something and . . . when you say Nashville, what you are really talking about is a lot of people from Texas and Oklahoma and the rest of the world who have gone up there. The powers that be in Nashville are not people who were born in Nashville, so you really can't geographically put all the blame on Nashville. It just happens that that is where all the folks wound up, that's where all the promoters and thieves from all over the country went when they found out that that was where the action was. Just like me in Houston you know. I was in Houston and I said hey it's happening in Nashville, let's go up there. So there were lots of people doing the same thing at the same time that I did and when I found that out . . . they were there already . . . they already had their plans set in Nashville the way they wanted things to be, and I didn't fit in to them too well. I laid back and stayed out of them and lived up on my farm in Nashville and I went into town once or twice a year whenever I had to record and I stayed out of politics, the local politics there and didn't get involved in any of the organizations that were there because I am not organizationally inclined. I don't . . . I can't be organized that easily.

PUTT: About a year ago there was talk of a movie about John Wesley Hardin which you were going to be in.

WILLIE: The guy never did get up all the money to do it I think.

PUTT: What about the movie that was made of the last [Fourth of July] picnic in Bryan?

WILLIE: They are working on releases now from all the artists, plus they are suing each other back and forth. So I don't know if the movie will ever come out or not.

PUTT: Well we went to see it that night. It was pretty fucked up because they didn't have the sound.

WILLIE: Yeah, there was no way you could tell anything about it, plus the 3-D that they had . . . did you see the 3-D night?

PUTT: Yeah.

WILLIE: That would give me a headache to watch that and I think they have decided to take out the 3-D now.

PUTT: They had some weird cuts . . . they would cutaway from a stage shot at night to a tit shot in daylight and back again . . . but I know it was tentative and I could see they had enough stuff to make a good movie out of it if they put it together right.

WILLIE: Yeah, I think it will be all right if it ever comes out. If they ever quit fighting and get it out. [It was ultimately released in 1979 as *Willie Nelson's 4th of July Celebration.* —Ed.]

PUTT: I know Leon (Russell) is a friend of yours and that you've known him quite awhile, but when I saw the movie Leon was really hogging the stage, especially with B.W. Stevenson and Doug Kershaw . . . if I'd been B.W. Stevenson and Doug Kershaw . . . if I'd been B.W. Stevenson I probably would have kicked his ass off stage.

WILLIE: Really, I think, not particularly to take up for Leon, but telling the facts, Leon was paid a good deal of money to MC the show, and he wasn't advertised as a performer, he was advertised as the MC of the show. And he felt like . . . well right off he felt like he should have brought his band, you know, he felt like he made a mistake by coming down as MC, he should have brought his band and performed. And he was really just trying to earn his money I think. He was just trying to be on the stage as much as he possibly could be. Knowing Leon, he would have much rather been back in the bus drinking beer.

PUTT: Yeah, okay. That explains it pretty honestly.

LANA (Willie's daughter): In this article here it says that you are the chunky granddad of progressive country. You went from father to granddad in about 3 weeks. Because there is another article from the *Houston Chronicle* last week that said you were the father.

PUTT: They said country granddad?

LANA: "Chunky granddad of progressive country."

WILLIE: Is that a man or woman that said that?

LANA: A man.

WILLIE: That's all right then, as long as it ain't a woman.

PUTT: Billy Joe said when he wrote "Willie the Wandering Gypsy and Me," that he didn't know you at the time, that he had just seen you and he wrote it without even knowing you. What did you think about that when you first heard it?

WILLIE: Oh, I thought . . . I think it's a great song. It's one thing to have a song written about you, but to have a good song written about you is even better. "Willie, the Wandering Gypsy" is a hell of a song.

PUTT: Yeah, it's a great song.

LANA: In an interview with Tex Ritter just before he died they asked him what his favorite song was. And he said that as of that date his favorite song was "Willie, the Wandering Gypsy and Me."

PUTT: I always liked Tex Ritter. Tex Ritter was the only cowboy singing star I could take seriously. Maybe Gene Autry.

WILLIE: Yeah, Tex was really the only one that I really felt could beat the shit out of the bad guys.

PUTT: And Lash LaRue, now he didn't sing . . .

WILLIE: Now Lash could do it.

PUTT: Did you hear about Lash LaRue getting busted in San Francisco?

WILLIE: No.

PUTT: He got busted for grass and they found a bull whip in the back seat.

WILLIE: Still carrying his whip around with him?

PUTT: Yeah, he used to dress in black and smoke cigars. He was ahead of his time.

WILLIE: Yeah, I liked Lash LaRue and Sunset Carson, do you remember him?

PUTT: Yeah.

WILLIE (to a friend): What do you say?

FRIEND: . . . have you got a disease?

WILLIE: This time of year I peel off and I look like a snake. I got burned in Hawaii.

PUTT: You've been in Hawaii?

WILLIE: I just got back.

PUTT: How was it?

WILLIE: It's beautiful, it's fantastic. We went out there and spent all of last week out there. The first day me and my wife, we layed out in the sun and burned up as you can see. And the next 4 days it rained, but even raining, it's a beautiful place. And it wouldn't have been any good for us if the sun had been shining, we couldn't have gotten out in it, because we were already burned up the first day.

PUTT: When you start to write a song, do you pick up the guitar and do it or do you carry something around in your head for a few weeks? How do you do it?

WILLIE: It varies. There's no set way. Sometimes I will sit down with a guitar and write a song. Sometimes I will be driving down the highway and get an idea and write it driving down the highway without a guitar and then try to remember it until I get somewhere where I can write it down or record it or something.

PUTT: How satisfying are your songs to you personally? Regardless of how successful they are with audiences or at making money . . . do they express the way you're feeling when you write them?

WILLIE: Yeah, they do. I've thrown a lot of songs away because they didn't.

PUTT: There'll probably be a lot of would-be songwriters hanging around your garbage cans if we print that. I read that Kristofferson said he really hated performing and all he cared about was the writing, but that he did the performing to keep the writing alive. Do you have any preference? Do you like writing better than performing or performing better or do you like it all?

WILLIE: I like it all. I enjoy performing really more than I enjoy writing. Writing is a kind of labor, even though it is a labor of love to a certain extent, it's still work to sit down and make yourself think about something long enough to write something that is going to be good and be able to call it a song when you get through. It requires a lot of concentration and a lot of thinking. I am basically lazy and performing doesn't require a lot of intelligence really, you just stand up there and you play. You don't have to do a lot of concentration. You just play what the crowd wants to hear.

PUTT: What about Austin or Texas audiences. You mentioned a while ago coming to Texas for that reason partly. Are they better than other places or different than other places?

WILLIE: I think their enthusiasm is probably the word that describes them, Austin and Texas audiences. They are very enthusiastic and if they hear something they like, they let you know enthusiastically. But if they hear something they don't like then they will also let you know.

PUTT: You've always been country . . . what do you think about newer people coming into country for rock and folk music and from different places?

WILLIE: I believe in order to play traditional country music, what we consider to be country music around here, in order to play Bob Wills . . . the way that it should be played, it helps to have been raised with that type of music instead of coming into it cold. Asleep At The Wheel does a great job of doing Bob Wills arrangements, but it would be impossible for anyone to have the same feel unless they were raised with that type of music. In order to do it right you have to have a certain feel for it . . . a natural feel.

PUTT: A couple of years ago you said that if anyone wanted to be a songwriter, they should go to Nashville or someplace where they can really do it. Is Austin getting big enough to attract songwriters and musicians now?

WILLIE: Honestly there aren't really that many publishers or people here to take care of . . . I don't know how many people are coming into Austin now with songs and wanting to record, but Austin I don't think is really set up to handle the number of people that come into Nashville, that's for sure.

PUTT: Of course, in Nashville, there is there problem that some guy gets off a Greyhound with a guitar, while some other guy is getting on to go back home.

WILLIE: That's right. I think the situation will take care of itself, because of supply and demand. Whatever, I think Austin is in a growing stage now, where it is a frontier really. It's a new music center and it is going through all the growing pains and all the problems and bullshit that anything new goes through, any kind of baby goes through.

PUTT: Is there a basic difference between Texas and Nashville music?

WILLIE: That's really back to labels again when you say Texas music and Nashville music. There is really no way to compare Nashville and Texas. Because the Nashville sound is all a recording sound. It has all come out of records up there. Texas people still record in Nashville and I am sure always will, because they have got some of the best recording studios in the world. Nashville is more recording and I think Texas is more live performance, live concert type oriented. The club scene is bigger in Texas than it's in Tennessee. There is only one place to work in Nashville and that's the Grand Ol' Opry. If you don't work there you can't get jobs nowhere.

PUTT: You have to go on the road?

WILLIE: Yeah, you have to go to Texas or you have to go to Oklahoma or Arizona or California, New York, but Texas is still . . . there are more places to work in the State of Texas than anywhere.

PUTT: There ought to be more TV coverage of Texas than there is.

WILLIE: Yeah, I think it will come too. I believe that all these things will happen as the scene grows and it gets bigger and more people start realizing that there should be more TV. There is somebody in the TV end of it who will say "Hey there ought to be more TV." But, those Lone Star shows that we did, I think they are going to be good. They are going to help a lot and help some of the television people to realize that there is something going on.

FRIEND: How's the interview coming along?

PUTT: Fine. I think I'm drunk.

WILLIE: We have a hell of an interview going. I'm interviewing him and he's interviewing me.

FRIEND: That's the way it ought to be.

WILLIE: Talking about the music thing that's going on. I really don't know, it's hard to say what questions need to be asked or what questions need to be answered. Like they kind of come up instantly, a question will come up and then there is an answer. I don't know what kind of questions should be answered about it or what should be asked about it.

PUTT: Do you think music, all kinds of music, is merging together?

WILLIE: The definition of music, my grandmother told me, was anything that is pleasing to the ear. And any other labels than that, I think are unnecessary. If I hear something that is pleasing to my ear, then it is music to my ear. And if it is not pleasing to my ear, it is not music, regardless of what label that you want to put on it. I think that you can just put it all in one big pot and call it music and either you like it or you don't like it. It depends on your ear. If your ear likes it, then you are relating to it somewhere. If it sounds good to your ear, it's music to your ear. And if it's not music to your ear, then it's not fucking music. That's all. It's just noise, and there is not anything else that you can call it if you don't like it. And if you do like it, there really is no other reason to call it anything but music.

PUTT: American music?

WILLIE: American music, if you are going to label it, that's a good label. But you really can't confine it to America, because I have made three trips across the big water and they yell and scream for country music over there. They yell and scream for the Wabash Cannonball and for Night Life and for Frauline and for Hank Williams and it could be that they have decided that American music is pleasing to their ear. But American music is as good a label as any to put on it.

PUTT: Someone suggested they give me a list of things I shouldn't ask you about, sensitive areas to avoid I guess.

WILLIE: That you shouldn't talk about?

PUTT: Yeah, but I knew it was bullshit so I didn't pay any attention to it.

WILLIE: You would have made it a point to ask those questions first. I'd like to know what I don't want to talk about. I really can't think of anything I wouldn't talk about, because I don't have any secrets.

PUTT: I read where Waylon said that he still listens to Hank Williams. Who do you listen to now, when you're at home?

WILLIE: Well, I'm almost ashamed to say that I don't listen a lot. I don't really listen to any one person and I very rarely put on an album including mine at home. I am always thinking about what I am going to do next, really, rather than what has already been done. Out of necessity, I usually had to figure out what I was going to do tomorrow today or what I have to do today in order to make it tomorrow in order to get things together, so I really don't listen to any particular . . . I listen to KOKE a lot. I listen to Sammy Allred. I listen to KRMH sometimes and watch the thing on TV on channel 5 or 6 where you get the news and weather going across the TV and there is some music playing in the background. They play some pretty good music there.

PUTT: Can you get Dolly Parton for the 4th?

WILLIE: It would be nice if I could get Dolly Parton. It's only going to be one day this year, so we are confined to a maximum of like 9 or 10 acts.

PUTT: I have heard that she's got a really shitty band together because she's got all of her relatives in it.

WILLIE: Yeah, that's what I heard too.

PUTT: The site [for the 1975 4th of July Picnic] at Liberty Hill, what is it? Is it a farm or something?

WILLIE: Yeah, it's right on the San Gabriel River. There are a couple of lakes on the property and there is about 500 acres there.

PUTT: They should get some good photographs this time.

WILLIE: Uh huh. They won't have to go from dark to light.

PUTT: Aside from the new album, you're going to put out some older stuff that wasn't released before. Is that going to be on your own label?

WILLIE: Yeah, on the Lone Star label.

WILLIE (looking through a copy of *Picking Up The Tempo*): Ray Wylie Crow calls who a cocksucker?

PUTT: Alvin Hubbard, I guess. We're stirring up a little excitement anyway.

WILLIE: Oh yeah, I believe in stirring up all the kicks you can.

PUTT: When did you figure out that you could grow long hair and a beard and put an earring in your ear and it didn't make any difference?

WILLIE: I always knew that. I always knew it didn't make any difference. I just had to do it in order to get the fucking attention. I knew it would draw some attention, definitely get some fire from certain areas and I couldn't get arrested up until then. Then I got arrested. I think that anybody that has ever had long hair and a beard and went into a truck stop knows how it feels to be a [*n*-word].

PUTT: Of course, if you've grown up behind truck stops you ain't all that worried.

WILLIE: No, you ain't worried about it and the [*n*-words] ain't worried about it. They go in truck stops.

PUTT: Sure they do.

WILLIE: It don't bother them.

PUTT: In fact it seems to be going the other way, if people don't quit whining about cosmic cowboyism, I'm going to put a gun-rack in my pickup and refuse to speak to anyone but old men and Mexican girls. I just bought a .357 magnum . . .

WILLIE: I've got one of those.

PUTT: Do you carry it around with you?

WILLIE: No. The last one I ever carried around with me, the Dallas Police Department got it.

PUTT: They never gave it back?

WILLIE: No. They kept saying they would if I would come up there. I said oh yall can keep it.

PUTT: But you have another one now?

WILLIE: Yeah, I have a .357. Of course, after I took it out and shot a box of shells through it . . . if I put myself in the right mood, I can still hear the ringing in my ears.

PUTT: Oh yeah, even with .38 specials it'll do that to you.

WILLIE: The first time I tried to shoot it, I had never shot a .357 before, and I saw them on TV using both hands, so I didn't know they were putting that left hand through the trigger guard and I did it like I used to do my old .22 like a rifle and I grabbed the barrel of that son-of-a-bitch and shot it and sound waves went up both arms. By the time they got to my head it went rrrrrmmmmmmmm . . .

PUTT: What kind is it?

WILLIE: Shit, I don't even know. It was given to me. Geno . . . it's a Colt.

PUTT: That's a good gun.

WILLIE: Great gun. Use ear plugs.

PUTT: Certain places up north now they put you in prison for shooting someone who's breaking into your house.

WILLIE: That's why we have got to be careful that we don't get into any of that shit down here in Texas. I don't think we will. I don't think there's ever any danger of Texas disarming. They can pass all the laws they want but they're not going to disarm anybody who wants to be armed.

PUTT: One of your earliest records which I suppose is already a collector's album, is the "Texas In My Soul" album, where you did Travis's letter and nothing but Texas songs. How did you decided to do that?

WILLIE: I just put together a bunch of songs that I liked about Texas.

PUTT: Do you like that album now?

WILLIE: Yeah, I particularly like . . . my favorite songs in there are the "Travis Letter" and "Remember the Alamo" . . . the whole album, but I like those two. They are my favorites. "Texas in My Soul" and "A Little Bit of Everything in Texas" and all those standards.

PUTT: I like the whole album. I guess at one time every kid in the state had to memorize "Travis's Letter."

WILLIE: Yeah, that's true.

PUTT: Well, I can sit here and drink beer all night long. If you've got some place to go, we can shut it down for a while.

WILLIE: Let's do and let me talk to those guys out there and if you've got some more questions you can come back out again.

PUTT: Thanks. I'd like to.

WILLIE NELSON: THE SECOND CROWNED KING OF COUNTRY AND WESTERN MUSIC OF TEXAS

Grace Mikel | 1975 | *Country Hotline*, vol. 10

This is another early example of Willie Nelson's cordiality with fans. Willie also graciously courted the press and accommodated interview requests. Of note is one of the first mentions of Nelson's concert durations, lasting anywhere from two to four hours. –Ed.

Willie Nelson, hero of the masses of Texas country western music fans came to Houston recently to visit his friends. When I say friends, that is just what I mean. As every Willie Nelson worshiper is quick to tell you, first of all Willie is their friend. I arrived at Gilley's Club at 7 p.m. and was greatly surprised to find every table in the club had been taken. Chairs were set up on the dance floor and still there wasn't enough seats to accommodate the great throng of people. Several hundred stood thru the concert while many more hundreds were turned away at the door. I met Willie out front and introduced myself and explained I'd like an interview if at all possible. Willie gave me a quick smile and asked if I'd like to do it right there! So with fans swarming all over him we got right into it.

This was his first concert in this area in some time and it was obvious he was as delighted to see his many friends as they were to see him.

Willie is a walking legend. His career spans many years. The beginning was filled with many disappointments and set-backs. He lived in Houston for awhile, and was even a DJ for a time. Down on his luck, he sold many of his songs for ten dollars each. Getting restless, again Willie moved on, hoping to find greener pastures in Austin. His first big break came when Faron Young recorded one of his songs, HELLO WALLS. The rest is history. What makes this man the great hero of the Texas country and western fan is easy to understand, as you watch Willie on stage. He performed for two straight hours, signing autographs all the while, bits and pieces of paper, hats, belts and everything the fans handed up to him. Then a thirty minute break, which was also used to meet the fans and sign more autographs. This is one super star, the other super stars can well take lessons from, as to how to treat their fans!

Willie did not hide out on his break like most artists do, and ignore his fans. He mixed with them. His concert was not a thirty minute quickie like the others, either. He had spent two hours on stage performing, took a thirty minute break and back for another two hour performance. It's no wonder Texans have crowned Willie Nelson their KING.

The Willie Nelson 4th of July Picnic each year has become a way of life for Texans. Many top artists are always on the line up with many more surprise guests dropping by.

I decided I would interview the fans at random and of all ages to find out what Willie Nelson meant to each of them. The answers were always the same. First, he was their friend. He was honest. He always had time for his friends. I worship the ground Willie Nelson walks on, was the golden thread that weaved itself thru every fan's opinion of their hero.

Willie's new album is called THE RED HEADED STRANGER, but a stranger Willie is not, to his thousands of friends.

Editor's Note—As we go to press we would like to note that Willie's annual picnic this year was an even bigger success than previous ones, with an estimated 70,000 attending.

THE MAN WHO BEAT THE SYSTEM

Patrick Carr | February 1976 | *Country Music*

By the beginning of 1976, Willie Nelson had switched to Columbia Records and had recorded and released his critically acclaimed album *Red Headed Stranger*. Journalist Patrick Carr's interview with Nelson captures his defiance of industry norms. It also reveals his commitment to family roots and music, and provides an in-depth look at Willie's journey, character, and influence. By 1976, Willie's hope to broaden his fan base with a younger generation began manifesting. On several occasions, he was pulled in as coheadliner for Bob Dylan's Rolling Thunder Revue, whose concert sales were lagging in the South. –Ed.

We begin with an ending of sorts. We are in Nashville on a drizzly night, packed into the Municipal Auditorium like so many high-rent sardines approaching the strung-out finale of the Disk Jockey Convention, 1975. Taken together tonight, we are perhaps the most professional audience any of these Columbia/Epic acts are likely to play for at least another year: all of us are Somebodies in the country music business, and we're all hip to the score. The Columbia/Epic acts bounce onstage and do whatever thing they do, three numbers each, one after the other. Tammy Wynette, Mac Davis, Barbara Fairchild, David Houston . . . it's very democratic but pretty soon it becomes obvious which artists are getting the corporate nod right now because all you really have to do is watch the company personnel pay or not pay attention. Nevertheless, it's a subtle affair.

But when Willie Nelson and his band of gypsies make their entrance backstage, looking for all the world like some flying wedge of curiously benign Hells Angels, subtlety goes by the board and it's plain that this year's Most Likely To Succeed slot has just been taken with a vengeance: a great shaking of hands begins. The impression is confirmed when Willie proceeds to get up onstage with his full band (all the other acts were backed by the Columbia band) and play a 40-minute set that, except for a quite seemly absence of illegal drugs and teenage nudity among the audience, might just as well be happening in Texas on the 4th of July. This is the ending of sorts, and what it means is that after telling the Nashville powers-that-be to get lost and leaving town just three short years ago, Willie Nelson has become the country music wave of the future and is now accepting Nashville's praise and promotional efforts on his own terms.

There is a postscript, though. Three or four hours later—after another couple of hundred handshakes, after attending a *very* high-rent Columbia party to which his band was not invited, and after behaving like a perfect gentleman through it all—Willie gets himself down to Ernest Tubb's Record Store and plays for two hours while most every other star in town is out at Opryland, all gussied up to celebrate the 50th Anniversary of the Grand Ole Opry amid great pomp and ceremony of the By Invitation Only kind. It isn't that Willie couldn't have shown up at the Opry—with his current Columbia-backed status, that's a silly notion—and it isn't that he's trying a reverse-*chic* move like one of Nashville's several dozen I'm-so-hip-and-isn't-this-earthy types might attempt. It's just that his old friend and musical hero Ernest was gracious enough to invite him, and that Ernest Tubb's Record Store is still the best place in town to get down and play straight honky tonk music for the friends and neighbors.

Apart from being a rebel against Nashville's creative restrictions, a culture hero, a real sweetheart, a person blessed with a highly sophisticated sense of humor, and the man who first made it possible for hippies and rednecks to co-exist under the protection of his music—all of which he is—Willie Nelson has always been one other thing. He has always been a writer and singer of the *classic* country honky tonk song, which is to say that he has always had a very precise, lonely, realistic understanding of the hard ways of this vale of tears in which we all live and suffer from time to time. This is the juke box Willie. Historically, this music came out of, more or less, his whole career up to today (which seems somewhat more optimistic when you consider the conclusions of the *Red Headed Stranger* album). It's the kind of stuff—like "Hello Walls," "Ain't It Funny (How Time Drifts Away)," "Pretty Papers," "Touch Me" and all those other perfectly morbid songs—that really say it to you when you're down and getting kicked. Willie wrote most of it in Nashville when he was a highly-reputed songwriter trying to be a singing star, simultaneously going through the usual business of divorce, marriage, divorce, marriage and consequent craziness (or is that vice versa?) and running with the likes of Faron Young, Roger Miller, Mel Tillis and other distinguished crazy people.

A segment of my Willie Nelson interview:

Willie (laughing): "I think a lot of people got to thinking that everybody had to do the same thing Hank Williams did, even die that way if necessary. And that got out of hand. I always used to think George Jones got drunk because Hank Williams did, like he really thought that was what he was supposed to do."

Me: "You ever do that?"

Willie: "'Course I did. That's the reason I know it's done."

Me: "You still do it?"

Willie: "I still get drunk, but I'm not really mimicking anybody now. I have my own drunken style."

Thesc days, see, Willie won't talk about the personal agonies of those Nashville years without humor, but it's all there in the songs which made him one of Nashville's most sought-after songwriters, and it came to a head during the year—his last year in Nashville—that gave rise to his *Phases And Stages* album. That year was a turning point, and it is chronicled in *Phases And Stages*. The album is an excruciatingly universal account of the way one man and one woman deal with their divorce ("That was the year I had four or five cars totalled out and the house burned down," says Willie), but it ends with a *very* significant song called "Pick Up The Tempo." It goes like so:

People are sayin' that time will take care of people like me
And that I'm livin' too fast, and they say I can't last for much longer.

But little they see that their thoughts of me is my savior.
And little they know that the beat ought to go just a little faster.
So pick up the tempo just a little, and take it on home . . .

For a man hitting the crucial age of forty, those are important lines. They speak of an affirmation of life and a determination to triumph over its emotional problems, and they represent Willie's decision to leave Nashville, move back home to Texas, and finally realize his potential—which is, in fact, exactly what he did. "I knew I only had a few years left to do what I was going to do, and I had to make a move," says Willie. "I wasn't going down there to quit. I was going down there with a purpose." The purpose, quite simply, was first to make himself a national recording star, and then to use that power base to make damn sure that people like him could be free to make their own music their own way without having to starve in the process.

Remember, Willie has a history in this department. It was he who first chaperoned Charley Pride into the country music concert scene, bringing him on stage in Louisiana—actually kissing him right there in the spotlights—and risking God only knows what kind of backlash in the process. The risk, once taken, paid off: Charley was accepted because Willie was behind him. Similarly, Willie used his high prestige and general likeability in country music artist circles to ease Leon Russell into the Nashville scene by surrounding him with Ernest Tubb, Roy Acuff, Jeanne Pruett and a whole galaxy of main-line performers when he was cutting the sequel to his "Hank Wilson" album. Willie can get away with heresy because more than any other artist occupying the often-queasy ground between country and something else, his country credentials are in order and—more to the point—he has never betrayed his roots.

So Willie arrived in Austin (where he was already a star), formed his present band around himself and his old compadre drummer Paul English (of "Me And Paul" fame), began booking his own dates and managing himself, set up that first media-shocking Picnic at Dripping Springs, connected with the local power elite in the person of Darrell Royal (coach of The University of Texas football team and a *very* influential citizen), and quickly assumed the role of main Godfather in the

Austin scheme of things. That, incidentally, is some gig: you don't know what a loyal crowd is until you've been to Austin and watched a whole clubful of liberated young things worship the ground good ol' Willie walks on to quite embarrassing excess.

Along the way—just before that first Picnic, in fact—Ritchie Albright of the Waylors suggested that he get in touch with one Neil Reshen, a New York manager and fixit person who at the time was looking to consolidate his country music holdings. Reshen already had Waylon as a client, and Willie followed suit. This action signified the arrival of the necessary teeth for the outlaw alliance Willie had been pondering for years, and it began a classic Beauty and the Beast operation that continues to this day.

An example of the dynamics of that Beauty and the Beast relationship:

Willie on Neil Reshen: "He's probably the most hated and the most effective manager that I know of. He *enjoys* going up to those big corporations and going over their figures. He's so sadistic, he *loves* to do it."

And once again, Willie: "At least you know where you're at with Neil. Nowhere."

And again: "Anyone who can learn to like Neil can like *anyone*. It's a challenge to like Neil."

"Willie, how're you doing on that?"

"I'm coming along, I'm coming along. I can stay around him a little while now."

Although the mere mention of Neil Reshen's name has been known to send secretaries to the bathroom and turn grown executives into violent monsters ("He's another of those guys I don't understand how he's lived so long without somebody really hurting him," says Willie), you have to admit that while Willie and Waylon ("It's like having a mad dog on a leash," says Waylon) may have been able to get out of Nashville's grasp without him, it's only through this man's unspeakably vicious yet effective manner of doing business, that the outlaw bid for independent power in country music has avoided bankruptcy and actually shown a profit.

So, with the active assistance of New York Neil, Willie *has* established the power base he was after. It is now possible for Willie to record with Waylon or Kris or Leon (he's planning a whole Willie/Waylon joint album), and what's more, with the formation of Lone Star Records, he can get people like Jimmy Day, Johnny Darrell, Floyd Tillman, Billy C, Bucky Meadows, his sister Bobbi and other Texas worthies into the recording studio and, since Columbia Records pays for promotion and distribution under a joint Columbia/Lone Star deal, actually get the finished product before the public. Like Willie says, "We're all together, and we have the same idea about what we want to do—which is to do our thing our own way. I'm trying to get these guys to do for themselves what they've been bitching about people not doing for them."

Willie's long affair with the business of honky tonk music represents one considerable side of his character which may be traceable to the fact that he and his sister Bobbi ("It's always been me and her") were raised without parents. Mr. and Mrs. Nelson divorced when Willie was a baby and Bobbi was three, and so for the first six years of his life Willie was with his grandparents. For the next ten years, he was raised by his grandmother alone, grandfather having passed away. That of course is a vast oversimplification, but the roots of his two divorces and highly creative loneliness must lie buried somewhere in there, just as the roots of his present, almost uncanny serenity must be located in the emotional steps he took to overcome his personal problems. Whatever, it is an absolute fact that the present-day Willie Nelson is most definitely *not* an individual still in conflict with himself.

In a sense, Willie Nelson now is in some sort of still-perceptive, still-creative cruise-gear, moving through a world of incredibly high pressure with almost perfect equilibrium. You can hear this feeling on the *Red Headed Stranger* album (a concept suggested and assisted by his wife Connie, with whom he does in fact seem quite happy) and you can see it when, dead center in the eye of one of this nation's strangest cultural hurricanes, he drifts through the absolute mayhem of his Picnic and somehow manages to be a rock-like source of calm and competence for (literally) thousands of the most outrageously *un*calm, incompetent hustlers, freaks and assorted weirdos ever assembled under one patch of Texas sky. It also shows when, in the middle of yet another night of pushing his ragged band through a set of half-tragic, half-boogie music and watching with a smile as his audience stumbles and whoops its way towards unconsciousness, it comes down to just him and his Spanish-style, gut-string amplified Martin, and for a while the most carefully emotional, beautifully balanced little collection of mood notes in the world go soaring through the rancid air. This is the musical legacy of Django Reinhardt, Grady Martin and other psychological gypsy guitar pickers from whom Willie developed his style; it is also the mark of a man who has *really* seen it all and can still look it straight in the eye.

Atlanta, Georgia: Willie is on a First Class trip. Laid out in the back of the limousine behind his big spade shades, he is relaxing into the ways of being a star with records on the charts. There'll be no more no-money dives to play, and for a while there won't even be any songwriting unless the fancy takes him. Willie explains that he's not one of those people who get headaches when they're not writing, and since his next two albums—a Gospel album and an album of Lefty Frizzel songs—are already in the can, all he really *has* to do is keep on showing up for Willie Nelson concerts.

There are also some interesting projects in wind, and they might even get done. There's the issue of a *Red Headed Stranger* movie, for instance ("If I had the money and any idea about how to do it, I'd be somewhere doin' it right now"), and the almost equally interesting notion of Willie, Ray Price, Roger Miller, Johnny Paycheck and Johnny Bush getting together to do a couple of original Cherokee Cowboy dates.

Tonight Willie's nose will be back on the grindstone as once again he takes the stage with his gypsies and plays for the sticky young drunks and dopers of Atlanta. Tonight, once again, he'll be up there doing "Will The Circle Be Unbroken?" and "Eileen Goodnight" with whoever wants to join in (this time it's Tracy Nelson and Linda Ronstadt and Mylon LeFevre), and tonight there'll be another endless hillbilly amnesia session up in the hotel room. Tomorrow there'll be another bloody mary morning when Paul, bless him, has paid the bills and checked us all out and onto the road again. But now, just for a while, Willie is thinking about his Gospel album and remembering that he was asked to quit teaching in Sunday school when they found out that Little Willie played the local Texas beer joints at night.

"Were you a good preacher, Willie?" I ask.

"Yes," he says, "I really was." For a moment, a kind of cold feeling has come into his voice. The only time I've heard it before was when I asked him to change his Razorback Chilli Team t-shirt for the magazine's cover photograph session, and, while doing it for me, he *did* let me know that he wasn't very pleased at what he figured was an attempt to soften his image for public consumption. He didn't really say anything about it, but he was angry, and for the first time I got a measure of how much he must have hated those Nashville executives who used to control his career and keep him where they thought he belonged.

This time, however, the anger is only a memory, and it passes quickly. But I'm wondering just how far he's had to come to cancel the past, and so I ask a serious question.

"Willie, are you a religious man?" I ask.

"Yes," he says. "Probably more than I ever was. Y'know?"

Somehow, when you really get serious about Willie Nelson, the answer is not at all surprising.

THE MYSTIC WILLIE NELSON

Nelson Allen | June 1977 | *Country Music*

Most prominent in the second of Nelson Allen's three interviews with Willie reprinted here is Willie's expression of loyalty to his musical peers. His ego does not necessitate sole credit or vainglorious music/film awards to bolster his public image. All he personifies is predicated on the authenticity of his music. –Ed.

I arrive at Willie's gate, considerably altered since I'd seen it last—a huge stone fence topped with barbed wire graced the front with some kind of electronic gate and voice box out front. I press the button marked *press* and get some guy on the other end, and resisting an urge to order a Moby Jack, inquire after Willie. "Willie's sleeping," the voice says. "Well, he told me to come out today," I say. "Just a minute," the voice says. That, I thought, is probably the lowest job in the country music business—answering Willie's box. Then Connie, Willie's wife who looks like a country singing star herself, suggests over the box that I try and get back in touch with Willie later. "He's sleeping," she says. "He was out all night long last night and didn't get home 'till seven this morning."

I know that, since he was out with me, but it's a few days later before we get together again. This time Willie and family are ensconced in the Ramada Inn while remodeling is done at the ranch. (I'd run into a man who operates a landscaping business a few days before and he told me Willie had called him up and said he wanted some landscaping. "What exactly do you want planted?" he'd asked Willie. "I don't care," Willie replied, "just put some stuff out there.") It's two o'clock but getting somewhat familiar with Willie's schedule I first go to the bar and call the room. "Willie's taking a nap," Connie says, "Could you come back around four?"

At four I knock on the door and am met by Willie himself and led into a large living room suite. Willie has on a fresh pair of overalls, a t-shirt, tennis shoes, black shades, and his hair is tied back still wet from a shower. "Sorry you had to wait," Willie says shaking hands, and I notice as always the one incongruous element to his otherwise laid-back demeanor—the horseshoe diamond ring on his right hand pinkie. Horseshoe diamond rings are the sole sign of achievement for successful car salesmen and all male country and western stars.

Except for a coiled and stuffed rattlesnake sitting atop the refrigerator, there is nothing in the place that doesn't belong to the Ramada Inn. Willie has a couple of phone calls to take care of before we talk. They have to do with his recent subpoena to appear before a Dallas court inquiring into illegal drugs (not a charge or accusation by any means), and Willie talks to lawyers and whoever else openly and totally unconcerned whether I overhear the conversations or not. Connie informs him that he's due to appear in San Antonio that night for an honorary award from a group of attorneys. "I don't want to go," he says but adds, "but tell 'em something good . . . like . . . like I don't want to." Willie turns to me waiting for the questions, waiting to give me some "different answers." I had told him once that "the questions are always the same." "The answers are always different," he'd said.

We had planned to visit a few places like the pool hall run by Willie's folks and the local golf course, but with the recent success it's been a while since Willie's had the time to really hang around Austin much—pitching washers behind Bully's, an east Austin bar, or playing golf with Darrell Royal, or just getting drunk with various Texas characters he's met through the years. Since the CMA Awards he's only been in town six days and more and more time is spent on the road. He purchased Porter Wagoner's bus, and it's been traveling from Atlanta to Jackson Hole to San Francisco and back again. Not long ago in Fort Worth he collapsed on stage. But no one has ever left a Willie Nelson performance disappointed, which is one of the reasons Willie scored so well when he first came to Austin. It was obvious from the beginning that Willie came to play. Lately he's been saying that he expects his career to peak soon as all careers do. He still gets nervous—the "only time" is right before he first climbs the stage. I asked him if it was true that he wasn't writing the sad country songs anymore because things were going good. "Yeah, to a certain point it is," Willie said, "I don't write the real sad tear-jerking songs that I used to write because I'm not real sad anymore."

ALLEN: *What happened to the movie you were going to do?*

NELSON: Well, originally this was Ty Hardin's idea. He went through three or four scripts before he found one that he really wanted to do and that he thought was the one that we ought to do. I told him I'd do it with him; I didn't know anything about the movie but I was just going to get into it to try and learn, because I want to do the **Red-Headed Stranger** (as a movie). I wanted to do that, so I was going to learn about movies and this was going to be my education. But then Ty bailed out on it, he thought the script wasn't strong enough. And then the guy that wrote the script was down there trying to get the show on the road . . . talking about maybe hiring another actor to play opposite me. It just got to be too big a hassle, too many things going wrong so I bailed out myself.

ALLEN: *Have you thought about how you would go about making the **Red-Headed Stranger** into a movie?*

NELSON: How I would make the film? Well, Jay Milner and a couple more people are writing the script and I've been getting copies of it for awhile and it looks pretty good.

ALLEN: *That album always seemed like a movie to me anyway.*

NELSON: Yeah, that's going to be the problem. I can imagine it being such a great movie, but whether or not we can get that on the screen is another question. It might not come out the way I think it'll come out.

ALLEN: *If you can get the right director . . .*

NELSON: Yeah, we need to get somebody that really knows what they're doing. If we aren't careful it could be like a bad fiddle player—if it ain't good it's terrible.

ALLEN: *You're on the road more now. How is life on the road?*

NELSON: Well, I enjoy it. I was on the road a lot before I moved back to Texas and I slowed down a lot when I first moved back to Texas, but before that for about 12 or 15 years in a row I went pretty heavy. I started out with Ray Price and played bass with him, and he worked his ass off all the time. We went all the way up into Canada with him and then flew over to Alaska. We did a 90-day tour one time of one-nighters. I'm used to living on the road and Holiday Inns are just uh . . . I feel more at home in a Holiday Inn than I really do at home because the home that I have now I haven't been in as much as I've been in Holiday Inns. They all look the same and you walk in one room and you say, yeah here we are again.

ALLEN: *Everything's right where you left it.*

NELSON: Right.

ALLEN: *Have there been any disappointments along with all the success you had recently?*

NELSON: No.

ALLEN: *I guess the disappointments were when you couldn't get them to promote your records?*

NELSON: Right.

ALLEN: *You were quoted recently as saying your career was about to peak. Did you say that?*

NELSON: Did I say that? It could be, it could be about to peak, but I don't feel like it is and I don't think that until I feel like it is that it is. But in some people's minds it may have already started a downward trend, it may be crashing.

ALLEN: *After you and Waylon won the CMA Awards . . .*

NELSON: No, Waylon and I are not going to be involved in any of the awards this year. Most of the awards that one of us is in, the other is in, and I don't want that and he doesn't either, so we're just both taking our names out of the pot. Because we don't want to be in competition with each other—we never have been—especially on national television. Just to sit there and look dumb while Waylon wins or I win, either way it's not right.

ALLEN: *With all your success, has it made it easier on people coming up, has it brought about any changes in the industry?*

NELSON: They tell me that it has. I don't know. I really don't know because the people in Nashville, most of them are still there. Now whether anybody who moves into town now has a better chance than he would have a year ago or five years ago, I don't know. I think . . . that his appearance is not going to hurt him as much as it would have a year or five years ago. People who walked into Nashville with long hair a few years ago, uh, I started to say they couldn't get arrested but actually that's the first thing they could get was arrested.

ALLEN: *Why all the new trappings, the voice box, etc., at the gate to your place? Why did that become necessary? Just too many unannounced visitors?*

NELSON: Yeah, really. And I only get two or three days off at a time, and when I do, I like to have complete isolation and privacy in order to rest—sleep for 72 hours or something.

ALLEN: *Is it becoming more difficult to just hang out around Austin like you did a couple of years ago?*

NELSON: Yeah, it is. It's hard to go anywhere and really just sit down and enjoy the evening.

ALLEN: *That's too bad in a way.*

NELSON: In a way it is but I know it's not going to last forever. Pretty soon I'll be able to go drink a beer.

ALLEN: *Have you given any thought to building your own club to hang out in?*

NELSON: No, I did that and wound up being . . . like I had an office to hang out in and everyone else hung out there, too. I opened up a pool hall so I'd have a place to go play pool and dominoes and I can't go over there.

ALLEN: *Why did you do that gospel album when you did?*

NELSON: I've been trying to get that album out for a long time. They kept putting me off from label to label. RCA wouldn't let me do one. They thought I needed to be a more established country artist before I could do a gospel album. I've done 32 albums and only one gospel album. I'd like to do several more and I probably will over the years. But this is just something I wanted to do and they wouldn't let me. They said you can't do that and I said yes I can. Another one of these things. But they didn't think gospel songs were commercial themselves and I knew they were because I knew that we were singing every night *Will The Circle Be Unbroken* and *Amazing Grace* and everybody would sing along. I knew that they would sell.

ALLEN: *There's a rumor that you disappeared for a period of time in the late 60's. Is that true?*

NELSON: I do that occasionally (laughing), I'm planning on disappearing in the next few minutes. How long a time did they say I disappeared for?

ALLEN: *About six months.*

NELSON: That's probably true. I haven't got to do that lately, but I'm glad you brought that up. It's a good idea. I can think about that for awhile.

ALLEN: *You don't want to say where you disappeared to?*

NELSON: Oh, no. I don't remember where I was. I really don't know where I went.

ALLEN: *Have you ever read or studied much of Edgar Cayce?*

NELSON: Yeah, I love Edgar Cayce. I really do. I think he was a smart man whenever he went to sleep.

ALLEN: *I read **Many Mansions*** [published in 1950, *Many Mansions: The Edgar Cayce Story on Reincarnation* was written by Gina Cerminara —Ed.] *years ago. Did you ever apply any of that to your own life?*

NELSON: Yeah, a lot of that. In fact, I belong to that ARA [Association for Research and Enlightenment —Ed.], that association there in Virginia Beach and they sent me all the literature and the books and everything that Edgar Cayce had . . . Well, not everything, I guess there's 15,000 readings that he had all together and they're all in the library there in Virginia Beach, and anybody that wants to see them can go over there and read them. He had so much to say about so many things that you can pretty well make a whole life philosophy out of what the man said. He went into reincarnation, he went into earthquakes, he went into pyramids, he went into the whole thing.

ALLEN: *Has it led you to fashion your own beliefs in a certain way?*

NELSON: Probably in a lot of ways it has. Between Edgar Cayce and a lot of the mystery schools that I've gotten interested in over the years like the Rosicrucians. There's a lot of interesting things there, food for thought. A lot of it makes sense. It's all based on reincarnation and karma and that's logical to me.

ALLEN: *Do you believe in reincarnation?*

NELSON: Yeah. It's the only thing that makes sense.

ALLEN: *Have you ever given any thought to who or what you might have been in a previous life?*

NELSON: No, I've thought about it, but I've never really cared, never cared enough to go ask someone who's supposed to be an expert on that kind of stuff. I never really cared to go back into past lives. I think people can . . . if a guy really wanted to be a singer and couldn't, but if he just kept trying and trying believe that if he didn't make it this lifetime he might make it the next lifetime.

ALLEN: *It's kind of encouraging.*

NELSON: It's a positive way to look at life. Everything moves in one direction, you either go up or back, you're either progressing or regressing, one of the two; you never stay in one place. I don't believe that everything ends pow and it's all over. That just doesn't make sense. You can't destroy matter, if you stop it here, it comes to life over here. You can't destroy energy.

ALLEN: *Do you have an interest in yoga, kung fu, martial arts?*

NELSON: Yeah.

ALLEN: *Is that something you were interested in or something you're still into?*

NELSON: I never have really quit. I still do yoga exercises practically every day. I don't do kung fu much, but I still practice a lot of stuff that I used to do.

ALLEN: *Where did you train for it?*

NELSON: In Nashville. There's a school there in Nashville. We used to go out to colleges and high schools there and put on exhibitions and try to raise interest . . . go out and break a few boards.

ALLEN: *Do they have belts like in karate and judo?*

NELSON: No, in kung fu you're either a master or a student. No in-betweens. I'm still a student.

ALLEN: *What is the difference between kung fu and karate?*

NELSON: I can't speak about karate because I don't really . . . but kung fu is probably 75 percent mental and 25 percent physical. It's a lot of mind over matter more than brute strength. And karate I think is more physical, building up callouses on your hands, and we didn't do that in kung fu. We didn't go into that heavy a physical thing. It's just concentration and believing that you can do it.

ALLEN: *Are the picnics over for good?*

NELSON: As far as I'm concerned right now they are. There are too many problems involved to try and put 'em on.

ALLEN: *There seemed to be both good and bad things come out of them. What did you like about them?*

NELSON: Well, it was good for me first of all. A lot of people know the name Willie Nelson that didn't know it then. That was one of the reasons that I put them on—to draw attention to myself. It was a big hype for Willie is what it was. But I think the shows were good. I know we had some problems with crowds, not the audience. I think we had more problems with the backstage people than we did the audience. The people backstage were harder to please. If they'd paid and walked in the front they would have had a lot better time. Everybody wants backstage and that's really not where it's going on. It's out front where the show is.

ALLEN: *It seems like you've been catching a lot of crap in your home state lately. Are you getting tired of all that?*

NELSON: Aw, yeah, I'm tired of it. A lot of that I don't even read. I look at the title and if it doesn't look too good I'll just pass on over that and look for some good news.

ALLEN: *You did read the Texas Monthly story?*

NELSON: Yes, I read that. Jan Reid's story about the death of redneck rock. ["The Coming of Redneck Hip" published in the November 1973 issue of *Texas Monthly*. —Ed.]

ALLEN: *All he did was talk about a term he'd invented anyway.*

NELSON: That's right.

ALLEN: *I don't know what he'll have to write about next time.*

NELSON: The reincarnation of redneck rock.

ALLEN: *That story was offensive. It was so contrived.*

NELSON: It was, it really was. He pissed me off right at first when he started calling me Cocaine Willie. Now he could have called me anything else but, uh, I just don't like cocaine and never have. In Fort Worth I was never known as Cocaine Willie.

ALLEN: *It kind of has a nice ring to it.*

NELSON: Oh, it sounded ok. It wasn't anything I wanted to sue him for but then when all that bullshit came up in Dallas those words came back to haunt me. They brought it up, well they called you Cocaine Willie so you're probably involved in some of that.

ALLEN: *I've heard that a lot of that came about because Gregg Allman released a lot of names when he was having trouble in Georgia.*

NELSON: I understand that happened but I don't think that my name would have been involved in anything that he would have turned in. The situation that I was in . . . there was a friend of mine that they were trying to get and they knew that I knew him and that I'd known him a long time and they knew we were good friends. So they just figured that I had to be involved in business with him.

ALLEN: *A lot of people wrongly think that there were dope charges against you when you appeared before the grand jury even though that wasn't the case.*

NELSON: Well, that was what I was talking about. It was just one of those guilt by association things. I'd known (this guy) for years and years and years when he was in the automobile business. He and I played poker together. He's still a good friend. I don't know what he did other than sell cars and don't want to know. It's none of my business. I bought cars and trucks from him and have records to prove it and that's the only business that I ever had with (him) . . . If they wanted to bust me on marijuana they could have done that years ago because everyone knows that I smoke a joint every now and then. Everybody also knows that I ain't got any for sale. I smoke it all. But that was a bad thing really because they were trying to get (this guy) and they just knew that I was involved with it. And there may have been some people who said I was, too, because a lot of people get arrested for one charge or another and they become a snitch in order to get better treatment. They'll say anything about anybody if it'll keep 'em from getting a long sentence.

ALLEN: *Do you think they called you up there because of who you are?*

NELSON: I think they probably did it to cause some publicity. Ray Price also, they mentioned his name and Ray Price is no more involved in dope dealing than I am or you are. He picks and sings. He makes a lot of money doing that. He makes $10,000 a night, so he's not gonna go out and mess up the whole thing over something stupid like that. He's got everything in the world going for him and there would be no reason to do a thing like that. Anybody with any intelligence at all should be able to see that. If they'd had any narcs or snitches around me, and I'm sure they have had, all they found out was just exactly the truth because I haven't got a thing to hide.

ALLEN: *Did you sever your connections with the nightclub Whiskey River over all that?*

NELSON: Well, that probably had something to do with it but I mainly just wanted to get out of the nightclub business. It's just a hassle. But that's a perfect name for a joint though. When I was thinking about really going into the nightclub business I was going to do a chain of clubs, the nightlife, and franchise them and all that.

ALLEN: *Tompall and Waylon are suing each other. Are you mad at anybody or is anyone mad at you?*

NELSON: No. I'm just laughing at both of 'em.

ALLEN: *Do you plan on building a recording studio now?*

NELSON: No, there's enough good studios around without me building one. If I put one up I'd have to use it all the time and I like to move around and use different studios.

THE NASHVILLE PEOPLE

Stacy Harris | June 1977 | *Countryside*

On June 10, 1977, Willie Nelson performed at the Oakland 1st Annual Country Western Jamboree, a concert squeezed in between two shows in Albuquerque, New Mexico, and Smithfield, Texas. Willie's tour itinerary was hectic, as he was able to fill in much bigger crowds since his appeal to the masses had broadened. On the concert stage, Willie successfully established himself as a multi-genre artist pouring out a long, impressive set of covers and his own song compositions. –Ed.

Despite all of the talk about "outlaw music," one of the genre's purveyors, Willie Nelson, doesn't necessarily see himself as being locked into an outlaw's bag. "I don't know what an 'outlaw's bag" is," Willie maintains, adding, "I didn't know I was an outlaw 'til I saw it in print. I don't know if it was really a promotional gimmick, or whether it was the media that first called us (Waylon, Willie, and Tompall Glaser) outlaws."

Still, be it myth or fact, Willie Nelson remains an outlaw, especially in the eyes of those who fixate on his sometimes shoulder length hair, cowboy hat, dress down clothes and tennis shoes. Then too, Nelson recalls, "I used to drink a lot and party a lot and talk a lot. I'm still doing it, but it doesn't cause as much reaction in Texas as it did in Nashville . . . Down there [Texas], people are used to me. I was born and raised down there, so I didn't upset anybody down there—we're talking about the '60s."

Willie's rebellious spirit, manner, and attitude may have been shared, but it was never affected by his fellow country artists. "It just seemed like it wasn't the thing to do in country music," says Willie. "I mean you *did* it, but you didn't get in the papers for it if you did it. You could maybe do it back stage and it'd be all right, but you didn't do it on stage. So that's the difference now, I think. We're doing things on stage now that we used to do back stage. People like to see it on stage better than they did backstage."

Older album covers show a young, clean shaven, short haired Willie Nelson. The pleasant looking young man from Abbott, TX was given, by his own admission, a fair hearing during those early days. "I've had doors slammed in my face every place else *but* in Nashville. I was accepted as a songwriter almost immediately in Nashville, and had a lot of success with 'Hello Walls' and 'Funny How Time Slips Away' and others, but I wasn't really that accepted as a singer. I was more or less known as a songwriter.

"In fact, I'm not that good a singer." Willie reasons that, "Some people sing and some people are stylists—and the people who can't sing had better have a style. So I don't consider myself that great a singer. I was glad I was being accepted as a songwriter."

Nelson feels his eventual acceptance as both a lyricist and a vocalist as "just a gradual thing that had to happen. I knew it would happen if I stayed with it long enough and just didn't run off and quit. I felt that eventually things would happen, because things were falling into place slowly, but the singing aspect just happened to be the last thing that fell into place as far as selling records."

Willie maintains that what he is doing musically these days is not a whole lot different from what he was doing during the lean days. More accurately, Nelson has changed with the times. Of his music, Willie says, "I don't care what they call it as long as they buy it, like it, and play it. I haven't changed . . . I don't like labels. The definition of music my grandmother taught me is 'anything that's pleasing to the ear.'"

Willie Nelson sees no plans to live and/or exclusively record in Nashville in his future. Sounding every bit the outlaw some would make him, the diminutive Texan adds, "I never stay anywhere. I can't afford to."

ON PICNICS AND THINGS

Stacy Harris | July 1978 | *Country Song Roundup*

The following article covers a two-year period in which Willie Nelson's annual 4th of July Picnic was essentially canceled, replaced by concerts at more easily controlled venues outside of Texas: the Tulsa Fairgrounds in 1977 and Arrowhead Stadium in Kansas City in 1978. The following year the event would return to Texas and the original outdoor format, taking place outside Austin at the Pedernales Country Club, which Nelson himself had recently purchased. Meanwhile, on July 4, 1978, Willie appeared on the cover of *Rolling Stone* magazine donning an Uncle Sam top hat, a sign that Willie Nelson had at last crossed over to become adored by the masses as America's counterculture.—Ed.

Willie Nelson, returning to Nashville for a TV taping, nursed a cold one backstage at the Opry House while ruminating about the prima donnas of the music business, promoters, and his cosmic cowboy cohorts.

"I haven't really seen one of my contracts lately," Willie notes, "but I know that I don't have any ridiculous riders on there. In the first place, I didn't know anything about that kind of backstage service—about having drinks and food and catering—when I was on the road playing out of Nashville before. We didn't have anything like that. It was unheard of for promoters to even think of anything like that. In fact, promoters today, in some of the shows that I've been around, *still* don't do that. I mean, they still promote the same old way. They don't furnish anything.

"Of course, it's nice if they have a catering service there, and some promoters just naturally do that now. It's just something that they do.

And if it's there I'm glad to see it, and I'm sure all the band is, but I don't demand anything."

Promoters who have only a surface familiarity with Willie Nelson (i.e. those who wouldn't know him from Waylon Jennings or Jerry Jeff Walker) and buyers who know nothing of Nelson's pre-Austin "straight(er)" days in Nashville may be a mite leery, considering the Texan's outlaw image. "Of course, from what they've read they have no idea what I do, because the outlaw thing is like you say, something that if they want to comment on it, I think it's funny. I laugh along with it. To me, it's a big joke.

"I'm just *not* an outlaw. There may be one or two things I do illegally. I speed occasionally. I go past 55 miles per hour, but not intentionally. I mean, I don't go around breaking laws all the time. I pay my taxes. I pay my rent. I do all that. I make car payments. So how they figure I'm an outlaw, I don't know. It must look good in print. It may sell some magazines. I don't really care. If they want to call me that, I'll go along with it."

Nelson's return to Music City was creating a stir at the time of our conversation, if only because he looked like a refugee from boot camp. "Well," Willie deadpanned, "I guess if they keep writing, I'll keep shaving now and then. It's not often that you can cut your hair and make the papers. No, it's just that it was time, I felt like, to cut my hair and shave. Then I got to thinking. Well, maybe they're listening to my hair instead of me, so it'll give me a chance to see.

"I've always had long hair," Willie points out," but originally when the long hair thing got to be an issue, I probably let mine grow a little longer than I normally would, because it *was* an issue and I knew it was a silly issue. So I was trying, maybe, to show everybody how silly it was. So I'd just see how long I'd let my hair grow, and I may do it again, but I like it pretty well any more. But there's no more significance in me growing my hair and cutting it off than anybody else doing it. I just cut it off when I feel like it's time to cut off your hair."

With a backward glance toward the success of RCA's rerelease of "I'm A Memory," a tune which Willie recorded a few years back, Nelson is anxious to rerecord some of his earlier compositions; ones which perhaps went unrecognized or were at least not fully appreciated in their time. "Of course," Nelson cautions, "there's a certain time limit, because of some of the different record labels, in order to do some of the older songs. If you do a song with a company, I think it's probably normal for you to wait five years before you can do the song again. In fact, it's in the contract that you have to wait, unless you get permission to do it.

"I'm with Lonestar–Columbia, which is a subsidiary of Columbia Records. I've been with them a while now, but all of the old songs were originally done on Liberty and RCA. I have to wait a little while before I'm able to do those old songs again, but I plan to do them."

Indeed, it seems that over the years Willie has changed record labels with the frequency that most people change socks. Nelson opines the traditional indictment of artists toward record labels when he indicates that "if I'd been having hit records, I never would have been unhappy with any of 'em. I'd have still been with the first label I'd signed with (Liberty) if I'd had hit records, but when you don't have hit records, I think you're *supposed* to be unhappy, and it's got to be someone's fault, either your own or the record company's. It's got to be one of the two. So I still wasn't sure whose fault it was for a long time, and I still don't know for sure, but I think by me moving out and at least jumping up and stirring around and doing *something*, I at least created a little energy that grew. And maybe started doing something different from what I was doing before."

With all the clout an artist of his stature can exercise, Willie admits he has the freedom to do "exactly what I want to do. I record the songs I want to record. I do them the way I want to record them. I don't necessarily record them any better today than I did back then; I just think that when you're having hit records, everything's OK and you love everybody, and when you're not, it's just not. And you gotta blame somebody, and these record companies are the first thing to blame, and whether they're at fault all the time is debatable, of course.

"If they believe in you and you have talent," Nelson explains, "then any record company in the world can sell that record, because it just takes salesmen, and you sell records like you sell any other product. You get a good salesman to go out and promote it and sell it, and that takes money. And if they believe in you enough to spend money, well then, they will do a lot more for you. If they don't have any money invested in you, well then, they will not have to do as much for you in order to get the returns, because there are no expenses.

"So if you come in and do a session, and you do one where they only spend two or three thousand dollars, they don't have to sell too many records to get their two or three thousand back. But if they spend $100,000 on an artist to buy him like they do a football player, well then, they have to do a big promotional job on this artist in order to get their investment back. At the same time, they make a start out of the guy—if he's good. If he's not good, they've blown $100,000."

The summer of 1977 has come and gone without Willie Nelson's traditional 4th of July picnic. Looking toward July 1978, Willie maintains that the picnics have been scuttled indefinitely. "I'll have to wait and see," Willie says with regard to future picnics. "I'm not planning on doing one again because of all the problems involved. It's too big of a hassle to go outside and do a show, because you lose a lot of control, plus you lose a lot of support from the local folks who don't want 100,000 people in their back yards."

While, on the surface, it seems that the picnic's problems could be alleviated with a change of locale, Willie Nelson insists that "It's hard to get a location. That's the thing. First of all, because there's always some do-gooder in town who wants to bitch about something. And as soon as something like this comes along, that gives him a perfect right—in his own mind—justifies him to speak out against it whether he knows what he's talking about or not. And these people can stop shows from being put on."

Nelson attributes the word-of-mouth success of his picnics with their demise, conceding that "You always lose a little bit more control each time you put one of 'em on, because they're a little bit larger plus you've got experienced picnickers now. They've been going every year for four years and they know how to do it. And they come and they bring their awnings and they camp out. And they get in free, because they know they didn't have to pay last year. So they come expecting to get in free.

"And you lose a lot of money," Willie continues, citing his 1976 fiasco. "I don't know that I'm going to tell you how much I lost, but I lost a lot of money . . . because I was unable collect the money when the people came. They came in so many big numbers, and also we didn't have adequate help out there to collect money on an outside festival. It just can't work with all the things that are wrong with it now. Maybe one day you can put a festival together, but there's going to have to be an enclosure where you can control the money, so you at least get your expenses back somewhere, and it's going to have to be sanctioned by the local offi— people; not the authorities, because you can buy *them*, you know, but the people themselves . . ."

Reconsidering, and deciding to talk more candidly about the 1976 picnic, Willie admits, "I lost $200,000. That's the cash money that I had into it. Really. I'm still playing dates working off the last picnic, and I still have people suing me. One guy caught on fire laying in his own bed—the paper I was served with said 'on or about July 3,' which he wasn't supposed to be there till the 4th anyway—and it doesn't cost that much to sue. I think it only costs something like six dollars to sue somebody, but it costs the person being sued hundreds of dollars to hire a lawyer and fight the case. So until they get all that worked out, I think I'll pass on the picnic."

Another catastrophic result of Willie's '76 picnic, underscoring his gun-shy stance toward future ventures, is the fact that "there was a kid that drowned there a day before the picnic started, also. Lots of things happen down there when people come early. They'll come two or three days in advance, and camp out and expect all kind of protection and the regular deal. But really, the show don't start till the day of the thing. But they're there early, and they get problems, and then they blame whoever's putting it on—or at least they *can*—and 99 percent of 'em *don't*.

Willie stresses that "99 percent come, and if there'd be somebody there for 'em to pay their money to, they give it to 'em and go in. If there's not, they walk in. I don't blame 'em. I'd do the same thing. Most of the people are all right. There's just one or two that cause a problem—and too big a problem."

Perhaps the largest single factor that convinced Willie Nelson to drop his plans for any future picnics was the bad rap the '76 gig got from disgruntled press people. In a tone of voice suggesting a mixture of muted anger and incredulity, Willie wonders, "How can you give press accommodations out there in the middle of a pasture anyway, when there's 100,000 people coming? I know there were a lot of things promised that shouldn't have been promised because there's just no way. There's no way. You have far more people backstage who expect special treatment than you can handle. If everyone would just come and not expect any special treatment, and just sit out front and watch the show and then let the people who are backstage put on the show, then I think it would be a lot better.

"If the press people were promised things and didn't get them," adds Nelson, "then I apologize for whoever's action that was, but you know how these things get out of hand. But anyone who's ever been to a picnic or an outside festival before should know it's going to be hot. It's going to be uncomfortable, and air-conditioned buildings—you're going to sweat in those. So there's really no way to give anybody protection or comfort during a picnic."

Surveying the aftermath, Nelson stresses that "the last thing in the world that I wanted to do was upset the press, because we needed the press. The whole point of putting it on was to get the press behind it and to make a big deal out of it. I don't know whether we started not living up to what we were promising the press, or if the press asked for something, maybe, that was impossible to give. One of the two happened, and a couple of the people down there were unhappy because they thought they had been mistreated. A lot of people wanted on stage. There's a rule that if you don't pick, you don't go on stage. I don't care who you are . . ."

Appropriately enough then, the death knell seems to have been sounded for the Dripping Springs, Texas, festivities which, one might say, are no picnic. Willie, looking relaxed in his Sir Thomas Lipton–like captain's hat, jeans, Emmy Lou Harris warmup jacket, and tennis shoes, puts it better when he says of the erstwhile annual bashes: "I'm enjoying not doing it." But it is Bee Spears who says it best, noting "I am, too—and I'm just the bass player.'"

A VOICE CRYING OUT OF THE COUNTRY . . .

Cliff Radel | April 19, 1979 | *Cincinnati Enquirer*

Cincinnati Enquirer reporter Cliff Radel most remembers Willie's intense gaze matching his for the duration of their interview. Nelson stays fixated and present, each interview, however significant, serving as an opportunity to evangelize his peculiar brand of down-home country gospel. –Ed.

Friday the thirteenth was running true to form. Everything was wrong. The hex was on. Bad luck was the only luck in town.

It had been that way all week. The car broke down. It rained. A mirror cracked. It rained. A check bounced. It rained. A cake fell. It rained . . . and rained . . and rained.

FOLKS BEGAN to wonder how long they could tread water. A neighbor saw an architect about an ark.

The phone rang night and day. The callers were either wrong numbers or salesmen pushing essential items like aluminum siding for dog houses.

The man I wanted to call didn't. It wasn't his fault. He was on vacation. And, as the people at Columbia Records say, when Willie Nelson goes on vacation, he vanishes.

There was an outside chance Nelson would call on Monday. Everything hinged on whether he could be found.

He couldn't be.

Tuesday was a repeat performance of Monday. So was Wednesday. So was Thursday. By Thursday night hope was running on empty. Willie Nelson was nowhere to be found.

A telephone call at 20 minutes past noon the next day changed all that. The man on the other end chased the bad luck with five words:

"Cliff, this is Willie Nelson."

The interview that wasn't was.

Hearing Willie Nelson's voice on the telephone was a shock. I opened my mouth and out came the words of a numb mind. "You're kidding!" I exclaimed.

"Naw. I wouldn't kid about a thing like that," Nelson replied. My shock disappeared and the interview continued.

WILLIE NELSON sings like he starts interviews. He is as straightforward as they come. There is no pomp, no frills, no artifice. He is what he is and nothing more—an honest voice in dishonest times.

That honest voice has quite a following. Every year millions hear Willie Nelson. His tours are cross-country treks. His records sell in the millions. Two Grammys came his way this year. Last year *Newsweek* and *The New York Times* crowned him King of Country Music.

Although a recent Columbia LP, *Stardust*, just went platinum (its million-plus sales far outstrip the competition) Nelson dismissed this King of Country Music business.

"King is a word that has been thrown around a lot," he drawled. "Elvis was a king and there were others. It all depends on who the subjects are. They all have their own king. But that's okay. It's flattering to be called a king, but not any of us is that far above the rest."

Don't be too sure, Willie. Not everyone can write standards like "Crazy," "Night Life" and "Funny How Time Slips Away." Then too, it takes someone special to perform those songs with a holely guitar.

The ravaged instrument Nelson plays on stage ""started out as a Baldwin. I busted it, accidentally, of course. It couldn't be fixed. The company went out of business. So, I had a friend take the guts and put them into the Martin classical guitar I'm playing now. That was about 15 years ago."

"OVER THE years it's gotten kinda battered. The hole is there because classical guitars are not supposed to be played with a pick. Through the years my pick and my fingernails have worn that hole. It looks kinda soulful, but it's just a hole."

Autographs surround the hole. The scrawls of Kris Kristofferson, Rita Coolidge and Roger Miller are most apparent.

Back when the guitar was new and holeless, a session musician told Nelson autographs "make guitars more valuable. So, I signed his and he signed mine. Then we went around gettin' everybody to sign them."

That session musician turned out to be a fair composer in his own right. His name is Leon Russell and he is playing piano on Willie Nelson's current tour, which visits Riverfront Coliseum Friday. Russell is filling in for Nelson's sister, Bobbi, while she records a solo album in Nashville.

The tour is not the only recent opportunity Nelson and Russell have had to work together. They just finished recording *One More For The Road* for Columbia.

"IT'S A double album with 20 songs," Nelson explained. One record is ballads like 'Stormy Weather,' and 'Tenderly.' The other side is uptempo stuff like 'Heartbreak Hotel.'

"We do standards. We got in the studio and started thinkin' about songs we both knew. Whenever we ran across one, we'd cut it."

One More For the Road is a sequel to *Stardust*, a collection of distinguished standards.

The media-proclaimed King of Country Music recorded such decidedly noncountry works as "Stardust" and "Moonlight in Vermont," "because those songs have been favorites of mine since I was five or six. My sister had just started to take music lessons and she bought all the old pop standards. As she'd learn them on piano, I'd sit by her and play them on guitar. The words were right there so I'd sing along.

"Those old pop standards," Nelson continued, "are some of the greatest music ever composed. Just like in the country field with 'Blue Eyes

Crying in the Rain,' there's thousands of them out there, waitin' for somebody to pick up and use. But people overlook them on their search for new material."

Nelson feels the past gets lost in the shuffle "because of money. New songs make more money for modern-day people than old songs. Which is fine, I write new songs, too, but when it comes time to record and you put your whole career on the line it makes better sense to do a song you know is good, especially if you're trying to get somebody to listen who has never heard of you. If you throw a new song and a new artist at them, it's asking too much of the normal ear to hear and appreciate anything that new."

NOT TOO long ago the powers that be in Nashville thought Willie Nelson was too much for the normal ear. He was respected as a songwriter, but scorned as a singer.

Although he wrote and recorded "Night Life" and "Funny How Time Slips Away," "it took a name artist to sell those songs. I couldn't do it. I tried. I put out 30 albums that flopped. I had a new style and new songs. There was no category to put me in. I wasn't country. I wasn't rock. I wasn't blues. No promotion department knew what to do with me."

The excuse he heard was that his voice and repertoire were "too different." Nelson could not quibble with that.

"My phrasing *was* different. By listening to all kinds of music I picked up phrasing by guys like Sinatra, the boogie and blues people and even Glenn Miller."

Nelson's "different" repertoire disregarded the artificial boundaries between pop and country—an idea held in common currency today, but a radical one 15 years ago.

"I'd sing 'Fraulein' in a beer joint and turn right around and do 'Stardust,'" Nelson recalled. "The people in the beer joint didn't mind. But when you tried to get that idea across to the people in Nashville, they swore it couldn't happen. It was beyond their conceivability that an audience would like 'Stardust' *and* 'Fraulein.'

"That's how stupid you can get sittin' behind a desk answerin' a phone all day instead of going out in the field and seeing what the people are doing," Nelson declared. "That's all I was doin'. I wasn't that smart. I wasn't a genius. I was just out there playin' music to the friends and neighbors and I knew what they liked."

The friends and neighbors liked Nelson, but the big boys in Nashville and the record-buying public didn't. He wrote wonderful songs, but it was up to the Patsy Clines and Faron Youngs to make hits out of them.

MAKING A name for others "was a bit hard to swallow," Nelson admitted, but wasn't "too disappointing. I was glad somebody sang 'em. I felt that someday, if the songs got established and I got established as a singer, the whole thing would work out in the end."

It sure looks that way. His perseverance has paid off with platinum albums, gold albums and Grammys. It looks like Willie Nelson was right all along. Even Hollywood thinks so. The movies are knocking on his door and he's letting them in.

Nelson just finished "The Electric Horseman" with Jane Fonda and Robert Redford.

"It's not a singin' part," he quickly pointed out. "It's straight actin'. I play Redford's manager. He has the part of a retired rodeo cowboy who does cornflake commercials. He wears a loud suit, gets on his horse, plugs the suit into the saddle, it lights up and he rides into ballparks at halftime to do commercials. He doesn't like this so he stays drunk most of the time. My job is to make sure he shows up on time."

NELSON'S FILM career does not end with "The Electric Horseman." There's "Sad Songs and Waltzes," "about a country picker who goes on the road and gets into a lot of trouble."

Who has the lead?

Willie Nelson, of course.

After that, Nelson's thematic album, *Red Headed Stranger*, will go to the movies. Then there's another Nelson vehicle, "The Songwriter." And after that Pete Axthelm's Willie Nelson biography will be put on celluloid.

With so much time being spent before the camera, Nelson probably won't have any left for the road.

Wrong.

"I'll always travel around and pick," he vowed. "I'm no movie star. I'm not quittin' anything. I'm just adding movies."

Since his work has received such wide acceptance after so many discouraging years, he could be having the last laugh on those who spurned his early efforts. He could be, but he isn't.

"I haven't got time to laugh," he said.

Willie Nelson was laughing.

WILLIE: THE GYPSY COWBOY GOES HOLLYWOOD

Michael Bane | May 1979 | *Country Music*

The late 1970s were busy for Willie Nelson. Commencing on the last day of 1976, Nelson swept through the American South with celebrated shows at the Austin Opry House, The Houston Summit, the Louisiana Superdome, and the Omni in Atlanta. On December 10, 1977, he appeared on *Saturday Night Live*. He also appeared in the film *The Electric Horseman* starring Robert Redford. On the heels of that was Willie's hope to adapt for film his record album *Red Headed Stranger*. By the end of the decade, Nelson was a prominent figure in the outlaw country scene. He released his album *One for the Road* (with Leon Russell), which reached the number twenty-five spot on the *Billboard* 200. He also released *Sweet Memories*, an album of older songs with a string section. Journalist Michael Bane captures a captivating journey through Willie's multifaceted career and personal life up to this point. –Ed.

It's the time of the preacher when our story begins, and, to be sure, it's been a long time coming. Forget all your country-rock-crossover-MOR clones—while nobody was looking, Willie Nelson sneaked in as the biggest star in country music, and now he's headed off into the sunset to become an international sex symbol, a la Kristofferson.

Right, Willie?

"Well," he says, in that soft Willie Nelson voice, "I don't guess there's any way I can avoid it, is there?"

Hardly. Ever since the Willie Nelson juggernaut spilled out of Texas and took the country by song and storm a few years back, Great Things have always been just around the corner for Willie. But Willie has a way of sliding out from underneath the brightest spotlight, and media folks have a notoriously short attention span. The net result was that, for the last couple of years, Willie's been popping up like a shark's fin on a mirror ocean.

But lately Willie's been taking on new frontiers. He just finished his first movie role with good buddy Robert Redford and Jane Fonda in a film called *The Electric Horseman*, and a second film, tentatively titled *Honeysuckle Rose*, directed by Sydney Pollack, is scheduled to begin filming in Texas around July. [It would ultimately be directed by Jerry Schatzberg, with Pollack producing. —Ed.] And the long-awaited filming of *The Red-Headed Stranger* album is almost ready to get underway—hopefully with Redford in the role as the Stranger.

And in his spare time, Willie operates the Texas Opry House in Austin, Willie Nelson Publishing in Nashville, Lone Star Records, and tours—or tries to tour—250 nights a year.

"Well, I don't think I'm going to make that this year," he adds, almost apologetically. "With all the movies and all, we'll be lucky if we get over 200."

Two hundred nights a year? Three movies ("Well, there's also this documentary about me that we're going to do this year. . . .")?

"Well, we all just love the road," Willie says. "We all enjoy playing music, so it's not really that hard a work. It is hard when you're doing too many nights in a row and you're not getting paid enough. That's hard. I mean, everybody likes to take a week off now and then, but any longer than a week and you start to get restless and want to do it again."

When you add up the performing dates and the movie filmings and the publicity operations and the miscellaneous comings and goings necessary to keep an operation like the Willie Nelson and Family band on the road, that doesn't leave much time for much of a personal life. What personal life that is left is scattered across three states—a couple of years back the press of stardom forced Willie to leave his ranch in Austin for the less celebrity-conscious reaches of Aspen, Colorado, and Malibu,

California. Connie, his wife, and his two daughters, Paula Carlene and Amy, now live in Aspen.

"It really wasn't that bad for me, because, you know, I'm gone most of the time anyway," Willie says. "But Connie was there and with people coming by all the time, it didn't give her much of a private life."

The ranch in Austin had, by last year, become something of a Mecca for the diehard Willie fans, and there are *no* fans quite like the diehard Willie fans. Living in a fishbowl would have been an improvement.

When Willie left Austin this time, it was with considerably more wailing and chest-beating from the community than when he left Texas before, in 1959 on the $150 proceeds from the sale of *Night Life*. In short, the Austin community felt betrayed—Willie was the most important mainstay of the much-vaunted Texas music scene: without him, quite frankly, there wasn't all that much of a scene. Or so some claimed. Willie himself is fairly fed up with hearing the myth of the Austin sound.

"There's still musicians there playing music," he says of Austin. "I never *did* think Austin was that much different from any other place. I don't think Austin is any different from Charlotte, North Carolina, or wherever. It's just some people who like music—that's all. Austin just happened to become my home town, and we stayed there for a long time and we played music there in a lot of different places for a long time. And then we started moving around a little bit. But I don't think that Austin either lost anything or gained anything by us either coming there or going, really. I'd like to say we're about even. . . ."

And Nashville?

"Well, I'd have to say the same thing. I don't think either town lost or gained anything by me being there," Willie laughs. Nashville might think differently. "I just don't think I made that much of an impression on either town. I don't know . . . maybe I made a few good impressions and a few bad impressions in both towns."

It's a question of myth, and Willie Nelson obviously doesn't subscribe to the Myth of Willie Nelson. The rest of the world can wear t-shirts that say "Matthew, Mark, Luke and Willie," and everyone else in the industry can either admire him for being a "canny businessman" or damn him for being a heartless, calculating bastard. Willie doesn't care one way or the other—what he does, how he perceives himself, is as someone who makes music.

"See, there's a whole generation of people who have never heard songs like *Blue Skies* and *Stardust*, just like they'd never heard country music before," Willie says, with all the fervor of a backwoods preacher, "We're bringing them those songs."

Sort of like a musical evangelist, I ask?

"Yea, I guess you could say that," says Willie. "Actually, Leon Russell's the evangelist."

At times, it seems like Willie Nelson is almost aggressively out-of-style. When **The Red-Headed Stranger** helped dump the country music industry on its well-padded posterior, and the pressure was on for Willie to produce yet *another* western morality play, he came back with a collection of his favorite gospel songs (exactly the sort of maneuver that causes record company executives to get early ulcers and die young). When the powers-that-be had gotten over the one, Willie delivered **To Lefty From Willie**, a collection of Lefty Frizzell songs Willie had long ached to record. And I can guarantee you that caused some sick stomachs in Nashville—I was at some of the meetings, and those folks were sweating *blood*. Lefty *Frizzell*, people raved. Who in the hell is Lefty Frizzell? And just who does Willie Nelson think *he* is? Lefty Frizzell, indeed.

Now Willie just laughs. The gospel album was successful, as was **To Lefty From Willie**. And so was his **Stardust** album, a collection of Willie's favorite songs from the '40s and '50s. So successful, in fact, that it's gone platinum—1,000,000 sales. This time, though, even the execs had learned. If it was anybody but Willie, said one well-placed source at CBS Records, Willie's company, we'd have serious doubts about releasing an album of greatest hits from 30 or 40 years ago. But Willie's different. Willie's stuff doesn't play by the rules.

"CBS is *real* nice," Willie says, laughing. "We're selling a lot of records."

And there's still lots of other albums that have been on Willie Nelson's mind for the last 20 years. "An album of George Jones songs, or an album of Kris Kristofferson songs, or a Hank Williams album, or a Bob Wills, or Carl Smith, or Webb Pierce. . . . There are really hundreds of songs, real good songs, that there's an audience out there that hasn't heard them yet. . . ."

And are just waiting for Willie the Evangelist to bring them the word.

What he's working on now is a duet album with good friend Leon Russell, a dream he's had since he and Leon first met in 1973 at the Dripping Springs Reunion. That meeting was particularly important for Willie, because it was at that meeting that Willie saw the artificial barriers between the music come tumbling down. They've been fast friends ever since, and, most recently, they've even managed a tour together.

"We [Leon and I] spent about a week together out in California a while back. and we did several songs—they're old standards; you'd know them all—everything from *Riding Down the Canyon* to *Tenderly. Heartbreak Hotel*—do you remember that? Oh gosh, of course you remember that," Willie says. It was late, folks. "Leon and I did a hundred and three songs in one week. Leon would sit down at the piano and I'd sing, and we did eighteen songs in one night. It was just kind of flowing real good. We'd just go through the books and find a song that we both knew, and then we'd just cut it. Most of those cuts are just one take."

He's even finding time to get back to a little songwriting, although not as much as in the times of dismal days past. "If I had a choice, I'd play four hours a day, seven nights a week," he recently told biographer Pete Axthelm. "The playing is the fun. The writing is the work. To write songs, I usually need a reason. Like not having any money. . . ."

"I've got an album of my own songs that I'm putting together to release one of these days," Willie says. "When I get to it."

There's also another concept album, a la *The Red-Headed Stranger*, that's been knocking around for a year or so. Called **The Convict And The Rose**, it had, at one point, gotten as far as having an album cover commissioned for it before getting shunted to the back burner.

"I still would like to do that one," Willie says. "Waylon and I had even talked about co-producing it. That could be sometime in the future, I guess."

What about that relationship with Ole Waylon, Nashville's favorite bad boy?

"I don't know. Everybody seems to be, if not causing trouble between me and Waylon, to at least try and say that there is trouble between us. But as far as I know, there's not. Some people don't like it when people are too good friends or are too successful. It doesn't matter whether you're in music or whether you're two good plumbers with the most business in town."

Some of Willie's ventures, though, do prove to work out better than others. A case in point is the struggling Lone Star Records, which recently ended a distribution deal with Phonogram. Previously, Lone Star had been distributed by CBS, Willie's company.

"Lone Star right now is going through some growing pains," he says. "We're looking for a home for the label. Actually, I haven't decided whether we're going to keep the label or change it to a production company and try producing some acts for several record companies rather than just one."

So far, Willie says, the problem has been that no one has been exactly sure what Lone Star Records was trying to do.

"They haven't been sure what to do with the music or how to classify it," Willie says, "Or how to sell it. They don't know what label to put on it."

How would Willie himself define Lone Star?

"Well, we're trying to give people who are playing good music like Steve Fromholz, Ray Wylie Hubbard, Don Bowman, the Cooder Browns, the Geezinslaw Brothers, Dee Moeler, Rusty Wier, B.W. Stevenson, all these guys, a place to be heard. I think there's a lot of talent down there that's going unnoticed. I just mentioned a few of them, but there's hundreds that people don't know about," says Willie the evangelist. "And I don't know how to expose them, other than just let time do it."

And, to be sure, record companies who signed deals with Lone Star did it with an eye on capturing Willie Nelson on down the line.

"Oh sure," he says. "Of course. And I'm sure that anybody who signed up the Lone Star label now would be doing it for the same reason, trying to get me. That's not what I want. I want these artists to be able to stand on their own and not have to ride on the coattails of anybody."

Meanwhile, the bright lights of Hollywood are giving their old come-hither glow, and who can blame Willie for having his head turned just a little? His role in *The Electric Horseman* is a good one: Robert Redford plays a tough rodeo cowboy, a la Larry Mahan, who gives it all up for the bright lights and deodorant commercials. Willie plays an old rodeo buddy who sticks with him as his manager—"It wasn't a hard part."

The role came about after Willie met Redford at Billy Sherrill's house in Nashville and rode out to California with him—"We hit it off pretty well," Willie says. Redford asked if Willie had ever considered movies, and when Willie said he thought he could handle it, Redford just nodded. Several months later Redford was on the phone, offering him the role in *Electric Horseman.*

"It's not all that different from being on stage," Willie says, "Except you've got to memorize your part instead of songs, and the songs are usually longer."

(The project of turning the story line of Willie's **Red-Headed Stranger** LP into a major motion picture has been approved by Universal Studios. Robert Redford is reportedly being considered for the lead role; he really liked the first draft of the script and is currently reading the second draft. If Redford does decide to do it, it will become an "A"-project at Universal and filming can begin in the summer. Rumors have it that celebrated director Milos Foreman [*Hair*] is being considered as a possible director.)

And lately Willie's been seen hobnobbing around New York with the likes of Burt Reynolds, Carol Lynley, and Candice Bergen (After spending an evening with women like Candice Bergen and Jane Fonda, moans Willie, one is never the same again).

"Well," he adds, "If Burt wants me to be in one of his movies, I'll say yes. And if Burt wants to get up on stage and sing with me again (as he did one beery evening not too long ago), that's all right by me."

FURTHER ADVENTURES OF THE GYPSY COWBOY

Nelson Allen | May 1979 | *Country Music*

This third interview by veteran country music reporter Nelson Allen (there are perhaps more not reprinted here) provides an intriguing behind-the-scenes look at Willie Nelson's life and career. –Ed.

Not long before Michael Bane spoke to Willie Nelson in New York City (a day or two before his concert with Leon Russell in Passaic, New Jersey), Texas writer Nelson Allen, a veteran Willie Nelson camp-follower, braved a backstage throng of whiskey-drinkers, well-wishers and autograph hounds to interview Willie between shows at the Austin Opry House (which Willie recently purchased for a reported $250,000).

Allen who described this adventure as his "last Willie Nelson story," has interviewed Willie numerous times over the past few years; and, as he's come to find out, it's not always an easy task: "I learned a long time ago that if you want to talk to Willie, you have to go straight up to him yourself," says Allen. "If you waste time going through channels or talking to whichever go-fers he's got, you'll never make it."

The following is a brief excerpt from their backstage conversations:

Allen: *Where are you living now, California?*

Willie: No. Here and Colorado. I'm dividing my time between Austin and Colorado. I'm down here but my wife and family are up there. I still like Austin.

Allen: *I read you had some trouble with your place up there.*

Willie: The IRS has a lien on my property up there, but it's no big deal.

Allen: *How's the Opry House doing?*

Willie: (He eyes the crowd.) It's holding up well and we may even be able to pay for it some day.

Allen: *Which movie did you just finish?*

Willie: Just finished working on one with Robert Redford in Nevada, *The Electric Horseman.* He plays an ex-rodeo cowboy.

Allen: *How do you like acting?*

Willie: Well, that movie was a comedy and it was a lot of fun. We got to improvise some, only once we got the lines down it was hard to remember to say them the same way each time.

Allen: *There are a lot of people local Texas bands, that aren't on your Lone Star record label. Why not?*

Willie: Well, we only had so much time and space to begin with. I think we'll do ok if we can get any promotion.

Allen: *Do you think any of these people can sell records?*

Willie: Well, somebody'd better get a hit soon. No, but really, I think any one of these guys can get a hit, even the Geezinslaws.

Allen: *You were quoted a few years ago as saying that your career would probably peak after a few years and taper off like Hank Thompson's or somebody's, but that doesn't seem to be the case.*

Willie: No, I don't think it is. I hope not. I always wanted to get it going and then never stop. That's what I always wanted to do. (Somebody hands Willie a Tequila Sunrise.)

Allen: *A lot of people seem to sort of look upon you as a sort of spiritual "advisor" or something; Gary Busey (star of* The Buddy Holly Story*) said recently that you were the one he talked to when he was having difficulties handling his newfound stardom.*

Willie: Well, I don't know if I've ever really helped anyone but . . . I enjoy being asked advice, giving my opinion.

Allen: *About the only thing I've heard you criticized for lately is that you're not writing as much these days. How do you react to that?*

Willie: Well, I don't care. I could do, and probably will sometime, another **Yesterday's Wine** (one of Willie's earlier albums that was recorded some years ago for RCA. It was a brilliant effort and far ahead of its time; it's been called country music's first "concept" album.) Or **Red Headed Stranger**, a whole conception thing again, but I wrote songs for forty years; sometimes when I was a kid, I'd stack up five or six songs a day, and if I want to take a little vacation now, that's my business.

Allen: *What was it like when you played at the White House recently?*

Willie: It was a lot of fun. It's not your average honky tonk.

Allen: *(Willie and I are both getting bored and the interview is about over, but I want to ask him one more question.) Have you made it with Linda Ronstadt yet?*

Willie: (The famous orange beard parts into a grin.) Did I what? (But by now, the Red Headed Stranger is already halfway out the door.)

Two days later, Willie Nelson flies out to Utah to make another movie.

BIKERS AND TEXAS: AN INTERVIEW WITH WILLIE NELSON

December 1979 | *Easyriders*

Willie Nelson's appeal also extends to biker culture. Willie knew this and was savvy enough to incorporate it into his concert festivals. One such example was when the Grateful Dead joined the 4th of July Picnic roster as a warm-up act on July 1, 1978. As state troopers swept the fairground with binoculars looking for a drug bust, the Dead jammed their homespun rock music. An attendee told *Country Music* magazine, "I giggle a little to myself when I try to imagine what was going through the minds of the people who came to see a Willie Nelson concert." Chances are Willie's audience appreciated the Grateful Dead as much as the Dead's audience dug Willie. –Ed.

When I got the call from our wandering photographer, Billy Tinney, I was skeptical. He was in Las Vegas and ran down some off-the-wall story about bumping into Willie Nelson and mentioning this rag. Willie actually knew of **Easyriders** and volunteered to pose in front of his Texas flag for a cover. He also volunteered to do this interview—blew Billy away. But Billy's been known to get a little blurred around the edges after a fifth of ta-kill-ya or so, so I didn't pay a lot of attention, at first figuring he'd been talked into a scam by some silk-suited cokespoon and had slipped over into fantasyland.

But damned if it all wasn't true, and the next thing I knew I was sitting next to the Cub, or resident photog, in a propeller-driven crate flying to Lake Tahoe to interview Willie. The Cub quickly drank himself into a stupor and was thus able to take the plane's constant shuddering and rattling in stride. I spent the time trying to go over the questions I wanted to ask Willie, but it's hard to write when your white-knuckled fists are locked to the armrests and you're begging the stewardess for a parachute.

Eventually, we found ourselves wandering the posh casino of Harrah's Hotel, where Willie was playing. Our grubby jeans and stained T-shirts looked out of place among the high rollers, but the pit bosses knew we were big shots when the Cub dropped three whole bucks playing the nickel slots. We had to operate on Willie's schedule the entire time we were there, which meant things never got started before 2 a.m., when the second show ended. Every morning would find me and the Cub clinging to our barstools, drinking our breakfast, adding additional stains to our T-shirts, and wondering if we could get through another day on a diet of booze, toot, and no sleep.

The interview took place in Willie's packed dressing room between shows. It was a glitter, star-speckled party atmosphere at first—Jane Fonda loved the **Easyriders** T-shirt the Cub laid on her. But I had to pull him over into a corner and talk him out of asking her to strip for an Ol' Lady Contest photo. Willie was gracious as always, and after excusing himself from the party, he gave us his undivided attention.

When I spoke to him, Willie had just finished one movie and was about to begin another. His records continue to sell millions, he had just completed a Christmas album, and he still found time to maintain a personal appearance schedule that would kill most entertainers. The story of Willie's career and success is too familiar to need retelling here, so the talk turned to motorcycles—the only thing I know shit about—and proceeding from that subject.

ER: You used to ride a motorcycle, right?

WN: Yeah, I've owned a bunch of bikes—everything from Harleys to Hondas.

ER: Did you start riding early, when you were a kid?

WN: No, I started later on in life, after I was grown. I'd always wanted one, even as a kid. But I could never afford one then. I was grown before I had any money. Unfortunately, I don't have the time to ride much anymore.

ER: When Paul Newman or Steve McQueen want to ride their motorcycles or drive their race cars, they have to face the opposition of entertainment executives who are uptight about the risks. Like them, you're valuable property—if you wanted to ride, would you face the same thing?

WN: Not with executives. I'd face it from my family, though.

ER: You've been called an outlaw and the name has stuck—both to you and to an entire movement in country music. The same term, as you know, has been applied to a segment of motorcycle riders—the sort of hardcore Harley riders we write for and about in **Easyriders**. Do you think there's any parallel to be drawn between the two?

WN: Definitely. I think that all bike riders are like pickers in the sense that they're both sorta looked down on by the community.

ER: Why is that?

WN: Well, a musician has always been a second-class citizen. I say always . . . actually, not so much now, but a long time that was true. He couldn't get credit, he couldn't get anything. He had no visible means of support, no *regular* job. A lot of bikers aren't nine-to-fivers, so they and musicians are treated the same—they're called loafers, troublemakers, everything.

ER: Is that why both groups, to one degree or another, feel alienated from society?

WN: Well, I think there's a freedom that certain people insist on having—like the cowboys, that type of person. Bikers have that same kind of image. Pickers have that image. A lot of people feel that way and want that freedom, but these people actually go after it—they try to live a free life.

A guy who has an eight-hour job where he punches a clock five days a week is generally a little envious of somebody who rides around on a motorcycle having fun. The same goes for the guy who rides around on a bus with a bunch of musicians playing music. You know, it's something the clock-puncher would like to do.

ER: So there's a mixture of envy in society's disapproval?

WN: I think so. The average person has mixed emotions about us.

ER: *Easyriders* has a substantial readership in prisons. You seem to be as popular with guys in the joint as you are with the public. Have you ever done any prison shows?

WN: Yeah, I've done a few shows in different prisons around the country. It's been a couple of years since I've done one. I think the last time I played was down in Texas, at Sugarland. I plan to do them as long as I can fit them into my schedule—I've got a lot of irons in the fire right now, so it's not easy. But I do a few benefits each year for causes I'm in favor of.

ER: At your July Fourth Picnic this year we met some Bandidos who are fans of yours. Do you have personal friends in motorcycle clubs or are they primarily just fans?

WN: I have friends in a lot of bike clubs.

ER: The audience you played to in Austin was young and hip. The people who came to see you here are somewhat older and obviously more affluent, but you do essentially the same show for both groups. What explains the fact that you cut across so many social and economic levels and are so popular with such a broad spectrum of people?

WN: I believe that people are people—period. They may dress differently and do everything they can to look different, be different, or act different, but as far as music is concerned they're all the same. Good music is appreciated by most people, regardless of how they look or how old they are or how much money they have. If you produce a sound that's pleasing to the ear, it doesn't matter how long the hair is. Whether it's over the ear or not, the same ear is there to appreciate the sound. Also, we play all kinds of music in our show. We haven't done anything brave—just play a lot of different kinds of music. And by doing that you attract a wide variety of people, all different ages and from all walks of life.

ER: You come from a religious background, a Baptist upbringing. What role, if any, did that play in accounting for your popularity?

WN: It had a lot to do with my learning people—learning what people want to hear and how to get their attention and what they respond to. You see, when you go to church every Sunday for most of the early years of your life, you learn how the preacher gets the congregation's attention and how he holds it. A preacher is a professional speaker, an entertainer, really. He's not usually regarded that way, but it's true nonetheless. He has to be a showman to sell his product.

ER: So you're saying that the religious influences played more of a part in your ability to project a performer than in the nature of the songs you write?

WN: I think you could say that. I owe a lot to those preachers I watched do their act all those years.

ER: So there's a touch of evangelism in the manner in which you relate to an audience.

WN: Or maybe there's a touch of show business in evangelism—or at least salesmanship, which is also show business. It all involves selling your product no matter what you're trying to sell or get across to the people. If it's religion, you've got to be good. Billy Graham is a great salesman. He used to be a door-to-door salesman.

ER: As you did, too—right?

WN: That's right. When you go from house to house and knock and you don't know who's behind that door, you learn a lot. Do that for a long period of time, and you learn a helluva lot.

ER: Were you good at it?

WN: Yeah, I was good at it.

ER: Would you agree that there's a religious thread running through the songs you write—a traditional morality?

WN: Well, I don't write immoral songs, so I must write moral songs—at least songs that I think have a moral. In my mind I write songs that mean something to me, songs I hope will say what I want to say. Being a positive thinker, I'm not going to write anything negative. So a lot of the things I write have what you might call a semi-religious effect on some people.

I believe that none of my songs present life as being hopeless. There's humor—wholesome stuff—in my mind when I write them. Even if the song is on a tragic subject, I try to say something about the lighter side of it.

ER: Do you think there's a 'lighter side' to songs like "Hello Walls," and "Bloody Mary Morning," and "Half A Man"?

WN: Well, yeah. Like in "Hello Walls"—when you put it in the blues rhythm, then you take it away from being too depressing and you add a little jump beat. That's what the blues is—depressing lyrics with a driving beat. The negativity is countered with a positive drive and the feel behind it. So people cry in their beer and listen to the blues but still don't despair.

ER: To what extent would you say drugs, including alcohol, have played a role in your life?

WN: I think drugs are medicines. In the Bible it says, "Physician, heal thyself." In other words, a person knows what's wrong with him and sometimes he knows what it's going to take to relieve that condition temporarily, until he can work it out. It's the same thing a doctor is going to do for him. A doctor is going to charge him for an office visit to do the same thing. If the patient knows what to do himself and is sure he knows, then he should do it himself. For most people drugs serve as a kind of self-medication.

ER: Does being from Texas mean something special for your music and your popularity? Is there something unique about being from Texas?

WN: Evidentally there is today—it hasn't always been that way. We Texans are boastful and we brag a lot, so over the years we've gotten a reputation for being bigmouths, bragging about this state we claim has everything in the world—which it does, you know. But for a long time they didn't believe us. I think now they say, "Those sonsabitches were right after all—Texans are okay."

ER: About Austin itself—recently you said that you really never thought there was anything special about the music scene there.

WN: Again, people are people. I think a lot of good people gathered in Austin and I got a chance to go down and play some music for them. A lot of good people are gathered in every town I've ever been in. In fact, I think you can pick a town and throw a dart at a map and we can get an auditorium full of people who will enjoy good music, if we can get them out of the house. In Austin, having a college there and having access to all those young people and all that peak energy made everything possible. It just happened to all come together there. That's where I happened to find the audience.

ER: Would you mark the 1972 Dripping Springs Picnic as where everything started to happen?

WN: I think that Picnic was probably the first big indication that there were a lot of young people who were into rock and roll but who were also able to enjoy another type of music as well. People love an underdog, and the Picnic has always been an underdog. There's always been a lot of reasons why there should not be a Picnic or couldn't be this time, and so forth. So each time we had it, it was like, "Well, I'll be damned; we did it again."

ER: One of the reasons your music hits home to so many people is the way you articulate difficulties and disappointments everyone has known. That experience comes from those lean years you spent before you were so successful and well-recognized. Do you ever worry that success will make you complacent and cause you to lose that connection with your audience?

WN: Absolutely. It's dangerous because it can happen to anybody in my position. And it would be easy, once you get a little bit of money, to quit work. But in order to stay ahead in the record business, in order to keep selling records, you need to keep putting on these shows and doing those one-nighters and working across the country and letting people know that you're still on the scene and still working and still enjoying having a big crowd come out and hear you. People will go where they know they're appreciated. And it works from the musicians' end, too. I think there's something built into most musicians and pickers—you know, it's their egos or they're hams or something. They enjoy an audience. They get off seeing other people enjoy what they do—and that's what keeps us all on the road.

ER: How much are you on the road these days?

WN: I don't know exactly. We're working more now than we ever were. I don't know how long that is going to go on, but right now we're doing over 200 days a year on the road.

ER: In a magazine article you were described as always carrying yourself "with a kind of fierce innocence."

WN: I think it's probably a fierce "So What?"

ER: Is that "So what" attitude responsible for your down-to-earth quality? You seem very genuine, very real, to people, and that has to mean a lot to them.

WN: Yeah, but I might be riding a trend, you know. I might realize it's a big audience out there with a bunch of longhairs in it and I might just be taking advantage of that opportunity.

ER: You're saying that you might have suckered a lot of people into believing in Willie Nelson. You might have run a scam on them, but even if it's fake, a lot of people are responding.

WN: Well, if I did anything, let's just say I crashed a party.

ER: You've achieved so much success that it's as if you don't have any worlds left to conquer. Beyond records and movies, is there anything that you haven't been able to do that you still want to achieve?

WN: Oh, something will come up—I really don't know what, but it will come up. I'm not bored at all with what I'm doing. Things are happening every day—I have to do double-takes all the time at what's going on in my life. But the future is always interesting. It's like riding a motorcycle—you always want to see what's over the next hill.

ER: Thank you, Willie.

WN: Thank you.

WILLIE GOES TO THE MOVIES: HONEYSUCKLE ROSE

Bill Oakey | March 1980 | *Country Music*

Willie Nelson's film career is as significant as his music. Over the years, Willie has worked in theatrical films, television shows, documentaries, and music videos. His appearances are as singular as his singing. To date, he has appeared over fifty times in various visual media. After *The Electric Horseman*, Willie took a starring role in *Honeysuckle Rose*, named for Nelson's tour bus, which is almost as famous as he is. It's a custom-made bus that serves as his home on wheels, equipped with all the comforts he needs while traveling. –Ed.

Dressed more stylishly "western" than usual, Willie and his band went through several takes of a new song, *On the Road Again*. The scene was intended to be a chic New York honky tonk, with plenty of smoke provided by a portable spraying machine. In reality, Willie and family were downstairs at Crazy Bob's Saloon, next door to the Greyhound Bus station in Austin, Texas. They were filming part of a sequence of concert scenes for *Honeysuckle Rose*, Willie's first movie as a leading actor.

The plot centers around a country singer on the road, who strays from his wife (Dyan Cannon) and falls for a younger singer (Amy Irving). Ms. Irving is also the daughter of Willie's best friend in the script, played by Slim Pickens.

Although the story is fictional, Willie reports that "the musical part of my character's life certainly parallels mine. Everything he goes through,

I've been through at one time or another. The movie covers thirty days in the life of a bandleader. I can't tell much difference yet in the transition from singing to acting, except that there's a lot more waiting around. Sometimes it takes two or three hours to change sets."

"I surprised myself in writing several new songs for the movie. We hadn't planned on that at first, but once we got into it, some ideas came to me. There will be four or five new ones, which will be included on the soundtrack album." Much of the concert footage was shot in the San Antonio–Austin area. In addition to established night spots, such as the Soap Creek Saloon, there is a Willie Nelson Picnic scene.

Willie explained that the discovery of Amy Irving as a singer took place during the film casting. "She submitted her resume for acting only. We had planned on using somebody else's voice, but when she sang at one of the rehearsals, we found that she was good enough to do it herself. She will be included on the soundtrack album. Mickey Rooney Jr., Hank Cochran, Johnny Gimble and his band, and Emmylou Harris will also perform in the movie and on the soundtrack. Ray Price was at the picnic, and he may be included too. By the way, he and I are doing an album together."

There is so much going on with Willie these days that it is easy to see why he would have to adjust to the slower pace of making movies. *Honeysuckle Rose*, scheduled to be released this summer, will follow *The Electric Horseman*, in which he had a small part.

Folks in Austin unfamiliar with moviemaking got quite a taste of it in October and November. The Warner Brothers film crew put out call after call for extras. Close to five-hundred in all were chosen. For thirty bucks a day they stood or sat in their assigned spots and hollered for Willie. Of course, some of those days were pretty long, but it was fun. When it was over, you can be sure that Willie was glad to be *On the Road Again*.

WILLIE NELSON: BEING A MOVIE STAR SURE BEATS WORKING

Bob Allen | October 1980 | *Country Music*

Bob Allen's interview with Willie Nelson contains a detailed description of the singer/songwriter's meteoric rise to fame and the changes he has experienced in his career. Of value is Allen's descriptions of Nelson's interactions with fans, colleagues, and industry executives. We also experience a grasp of Willie's journey and the unique challenges he encounters as a public figure. In this article, I've corrected the name of the film *Barbarosa* (1982) which was misstated in *Country Music* magazine because of a transcription error. –Ed.

After national exposure in a film with Robert Redford, and more recently, in a starring role of his own in *Honeysuckle Rose*, the quiet days are gone forever for the Red-headed Stranger . . . but *who's* complaining!?!

Several months from now after the picture of Willie Nelson sitting on a wooden fence in front of a pastoral Texas outdoor scene has appeared as part of the promotional campaign for his recently released feature film, *Honeysuckle Rose*, only a few people will know where it was really taken: in the parking lot of a nondescript beachfront motel in the suburban outskirts of Fort Lauderdale, Florida.

But *that* is the reason why Willie is perched on a small "portable" Hollywood facsimile of a wooden fence on a patch of grass next to a busy dual-lane thoroughfare, in front of a Best Western Motel in this rather early, but very hot Sunday morning in Southern Florida.

The theory is that Willie Nelson doesn't have time right now, in the middle of a tour, to come to Hollywood for this photo, so instead, Hollywood has come to him: A contingent of photographers and executives have flown in the night before and brought with them, the pieces of the ready-to-assemble fence on which Willie is sitting. Later, back on the West Coast, through the wonders of modern photography, the photo of Willie will be touched up slightly; a bucolic scene of hay bales, moo-cows, horses and cowboys and cowgirls will be superimposed over what is now mere asphalt and parked cars. More fence will be stripped in, until it looks like that one little section on which he's sitting stretches all the way to the Texarkana border.

Even though it's only about 10:00 a.m., a small crowd quickly gathers. Cars that pass on the busy street honk their horns and the drivers lean precariously out with huge smiles on their faces, giving ol' Willie the universal power sign of the raised fist.

"Hhheeeeeyyyy Willllleeeeee!!!!!"

Willie smiles quietly at them and returns their acknowledgments with his own clenched and raised fist. It's obvious he doesn't mind being recognized like this. In fact, he seems to rather enjoy it.

But still, there's something slightly incongruous about it all: dear old Willie, his slender, well-carried frame perched up there like a parrot, with a Best Western Motel behind him, cars whizzing by in front of him, and the hot Florida sun beating down causing beads of sweat to form on his brow and under that freshly-pressed, expensive cowboy shirt he's wearing, while his air-conditioned tour bus sits idling a few yards away, ready to whisk him off to his next show, clean across the state in St. Petersburg on the Gulf Coast.

Perspiration is also forming on the brows of the two young photographers. One of them appears to be uneasy about something. His camera stops clicking. He looks up at the sun, then looks at the ground and then looks at Willie. He is not happy with Willie's tennis shoes.

"I think you should have boots on," he decides after a long, pregnant pause.

Ol' Willie, whose movements are slow and deliberate anyhow, looks down from his perch at the ground, then he looks up at the sun. His eyes narrow into slits and he locks the photographer in a scowl that would send Charles Bronson running for cover.

"What makes ya think that?" he says ever so softly.

The photographer backs off a bit, throws up his hands in a conciliatory gesture. "Well, it's uh . . . it's *fine* with me . . . it's great . . . if you're comfortable with the image . . ."

"I am."

Far from ever being replaced by cowboy boots. Willie Nelson's blue sneakers will probably some day be set in bronze. Because here lately, travelling the road with him, one gets the distinct impression that the whole world is now waiting to embrace him just the way he is—blue jogging shoes and all. To steal an applicable phrase from the late John F. Kennedy, the quiet days are gone forever. When Willie's on the road anymore, it's nothing like the tours of earlier years when he could check into a hotel under his own name, and walk around outside the club before the show to kill time. Nowadays, as soon as he signs his name to a room service tab, it's all over: Word spreads through the hotel that he's cloistered away on the grounds and a quiet, hushed excitement spreads through the lobby.

And funny things happen. Like the time on an earlier date of this particular swing through the Southeast when Willie happened to check into the same motel where two busloads of kids from a high school marching band were staying. The students and their instructors got word from the hotel management that Willie was on the premises, and then proceeded to roll out their instruments on the front lawn and play a command performance just for him. Willie was so amused and delighted by it all that he returned the favor by sticking around to pose for snapshots and sign autographs.

Things like that just seem to happen to Willie everywhere he goes these days: every mayor seems ready and waiting to give him the key to his city. (He was recently presented the key to one good-sized Southern metropolis by the mayor, only to later pass it on—with equal formality—to the nine-year-old sister of one of his soundmen who had come to see his show.) People line up to get their photos snapped with him and offer him the use of their houses for the weekend. During his stay at the beachside motel in Fort Lauderdale, a large speedboat called the "Hot Lick" was quietly placed at the disposal of Willie and his travelling Family. Several times when he set off to take his daily run down the beach, he was waylaid by well-intentioned fans bearing joints and cold cans of beer.

Except for some weird scenes in the parking lot—where crowds inevitably gather around the four tour buses that haul Willie's Family around the country as soon as they pull in—and backstage, where the "lunatic fringe" sometimes congregates. Much of the adulation for Nelson still remains more of a reasonably calm veneration than a dangerously heated frenzy.

Nelson's own appraisal of his new role as a latter-day cultural hero is amazingly realistic—almost self-effacing. "It's a big responsibility to know that maybe just one person might be influenced just a little bit by what I do," he told me in his usual soft speaking voice one afternoon sitting in his tour bus as it carried him and his band through the suburbs of Fort Lauderdale on the way to a one-nighter at an auditorium in a town somewhere out near the Florida Everglades. "But to think there might be thousands is a little bit scary . . . especially when I don't consider myself as that much of someone to pattern their lives after . . . But," he adds, "I feel like I've made all the mistakes and I hope I've learned from them."

An objective look at the present state of Willie Nelson's nearly three-decade-long musical career indicates that he's not only learned from the errors of his ways, but he's in fact, gone a step further and turned them all into triumphs. For at least the last three years, some journalists have been subtly predicting that his career was bound to peak any second now, and that it would be all downhill from there. But, the fact is, it just seems to be gaining more and more momentum—almost by the day.

In fact, throughout Willie's entire organization, there is a strange new feeling during this late Spring tour. It is a feeling that things had reached a new level that everyone involved is just learning how to deal with. Security is tighter and the whereabouts of Willie at any given time is a well-kept secret. (Some members of his crew even wear t-shirts insisting, "I DON'T KNOW WHERE WILLIE IS!") Calculated strategies now have to be developed to get Willie swiftly through the choking backstage crowds and into his bus after the show. There seems to be shades of Elvis Presley everywhere; there are now hulking security men who keep watch over him from the shadows in back of the stage, all through his performances.

The point is, things *have* changed. Members of the band now find themselves being chased through hotel lobbies by teenaged girls; and inside the auditoriums during the shows, there is a tense, restless electricity that just wasn't there a couple of years ago.

"Goin' out and openin' for Willie on a show sure ain't the easiest thing in the world," singer/songwriter/comedian Don Bowman, a long-time Willie Nelson sidekick sighs as he sits in the air-conditioned comfort of his hotel suite complete with a picture window over-looking the ocean, the morning after one such concert in West Palm Beach. "This tour's been the wildest of all. It's like . . . the crowds . . . Well, you saw 'em last night, up standin' on their chairs before he even hit the stage . . . The only thing there is to compare it to is Elvis."

The electricity of his live shows, though, is merely the most obvious evidence of the fact that Willie Nelson is in high gear, and clearly on his way to becoming a household word. He's walked away with both the Country Music Association's and the Academy of Country Music's *Entertainer of the Year* awards in recent months, and he's selling more records than ever before. All of his recent albums, including **Willie And Family Live, Willie Nelson Sings Kristofferson** and **One For The Road** (with Leon Russell) have reached either gold or platinum (million-sales) status. His two most recent, **San Antonio Rose** (with Ray Price) and the soundtrack from **Honeysuckle Rose**, both headed right for the top of the country charts. During the mid-summer of this year, he had six different albums simultaneously in the charts.

Then there's this whole new dimension to his career which probably has more to do with all the craziness on the road than anything else: his successful involvement in and national exposure from films like *The Electric Horseman* and the $11 million Warner Brothers release, *Honeysuckle Rose* in which he recently made his debut in a starring role. Soon he will begin filming *Barbarosa*, in which he takes his first *non*-musical dramatic lead opposite Gary Busey of *The Buddy Holly Story* fame, whom Willie has known since back in the days when Busey played drums for Leon Russell. "Ever since I was a kid, ever since I first saw Gene Autry, there was no doubt about what I wanted to be," Willie smiles: "A cowboy movie star."

Yet, there's still more. In addition to the movies, the records, the sold-out tours, there's his songwriting, which Willie has gotten back to with the new material written especially for *Honeysuckle Rose*. There's his publishing companies, production companies, music clubs, golf courses, restaurants, stores and other business enterprises. All the details and responsibilities that come with each of these would be enough to drive most grown men crazy. How in the *world*, Nelson is asked one night as he sits peacefully backstage between shows, in a small, ridiculously crowded and noisy dressing room, sipping a Budweiser and toking contentedly on a joint, does he keep up with all this?

"Ah, it's not that time-consuming, really," he replies softly (as if to say, "Aw, shucks, anybody could do it!"). "Those kinds of decisions (like last-minute photo sessions) don't really come up that often. And when they do, it's kind of a pleasure to be diverted from whatever I was thinkin' about anyway."

Don Bowman has known Willie through the lean times, at least since the early 1960s when they played a series of shows together in Texas to support the campaign of former U.S. Senator Ralph Yarborough. ("You talk about *hot*!" Bowman laughs. "*Hot*, we were *not*! I remember we played some auditorium in Austin. You know: 'FREE CONCERT: WILLIE NELSON.' And the only people that showed up was me and Willie and Paul (English) and Senator Yarborough, and a couple other dudes we had to call at home to come down and open the building! We were not exactly overrun! But we had the nicest hotel suites in town and we just stayed stoned for 18 days. Wasn't no reason to straighten up. We got paid for that first gig and the check bounced, bigger 'n hell. . . . But God, did we have alot of fun!")

Bowman maintains that there is nothing put on about Willie's almost impenetrable calm. Still, after all these years, even he expresses quiet amazement over Willie's ability to keep his cool amidst all the madness.

"Willie's the only person I've ever seen . . . well, Bobby Bare comes pretty close. . . . He just doesn't get upset. I mean, if he really wanted to get into it, he could drive himself crazy in about 20 minutes! But all he wants is that guitar tuned and waitin' for him when he hits the stage every night. That's all he worries about.

"And another thing I've noticed," Bowman adds, "is how much more confidence he has now. I've noticed it standin' backstage and I told him the last time we talked: I can hear songs of his I heard fifteen years ago, and I hear 'em now and hear all kinds of highs and rolls and runs and deep notes that he was afraid to try and sing before.

"But now, shit!" Bowman laughs, "he's won every damned award they can give away! I mean goddamn, even he's got to know that he can do any damn thing he wants to now!"

[The article prints several lines from "On the Road Again" here that have been cut. —*Ed.*]

"My wife Connie helps me a lot mainly just by being a good critic," Willie tells me that afternoon as we ride toward the Florida Everglades in the tour bus. He glances around the rear compartment of the bus before making his next remark, as if he is afraid it might be taken the wrong way if overheard by the wrong person. "She'll give me good honest opinions . . . which are sometimes very hard to find."

A little while later, what Willie says is illustrated when a couple of young Warner Brothers film executives come on the bus for an impromptu meeting to discuss the advertising campaign for *Honeysuckle Rose* and the accompanying soundtrack album.

The Warner Brothers fellows are smooth—so smooth you might think they were born with martinis in their right hands. They dwell in an uncertain world where those drawing six-figure salaries and riding high on huge expense accounts can suddenly find themselves cleaning out their desks if *their* pet project dies at the box office. These guys are disarmingly like the cliched Hollywood types so often depicted in TV comedy shows. As Willie and the execs gather around the small wooden picnic-type table in the bus, there is much heavy-duty *stroking* going on on the part of the executives. This is an industry term, stolen from the glossary of pop psychology. It is the oft-practiced strategy of winning the favors of, and putting at ease, a ranking individual by massaging his ego and reassuring him of his own overwhelming importance in the scheme of things through the use of lavish, yet subtle compliments.

The Warner Brothers executives have brought with them, proposed sketches for the movie posters for *Honeysuckle Rose* and the album cover art for the film's soundtrack, to be approved by Willie. A large joint is passed around among Willie's contingent and Willie takes a healthy toke from it as the movie execs come on strong with the strokes:

"Now *this* one will be used for the poster and the advertisement," says one of the Warner Brothers people. "It'll make a great ad! It will be run in *Time, Newsweek, The New York Times. . . .*" The man's eyes seem to glaze in awe at the gravity of his own words as he recites an impressive shopping list of national publications.

Willie doesn't bat an eyelash or even lift his intent gaze from the sketches. He just takes another long, thoughtful toke on the joint. "And this'll be for the album cover?"

"That's right! . . . I'm telling you, *everybody* at Warners is *up* on this project," the executive adds in smooth, reassuring tones. "It's going to open in cities all across the country before all the kids go back to school!"

Willie's expression does not change. His eyes maintain their skeptical but approving focus on the album cover art. Smoke trails softly out of his nostrils. "Hmmm," he replies absently, "I'll have to have a hundred picnics this year—one in every town. . . ."

"I'm telling you," the Warner Brothers man adds with an extravagant wave of his hand that causes his expensive digital watch to glint in the early evening light. "*This* is going to be the *biggest* movie Warner Brothers has had in a long time!"

The inscrutable concentration in Willie's eyes does not relax. He takes another drag on the joint, passes it along and looks across the table at the man with a very distant, noncommittal smile.

"I sure hope so," he says softly.

A few minutes later, word is passed to Willie that it's time for him to head for the stage. There are 6,000 people waiting impatiently for him inside the coliseum. He quietly excuses himself from the meeting and heads directly for the backstage entrance and on to the stage where his battered guitar, along with his band, is already waiting for him. The applause from the 6,000 Florida fans is deafening, and like Don Bowman said, a few of them are already up on their chairs.

At the end of the show, nearly two hours later, with routine clockwork two ranking Family members wait for Willie just off the stage behind the huge Lone Star State flag as he makes his exit. They hand him a lit joint so he can enjoy a few quick tokes before he goes back out to do his encore.

After the show, there is no autograph signing in the parking lot like there would have been a year or so ago—the crowds are just too big and too unpredictable now. Instead, Willie is ushered quickly through the hopelessly crowded backstage corridors by a T-formation of the same hulking road crew members who have been watching and waiting silently in the backstage shadows throughout the entire performance. In the parking lot, Willie hops into a chauffer-driven Cadillac Eldorado with Don Bowman and Paul English and they disappear into the night with the roar of the audience and the final stanzas of their song still ringing in their ears:

[The piece ends with the same quoted lines from "On the Road Again." —Ed.]

WILLIE

Bob Millard | September/October 1983 | *Country Music*

Many mainstream interviews publish retreads of well-known facts and anecdotes of key celebrity figures. This is especially problematic with those who are always in the public eye. Willie, with his prolificity of songs, albums, movies, and books, is one of those who could risk overexposure but somehow does not. Willie's life is so varied and vast with unique experiences that it is possible to come out of each interview with entirely new information given by Willie. He is ever candid. He is not afraid to tackle those tough questions concerning his private life: IRS seizures, ex-wives, drug busts, and a host of domestic squabbles. He is, as the saying goes, an open book. –Ed.

Now that everybody who watches TV or lives within fifty miles of a newsstand knows all about Willie Nelson's taste in breakfast food and his feelings about double dating and the color of his bathtub, we thought that, as in the past, we would let you country music fans know what the man thinks about more substantial matters—music, for instance, and the odd path by which he arrived at his current super-celebrity. This time Bob Millard caught up with Willie in Nashville, and the following discussion took place:

CM: Tell us a little bit about when you got to Nashville. Obviously you were ready to do some new things, but did you know what you were going to do?

Willie: I really didn't know that much when I came to town. I knew a lot less than probably what I thought I did, really. But I felt like I knew what I wanted to do, and I felt like I could write songs pretty good, and I felt like I could play the guitar, and I felt like I sang okay. I wasn't here too long, though, until I began to get my confidence shook a little bit and started thinking, "Well, maybe I'm not as good as I thought I was"—and maybe I wasn't, you know. But you can get sobered up pretty quick when you come to Nashville expecting things to happen overnight. You find out fairly soon that it doesn't work that way.

CM: So there was a rude awakening at some point?

Willie: Well, it was definitely an awakening that it was going to take longer than I thought to do what I had in mind, and I didn't know whether I had that much time or not, really.

CM: Why? Did you think you were going to run out of bucks?

Willie: Well, I thought I'd run out of time. I was pushing forty and things weren't exactly happening. I'd had a lot of success as a songwriter, but I wasn't selling any records, so I'd just about come to the point where maybe I wasn't going to sell any records and maybe that was it. Maybe I should be satisfied being a successful songwriter, and let it go at that.

CM: But you didn't.

Willie: No, I didn't. I decided to go back to Texas. I knew that I wanted to play music. I knew that I wanted to sing and wanted to get out there with my band and travel around. Whether I was selling any records or not, I knew I still wanted to do that, and it just made more sense to go back to Texas where I could do that—work Texas, New Mexico, Oklahoma, and make the circle a little smaller. You know—"I'm still doin' what I want to do and I'm still not makin' a great deal of money, but I'm makin' enough money to keep the band together and pay my bills, and the songwriting money is still coming in, and if I can every now and then get a few songs recorded by a couple of major artists, well, I can make it okay." And that was what I'd really decided to do.

CM: Were there one or two people in Nashville who really helped you get going, helped you do what you wanted to do here?

Willie: Well, Billy Walker and Hank Cochran were the ones that first opened up their doors and said, you know, "Come on in and we'll feed you and give you a place to stay until things start happening." To me, now, that's the kind of help that you never really forget.

CM: You worked with Chet Atkins while you were at RCA. He and Don Law and a couple of others people in town brought the horns, the strings and the voices and everything to Nashville, and they called that "The Nashville Sound." That didn't work too well for you—or did it?

Willie: No, it didn't, but it worked great for a lot of other people. It was a way for a lot of other people to go. By the time I got to town, I think it had been used a lot, excessively, and it was not as powerful a way to do it by the time I got to town. I think by then it had got to the point where it was time for the pendulum to start swinging back the other way and go from more to less.

CM: That sort of production didn't really allow you to do the sort of unique phrasing things that you like to do, did it?

Willie: No. I feel that the way that I can be heard best is as close to voice and guitar as I can get, with just a few things to complement it in the background—nothin' elaborate, because I think what I'm trying to sell is a lyric and a style which can be covered up real quickly and easily if you're not careful.

CM: When you were looking around in Texas and seeing your audience changing, you sort of decided to help that gel with your 4th of July Picnic, didn't you?

Willie: Well, another kinda gut feeling I had was that those outdoor concerts were a great way to bring together a few of the young country music fans and put 'em in with some of the older country music fans, and let everybody get a look at each other. I saw that working at the first Dripping Springs Reunion there in Texas, and decided that that would be a good vehicle for that, and also a good way for me to be heard by all these different people. Guys like me and Kris Kristofferson and Waylon Jennings and Charlie Rich and Billy Joe Shaver, Jerry Jeff Walker, Lee Clayton and all of the people who were trying to get something started back in those days—that was a way to get everybody together to listen to what we were doing.

CM: You really broadened that. You brought in people like Leon Russell . . .

Willie: Yeah. Leon was a big help to what I was trying to do back then because he had the young people listening to him and he was the big rock and roll star at that time, but he also did an album called *Hank Wilson's Back* where he sang all those country songs, so he found out too that there were a lot of young long-haired country fans out there. And he loves country music. So when I was puttin' on this first 4th of July Picnic and asked him to come down, he came almost immediately because he wanted to sing to those people too. He saw the same thing that I saw happening.

CM: I've got to ask you about this story; I just read a reference to it. Here in Nashville you were married to a Cherokee lady who didn't like your drinking, jumped into your bed and beat the hell out of you one time?

Willie: Yeah. I was here in Nashville when all these crazy things happened. But she's a great lady. She and I get along fine—we got three kids together, they're grown, they've got kids of their own—but back then we were young and I was crazy, and I was always comin' home, getting way out of line. So one night she decided she'd had enough of that. I came home drunk and passed out—we'd had a big fight and I'd passed out on the bed—so she sewed me up in the sheet and beat the hell out of me with a broomstick, packed all her clothes and mine, and left. By the time I got out of the bedsheet, she'd already gone. I didn't have anything to wear except the shorts that I had on, and it was snowing, cold. She knew how to handle me.

CM: *Red Headed Stranger* put you way, way up there. How did you come about doing that? That was, I understand, kind of an orphan project over at CBS.

Willie: Well, that was my first album for CBS. And it was the first time they let me do it the way I wanted to do it. When I got through with the album, I turned it in, and I said "This is it: Put it out." And it was a little bit different, I think, from what they expected. They expected a big production, you know, and it wasn't that at all. It was the very opposite from a big production. I'm sure that to a lot of those guys it sounded like a demo session, so they didn't take it very seriously. Fortunately, they went ahead and put it out and promoted it, and it did okay.

CM: Wasn't that a big gamble?

Willie: It probably was, but I didn't have anything to lose anyway. It was my first chance to do something and to show CBS that I could do something in the studio, and I believed in it that much. I believed in the song "Red Headed Stranger," and I believed in the story, and also I thought that what I had put together made sense. I believed in it a lot. I believed that if CBS got behind it and promoted it, it would sell. I knew that if it did, the next one would be easier and the next one would be easier still. But I knew this one was going to be difficult to get through because it was simple, it was not anything that CBS was expecting. I can understand why they were kind of taken aback when the tape came in and it sounded like a demo session, but fortunately, they went ahead and got behind it and it all worked out.

CM: They didn't want to say "Oh, c'mon, Willie, let's put some strings on this?"

Willie: Well, they may have wanted to say that, but they never did say that to me because they knew how I felt about it and they knew that when I handed it in, that was the way I wanted it. So no, they didn't try to influence me in any way. Whether they agreed or disagreed, they were either gonna prove me right or wrong—and either way, you know, they couldn't lose.

CM: The will to take the risk at that time has to be part of what looms in your "rebel" and "outlaw" legend. Do you feel much like an outlaw now?

Willie: As much as I ever did. Yeah, you know, it's still difficult to do things the way you want to do them. There's always somebody out there tryin' to get you to do it the way they want you to do it. Which is okay. It's normal, and I know how to live with that, but I still feel that the problems are there today as much as they ever were.

CM: The *Wanted: The Outlaws* album sort of hung a name on you. Did you care for that name at all?

Willie: Oh, I didn't mind it. Up till then, they wasn't hanging anything on me. So at least they were talking about me, and they were talking about Waylon and Kris and Tompall and all those and calling us "outlaws," and that was great. At least we had a side to fight on then, and there was a team developing—whereas up until then it was just a lot of different guys out there trying to do things separately. Once we got together and started trying to do them, then we were "outlaws." They put a label on us, and we were more effective.

CM: That wasn't just a marketing term?

Willie: I think it started out to be a marketing term, but it wound up to be a very good tool for us to use. I mean, we didn't have to say the word "outlaw"—we just had to show up with our long hair and our beards, and all of a sudden, "There's another outlaw!" And that's great. At least we got some recognition and some attention.

CM: When you got back to Texas, you were looking around and seeing long-hairs in your redneck crowds and rednecks in your longhair crowds. Where did you start putting two and two together?

Willie: Oh, places like Big G's in Round Rock, Texas, which was probably one of the strongest cowboy-redneck strongholds in the world. When I saw young cowboys coming in there with their hair down to their shoulders, I knew that things were changing and that here were some more rebels or some more outlaws—if you want to call it that—that were venturing out there doing what they wanted to do, taking a chance on being ridiculed or causing some trouble or whatever. But it was just some people that believed in freedom and that weren't afraid to live their own lives and do what they wanted to. And I saw this type of movement and I naturally wanted to be a part of it because I could relate to it very well.

CM: So it wasn't just you saying "I think I can sell this." It was reinforcing your own . . .

Willie: Absolutely, yeah. I knew that I was not alone, that there were other people out there that had the same problems in different areas and under different circumstances. Basically, the same things that I was running into in the music business, they were running into in school, in college and in their daily lives.

CM: Those pop ballads and concept records that you've done—"Always On My Mind," *Stardust*, "Somewhere Over the Rainbow"—they seem so far away from the mystical cowboy thing that *Red Hearted Stranger* was. . .

Willie: Well, they don't to me. I see all those things related pretty well. The *Stardust* album to me was just as much an outlaw movement as *Red Headed Stranger* because here were a group of pop standards being recorded by a country outlaw, and it's kinda hard to understand how that could be successful. But on the other hand, in my mind I knew that those were ten of the best songs I've ever heard in my life. and I couldn't imagine anyone with any ear for music at all that couldn't hear those songs as being incredible songs. The young people that I was seeing scattered out in the audience, who were listening to music and listening to what I was saying—*they* liked "Funny How Time Slips Away" and they liked "Nightlife." Those songs had some chords in them, and they were fairly progressive, so why wouldn't those same people like "Stardust," and why wouldn't they like "Georgia"? This is what I was thinking about. I knew they would. I knew that if they thought *my* songs were good, wait till they hear some of Hoagy Carmichael's songs, or wait till they hear some Johnny Mercer, or wait till they hear some Irving Berlin! If they think I can write songs, wait till they hear *these* guys write.

CM: You've sort of taken all the Hoagy Carmichaels and the hard-country cats and the Django Reinhardt guitar people, and you've really melded a lot of things into your own stuff, made it your own. You take left field and reinvent it, and it's right there where everybody wants it once it comes out.

Willie: Well, I don't believe that I'm that much different from anyone else. I don't think that my musical likes and dislikes, musical tastes, are that much different from the normal guy walking down the street—whether he's white, black or striped. I think our basic emotions are the same, and I believe that he will like a lot of the things that I like, so I figure that all I have to do is record what I like.

CM: Works pretty well.

Willie: So far.

CM: You got real sick a couple of years ago. Your lung collapsed on you. You hadn't really been doing a whole lot of songwriting for four or five years immediately before that. Did that really change your perspective? When you came out, man, you went into the studio. You couldn't tour, but you just really went to work.

Willie: Well, I had all that energy and I wasn't touring. When I got sick, I cancelled a whole slew of dates, and I was only sick for a couple of weeks, and there I had six months of dates cancelled. I'm a pretty active guy. I can't just sit around. So I did a lot of writing and did a lot of studio work, just to keep busy and keep moving. And during that time I did a lot of things. I did an album with Roger Miller, did one with Webb Pierce, did one with Merle Haggard, did one with Waylon, and did a couple of my own.

CM: Your accident. When you were out there in the surf and your whole side collapsed and it looked like you might drown, did your life flash before your eyes?

Willie: No. (*laughs*) I pretty well knew what had happened and I don't know why—I just felt like my lung had collapsed—and I was close enough to the shore where I knew I wasn't going to drown, and my two kids were there with me, so I wasn't really worried about dying. I was hurting like hell and anxious—*very* anxious—to get out of that water and get to the beach and lay down, which I did. I laid there for about thirty minutes before I could get up and get enough breath together to walk back to the motel room, and then the paramedics came and took me to the hospital. But no, I wasn't worried about dying really.

CM: About a month after that, when you were pretty well out of danger, Lee Clayton came into a party with a big bag of "Maui Waui" saying "You gotta try this, it's the same shit that collapsed Willie's lung" (*laughter*).

Willie: You know, I smoked about three or four packs of cigarettes a day—regular cigarettes—for 25 years, which I know weakened my lungs a lot. But I quit smoking those cigarettes, and I didn't smoke a lot more weed, because smoking is just a lot of picking something up and putting it in your mouth anyway. In the end I decided to double up on the weed and cut down on the cigarettes. I figured it'd be healthier for me. And in the long run it probably is, 'cause I know those other cigarettes will kill you.

CM: Maybe having the energy and having nothing to do is why you got real creative again?

Willie: I think so. I think that's exactly what happened—plus I wasn't smoking nothing. For several weeks there, I didn't take a hit of nothin'. So I had a lot of energy there that I wasn't used to, and my mind was clear, and I was lying there saying "Well, now what are you gonna do for the next six months?" So I started writing and I started getting very active in thinking about writing and studio work, and I got a lot done in that period of time that I would normally have not gotten done. So all in all, it was a very successful sickness that I came up with.

CM: Are you still on that hot streak, writing a lot?

Willie: Well, no. I've settled back to not writing much again, which is okay 'cause I got a lot out of my system on *Tougher Than Leather* and I quit going around telling myself I'd never write again. At least *that* thought is out of my mind. At least I know I will write whenever there's a reason to do it or time to do it.

CM: What makes you want to write now? Anything?

Willie: No. I haven't got any burning desires to write today (*laughs*).

CM: Do you have *any* burning desires? You know, you're lauded all over, and you're at the pinnacle of your career. Is there anything left to challenge you?

Willie: Well I'm sure there is. I couldn't put a name on it right now. I mainly want to keep doing what I know how to do, keep working those tours and making records. I know eventually the records won't sell as well as they're selling now and the tours won't draw as many people as they're drawing now, but right now we're doing real good and I'm enjoying it all and I'm just going to ride it as long as it lasts.

CM: So there's no thoughts of saying "Well, I've had quite enough of this" and rockin' back and going to live in the Rockies somewhere?

Willie: I can't do that. I'll take off for a while, but then I'm ready to go back to work again. I knew a long time ago that I wasn't in this for the money because I did it so long *without* money. I know that I do what I do because I enjoy doing it.

CM: So that song "On the Road Again" is real true.

Willie: Yeah. It's very much true.

CM: Were your folks musical?

Willie: Yeah, my parents and grandparents were all musical. My grandparents taught me a lot about music, music theory, chords and rhythms and what have you. They used to sing gospel along with the Stamps Quartet and the Stamps Baxter Quartet and all those old books, all those old songs. I used to sing out of those books, too, and we used to get together and sing gospel songs a lot. I enjoyed that.

CM: There's a lot of country stories about "Boy, if my folks ever caught me slippin' off to that honky tonk. . ." I guess if you were nine years old when you got into your first band, your folks must have encouraged you?

Willie: Well, my grandmother was not too happy about me playin' around those beer joints, you know. But on the other hand, she knew I loved to play music, she knew I was gonna play music and that's what I was gonna do, so she didn't try to stop me. She *did* ask me if I wouldn't go on the road until I got grown, you know—so here I am, nine years old, playin' in this Bohemian polka band, and I go six miles down the road to play for this dance, and she's upset because now I'm goin' *on the road.* (*Laughter*) Six miles down the highway is *on the road* to her.

CM: In Texas, were you influenced by Mexican music?

Willie: I'm sure I must have been, because I was exposed to it all the time. I lived across the street from Mexicans and listened to their radio all the time, so I'm sure I must have been influenced by it. And besides, I really do like Spanish music and Spanish-flavored music.

CM: Which led you naturally to the polka band that you joined. . .

Willie: Well, around that part of the country, around Abbot, there were a lot of Czechoslovakians and a lot of Bohemians, and their music was polkas and waltzes—that's what they loved to dance to, and they would have big dances, wedding dances or anything that come up. Any kind of special occasion, they'd throw a dance, and so there was always a lot of Bohemian dances. If you wanted to play Bohemian dances, there was a lot of work. So I started out playing in this Bohemian dance band, playing a non-amplified rhythm guitar along with a lot of drums and horns—so it was several years before anybody found out that I wasn't really that great a rhythm player.

CM: After that, you went on to work with your brother-in-law, didn't you?

Willie: Well, my brother-in-law was a guy named Bud Fletcher, and he had married my sister when she was still a junior in high school, and we formed a little band. He would book us into clubs, schoolhouses and what have you around Central Texas—in fact, all over Texas.

CM: I understand that you played a lot of tough little clubs. It must have been kind of rough for a kid that young.

Willie: Well, I saw a lot of fights. There was usually always somebody getting' drunk and starting a fight or throwing a beer bottle. But it didn't involve me—I mean, I was a kid, and you know, nobody was fooling with a kid. But you could get in the way and get stepped on a lot. That was about the most dangerous thing that could happen to a kid like me. But there were a lot of rough clubs back then.

CM: Were any of the clubs the kind that have chicken wire and stuff in front of the stage to keep you from getting beer bottles between the eyes?

Willie: That was later on, after I moved out of the area around Abbott, when I moved up north to Fort Worth and started playing in clubs up there. Those were really rough clubs up there, and I was older too, so I was more involved in everything that went on. There was one particular club where not only did you carry a pistol in your guitar case, but the musicians insisted that there would be some chicken wire put up in front of the bandstand so that we could play our music without having to worry about people out there throwing beer bottles at each other and hitting us.

CM: Hank Williams, when he changed band members, used to take them down to the pawn shop and let them pick out their own blackjack when they were gonna go play Texas.

Willie: (*laughs*) Yeah.

CM: You didn't really come up the easy way then, did you?

Willie: No, I can't remember anything being easy. It was all pretty tough back then.

CM: You got sued last year, I think, for playing a three-hour set at a State fair. Did people there complain about you playing a long set?

Willie: The people never complain. Occasionally, one of the promoters might complain. Sometimes, working those fair dates, if there's a complaint, it normally comes out on the midway somewhere where the guy who's running the ferris wheel or whatever would like for the show to let out so he can get some of the people through there. Casinos in Vegas and different places normally want you to do a short show so that the people can get out there and start losing their money quicker. But the people themselves never complain. They'll appreciate it if you give them a nice show.

CM: Your new album, *Tougher Than Leather*—doesn't that sort of take off from *Red Headed Stranger* and get even more mystical?

Willie: I guess you could say that. It deals more directly with reincarnation and that theory.

CM: Where did you get reincarnation as an idea?

Willie: I grew up in church. I grew up in the Methodist Church, and switched over to the Baptist Church when I was a teenager, and then I started lookin' around at other religions of the world. I came across all the reincarnation religions and started comparing them with the religions that I had been involved in, and found out that they were the same. There was really no difference—basically, they all followed the golden rule "Do unto others as you would have them do unto you" and "You reap what you sow." Those were the main bottom-line ideas of all religions that I ever got involved with. I really felt like I could relate more to the ones who outwardly believed in reincarnation: I really saw that that was a more just belief. To say that we're all born equal and live one time and die just didn't show the merciful Creator—to me it showed a very *un*merciful Creator. To look around and say "Well, let's let this million or so be goin' blind over here, and we'll let this million or so people be born in a depressed area, and then we'll let these nice folks over here be born to rich parents"—I saw a lot of inequality going on there, and I didn't believe that that was the way that the great Creator intended for it to be, and the only other thing that made sense was reincarnation.

CM: You're in a good incarnation now. Steve Young is into this, and he believes that he was a Confederate officer who got killed. Do you have any beliefs about where you may have been before?

Willie: Oh, my imagination, you know—if I want to let it run away, I can imagine all kinds of things, and very possibly they're all true, but mainly I'm concerned about what I'm doing this time more than I am about what I did last time or what I'm going to be doing next time. I think all those things take care of themselves, and since there's no way to know for sure, then I don't worry about it. But I do know what I am doing this time, and where I am this time, and to me that's more important.

WILLIE NELSON

Jim Hatlo | December 1984 | *Frets*

Willie Nelson has always marched to the beat of his own battered guitar. Long before he became a music legend, Nelson quietly defied expectations through his singular voice, phrasing, and choice of instrument and style. In a time when country pickers favored bright steel-string twang, Nelson chose a nylon-stringed Martin N-20 classical guitar and called it "Trigger." He flatpicked Trigger like an old jazz man. This approach set him apart from his peers. It makes his music singular and unmistakably his. As this profile reveals, Nelson's musical journey is vast and varied. He still thinks of himself humbly and honestly as "just the guitar player, sometimes." This piece delves into the man who lets Trigger do all the talking. –Ed.

Willie Nelson is a man of surprises. "Improbable" is the mildest word that describes the course of his career from sideman to superstar, a career marked by so many odd twists, turns and bumps that the story would be hard to pass off a convincing fiction. It isn't out of character, then, that as an instrumentalist he plays a type of guitar that country bandleaders aren't supposed to play, uses a technique usually reserved for another type of guitar altogether, and first chose to do so for one of the least likely reasons.

In place of the obligatory pear-monogrammed steel-string, Shotgun Willie packs a Martin short-scale N-20 *classical* guitar, one of perhaps only 277 ever built. In country circles, let alone the string music world at large, Martin classicals are about as common as Porsche limousines.

And while manicured fingers are considered *de rigeur* for the playing of classical guitars, Willie uses a flatpick—which accounts for one of his instrument's trademarks. In the soundboard, a ragged gash extends from near the lower quadrant of the soundhole rosette down almost to the treble end of the bridge saddle. Classical guitars traditionally do not have pickguards. Wille's instrument, after 15 years of flatpicking, provides an object lesson in why steel-string guitars usually *do*.

Even if the famous auxiliary soundhole, surrounded by pick-abraded bare wood, with skeletal brace ends and edges peeking through, never had formed on Willie's N-20, there would have been no question of the guitar's identity. Besides its battle scars, the soundboard bears the autographs of such artists as Roger Miller and Johnny Bush, along with other graffiti left—at the owner's invitation—during Willie's days as a Nashville songwriter who couldn't quite go over the top as a performer.

Why did Willie Nelson start using a classical guitar in the first place? Test your musical intuition by choosing one of the following: Willie switched to a classical guitar because he wanted to *(a)* favor a weak left hand by changing to the lower tension of nylon strings; *(b)* inject an element of mariachi music into his Texas-based country stylings; *(c)* get a guitar that was strikingly different from those of his performing peers; *(d)* sound like France's Gypsy jazz guitar virtuoso, Django Reinhardt.

The correct answer is *(d)*.

Any similarities between the style of Nelson and the style of Reinhardt are purely intentional. "I wanted to look for a guitar that I could use to find that tone that Django was getting," Willie says, referring to the sound of Django's unusual Selmer-Maccaferri steel-string acoustics. "The guitar that I am using now is the closest that I could find to that."

Most guitarists would figure that Willie was drawn to a nylon-string instrument because of its comparatively easygoing action. But he says that in fact, the opposite is true.

"The action is really a lot slower than what you'd get on a regular Fender electric or something, which I used to play all the time," he explains. "I played a lot of Fenders and a lot of Gibsons—all electrics. I really didn't play the acoustic guitar on stage then, for the simple reason that the fingering was more difficult. But finally I sort of settled for the harder action to get the tone I wanted."

As a performer, Willie also settled for harder action to get the kind of results he wanted. For years he channeled royalties from a successful songwriting career into a money-losing band, so that he could play his music the way he wanted with his "family" of loyal sidemen. He went against the Nashville grain in the early '70s, switching to a non-country label, recording in New York, and moving his base of operations to Texas. That earned him the label "outlaw," but it helped launch a new wave in country music that eventually overflowed into the rock and pop markets and carried Willie Nelson to megastar status. At present, his roll call of recording credits includes no less eight gold albums, six platinum albums, one double platinum album, and one triple platinum album.

Ironically—or perhaps, characteristically—the triple platinum album isn't country at all. It is *Stardust*, Willie's 1978 tribute to the standards (like "Stardust," "Blue Skies," "September Song," and "All Of Me") that he heard and loved as a boy in the 1940s.

Born in the teeth of the Depression in April 1933, Willie grew up in Abbott, Texas, south of Fort Worth. His mother left home when he was six months old, and he was raised by his grandparents. His grandfather, a blacksmith, gave Willie his first guitar lesson at age six. Willie's grandmother, who wrote gospel songs, also played guitar. "I started out with a thumbpick," Willie recalls, "because that was what my grandparents used, so I was taught that way. But later on I began to hear players like Eldon Shamblin [of Bob Wills' Texas Playboys], and they used a straight pick. So I changed because that music was more what I wanted to play. When I was a kid I used to play the mandolin—fool with it a lot, and the banjo, and everything that had strings on it. I usually could get some sort of sound out of them. But I never really tried to get good on anything other than a guitar."

His older sister, Bobbie (now the pianist in Willie's band), was taking piano lessons, so the sheet music she brought home supplemented the songs he heard on the radio—World War II pop hits like "Coming In On A Wing And A Prayer" and "Don't Sit Under The Apple Tree (With Anyone Else But Me)." Through radio he also drank in *Grand Ole*

Opry country music, western swing, and jazz. As he grew bigger, Willie earned $3 a day picking cotton with black field hands. What made the work bearable for him was the blues and work songs they sang.

At age 10 Willie made his professional debut, playing in a Bohemian polka band for $8 a night. He began working in a small group with Bobbie on piano, their father on fiddle, Bobbie's husband on bass, and the local football coach on trumpet. Gradually he evolved a guitar style influenced by such players as Johnny Smith, Hank Garland, George Barnes, Barney Kessel and Django Reinhardt. "I liked those rhythms that Django's band laid down, too," says Willie, "the stuff his brother Joseph played on rhythm guitar." Perennially eclectic, he also was drawn to the music of flamenco guitarist Carlos Montoya. "The Spanish flavor was something I always enjoyed anyway," he says, "so Montoya was one of my favorites from the beginning."

After high school he served a short stint in the Air Force during the Korean War, then spent the '50s working as a door-to-door salesman (variously selling vacuum cleaners, Bibles, and encyclopedias), a plumber's helper, a used-car salesman, a janitor, a Sunday School teacher, and a disc jockey, all the while playing in bars and honky tonks. And writing music. One of his first successful songs was "Family Bible." He sold the rights to it for $50, so he could buy groceries for his family. In 1959 he wrote his classic "Light Life," which would eventually be recorded by more than 70 different artists and sell over 30 million copies. But two years later he sold the rights to it for $150, which he used to buy a second-hand Buick. He used the Buick to move to Nashville.

Willie's work won quick recognition in Music City. Songwriter Hank Cochran heard Willie one night in Tootsie's Orchid Lounge, the bar that served as the unofficial artists' club room for the neighboring Grand Ole Opry, and signed him to a publishing contract. Singer Ray Price, who with Cochran was a part-owner in the publishing company, also was impressed. He made "Night Life" his theme song, and hired its author as a bass player.

Soon vocalist Patsy Cline had a huge hit with Nelson's "Crazy," and Faron Young had another with Willie's "Hello Walls." Liberty signed Willie to a recording contract, and he scored his first Top Ten country hit in 1962 with the single "Touch Me." He became a regular member of the *Grand Ole Opry* in 1964, and the following year he signed with RCA. But though he recorded more than a dozen albums for RCA between 1965 and 1971, Willie didn't enjoy the kind of success that other artists were having with his material.

One reason was his phrasing. Intrigued by crooner Frank Sinatra's knack for singing off, or against, the beat, Willie had adopted the technique in his own music. (That kind of phrasing often turns up in Willie's guitar solos). But his producers saw Willie's use of rhythmical license as a liability, not an asset—and often remixed his studio tapes to get his voice back *on* the beat.

The results weren't impressive, commercially; and artistically they were frustrating for Willie. His substantial songwriting income allowed him to hold his road band together, however, and they kept the faith in live performances. "The music I played on a bandstand was better than the music I played in the studio," he once told Al Reinert of *New York Times Magazine*. "For one thing, I'd be using my own band, and we'd have a better feel for it—be more relaxed. We'd have an audience to play for, and it was just a whole lot more fun."

In 1969, in the middle of his second divorce, Willie's Nashville house burned down. His guitar was one of the few things he was able to save from the flames. While Willie's home was being rebuilt, he moved back to Texas—and stayed. He made the relocation official in 1972. Meanwhile, Willie and his band began hitting the Southwest tour circuit again; and with the expiration of his RCA contract, he left the Nashville studios behind as well. In 1971 he signed with Atlantic, which was venturing into the country market. It was a good move for both parties.

Given a free hand, Wilie took his own band to New York to record *Shotgun Willie*. Finished in less than two days, the LP brought their "outlaw" sound out into the open. Within six months, sales of *Shotgun Willie* had surpassed the sales of all his Nashville albums combined.

From there, the successes began to snowball. *Phases And Stages*, completed in 1974 as Atlantic wound down its country operations, sold 400,000 copies. Meanwhile, the Nashville songwriting fraternity saluted his earlier contributions to country music by inducting him into the Nashville Songwriters Hall Of Fame in 1973.

Willie formed his own record company, signed a distribution agreement with Columbia, and in 1975 released *Red-Headed Stranger.* From that came the single, "Blue Eyes Cryin' In the Rain," which gave him his first Top Ten country hit in 13 years and won him his first Grammy Award. (It also documented a rare reversion to fingerstyle playing on the guitar solo. "I didn't use a pick on that one," Willie says. "Sometimes I use my thumb by itself, to get a softer sound. On 'Blues Eyes,' that was strictly thumb and fingers.")

Red-Headed Stranger was certified gold in March 1976, and before the month was out Willie shared in the plaudits as RCA's *The Outlaws*—a compilation featuring the music of Willie, Waylon Jennings, Jessi Colter, and Tompall Glaser—also earned gold record status. Honors and hit records came almost predictably thereafter. Among his laurels to date are eight Country Music Association awards, including Best Album (twice), Best Single (twice), Best Vocal Duo (with Waylon Jennings in 1976, with Merle Haggard in 1983, and with Julio Iglesias in 1984), and Entertainer of the Year—a title conferred on him in 1979 by both the CMA and the Academy of Country Music.

Willie no longer has to worry about breaking even outside the studio. This summer, Willie Nelson & Family was No. 14 in *Billboard Magazine's* list of top-grossing concert appearances (a roster on which the much-hyped Victory Tour by the Jacksons sewed up 6 of the top 12 spots). Willie also is listed as one of the top ten money-earners on the Las Vegas showroom circuit (along with his old idol, Frank Sinatra).

But despite all the justifiable to-do about his gilt-edged performing status, Willie still prefers to think of himself first and foremost as a picker.

"What I always liked to do was be the guitar player," he says. "Somewhere along the say, I started being the singer. I'm not sure how that happened. I think one night the front man didn't show up, and I wound up fronting the band and doing the singing. And I don't know if that was really the best day of my life! I really do like to be just the guitar player, sometimes. It's very enjoyable when the only responsibility you have is playing the guitar.

When you are playing lead, what's going on in your mind? Are you thinking of the chord changes or melodic patterns on the fretboard, or modes related to the key of the tune, or positions you like to work from?

Not consciously. I think probably if somebody put a computer on me, they'd find I use a lot of things the same way. But consciously—I just play off the top of my head. On the songs that I do a lot, I guess I'm subconsciously aware of the chord structures and I just play whatever notes I hear that fall within those. I really don't think about all that. I guess I'm playing from somewhere else.

Do you work out solos ahead of time? Often, when you're fronting your band, your solos will restate the melody. But in some situations—on the Angel Eyes *album, for example—you'll take what sounds like a more spontaneous lead break.*

It's all how I feel at the moment. I really am not confined to playing anything the same way. I don't have any arrangements that I try to follow, other than the basic things that are always there in a tune—the stuff that you can't get around. Whenever anyone in the band takes choruses, they just play what they want to play.

Back in 1976, when you were interviewed by our sister magazine Guitar Player, *you said that in doing solos you didn't get into a lot of minor scales, because you felt you were major-chord oriented. Now that you're playing things closer to mainstream jazz, is that still true?*

I think so. I love minor chords, and I have written some songs with minors in them. But basically, the songs that I listened to and learned in the beginning were major-chord songs.

Is that when you developed your feeling for standards like "Stardust"? Would it be fair to say that growing up with that kind of material helped you learn how to put together well-crafted melodies?

I think it very well could have. I was always exposed to those songs through the radio and through music that came into the house—sheet music, and so forth. I love good melodies, so I'm sure that had a lot of influence on me.

Through albums like Stardust *and* Angel Eyes, *you've probably influenced a lot of younger musicians yourself, giving them their first exposure to standards and jazz. Do you have any other styles of music up your sleeve—material you might record in the future?*

There are some of the older styles I still haven't done, like Stephen Foster songs, and old Sons Of The Pioneers things—the real cowboy songs like "Leaning On The Old Top Rail" and "Empty Cot In The Bunkhouse Tonight." All of those classics are still there to do.

Often you're functioning as a rhythm player. In your opinion, what goes into really playing rhythm as well as it can be played?

I think you have to know the chord forms. I think guys like Paul Buskirk and Homer Haynes are two of my favorites because of their styles. [*Ed Note: Mandolinist Paul Buskirk and guitarist Henry "Homer" Haynes (half of the team of Homer & Jethro) had strong elements of swing in their music.*] It's 4/4 rhythm and it's done without drums. Or it can be done with drums; but I really like the sound of the kind of rhythm section where you just have an upright bass and the rhythm guitar.

Does a rhythm guitarist need a special sensitivity to where the lead player is going?

Yes, I think that's an innate thing that most good rhythm guitarists know, because most rhythm guitar players are also lead guitar players, to a certain degree. So you just have to have a feel of when to play and when not to play, or how loud to play.

When you're chording, do you ever use your thumb to fret notes?

Yeah, a lot of times. I do that especially in open-chord rhythms. For instance, on a [first position] D chord I'll use the thumb on the low *E* string to play an *F#*.

You generally use Fender medium flatpicks on your nylon-string guitar, instead of fingerpicking it. How often do you change picks? Some steel-string players have told us they go through a half-dozen a night, because the picks get worn and start sounding scratchy. But it would seem that nylon strings would be easier on a flatpick.

I guess a normal person probably would be able to make them last longer, but there's one tune we do each night—"Bloody Mary Morning"—where I'll go through a pick every time I play it.

You can hear the difference? The pick starts to sound rough?

No—I just break it.

Do you play with the point of the pick, or do you turn it and use the rounded corner for a mellower sound, as some players do?

I try to keep it on the point, but in the course of "Bloody Mary Morning" I play every side of it, I think! I use up a couple of picks a night, because "Bloody Mary Morning" will take care of one, and "Whiskey River" will eat up another; so I'll go through at least two picks, maybe three, every show.

You used to use ball-end La Bella nylon strings. Are you still staying with that brand?

As far as I know, I am. The strings are automatically changed on my guitar every few days by a guy in our crew, and I'm not sure if he is still using La Bellas or not. I can't tell any difference.

Are the strings changed on a regular schedule, or does the frequency just depend on how often you're performing?

I think probably every three or four days he'll change the strings. And we keep another guitar handy, with the strings on it already stretched, so that we kind of rotate them. When you put new nylon strings on a guitar, you're always retuning them as they stretch out. That happened to me a lot of times on stage. Boy, it was hard, especially under those hot lights. Finally, we got real brilliant here and figured out that if you stretch them a few days *before* you put them on, you wouldn't have to do that. I don't know why we didn't think of it years before, but better late than never!

Are there certain strings you're more likely to break than others? Some players find that the G string is the first to go, for example.

I very rarely break strings. In fact, I don't remember the last string I broke. The picks go before the strings do, because the nylon strings are more flexible.

The nylon strings are one of the things that set your sound apart; but the way you amplify your guitar has a lot to do with that, too, doesn't it?

I think so. It's a Baldwin amp with a Martin classical guitar—which is kind of a bastard situation. I've tried other combinations, and I don't get the same sound that I do with this one, which was really accidental.

Didn't the pickup itself come from a Baldwin guitar that got broken?

Yeah, I had it taken out of the Baldwin and put in this one years ago, by Shot Jackson's place in Nashville [*Ed Note: In the late '60s, after Baldwin acquired Gretsch and began marketing a line of guitar amplifiers, the company briefly offered a classical guitar model with a ceramic piezo-electric pickup, and a companion amplifier designed for a "natural" tone response.*] I've never changed it. I've tried to keep everything exactly the same, and the amplifier is still the same one. They don't make Baldwins anymore, you know. Each time I come across a used Baldwin amp, I try to buy it so I can use the parts for replacements on this one. I've got a couple of them.

You've had a lot of work done on your guitar to keep it in service through all your years of touring. Who handles the repairs?

A guy named Newman, in Austin [Newman Guitars, 200 Academy, Austin, TX 78704]. He has a guitar shop in the Opera House in Austin, and he's been fixing my guitar for years.

Does your road crew take special precautions with the guitar and amp, since those are really one-of-a-kind items?

They have nice sturdy cases for both. Steel cases. They take real good care of them.

Do you carry any other acoustic guitars on the road with you, or keep some at home that you just use for recording?

I have a couple of guitars around the house, and sometimes I have one on the bus just to fool around with, but my stage guitar is my main guitar. The others are a variety of things—just whatever is available. It varies from one day to the next, really.

How many days a year are you on the road?

I think probably somewhere between 200 and 250. That's this year. It's been like that practically every year, and each year I say, "Next year I'm going to slow down." But I still like doing it. I just enjoy playing music a lot.

THE PICNIC

Michael Bane | July/August 1985 | *Country Music*

At Willie's first 4th of July Picnic concert, both rednecks and hippies flocked in attendance—and his drummer, Paul English, got married. Despite Willie's family-oriented outlook for the original festival, there was an ongoing problem with recreational drug use and partial nudity. Over the years, Willie course-corrected and made his gatherings more safe and secure. –Ed.

The wind was the wind off a blast furnace, a hot, dry sirocco that rolled across the flat plains of Texas to spray a fine abrasive grit into every crack and crevice of rock, tree and human being. It was the kind of wind, wrote Raymond Chandler fifty years ago, that cancelled all the bets.

"Meek little wives feel the edge of the carving knife and study their husbands' necks," he wrote. "Anything can happen. You can even get a full glass of beer at a cocktail lounge."

Willie Nelson squinted out across the crowd, blinked in the relentless sunlight, grinned a classic Willie Nelson grin. The wind blew fine white dust in little ripples across the newly built stage; the speakers whined slightly, a hum not unlike the space shuttle getting ready to blast off.

"Hello and welcome," said Willie Nelson. "Welcome to my Picnic."

The crowd, all denim and leather even in the hot Fourth of July sunshine, roared their approval, and Willie Nelson, the absolute undisputed world-champion country music singer, well, he sang "Whiskey River."

Perhaps the most amazing thing about the 1984 version of Willie's summer extravaganza, held in a natural amphitheater on the outskirts of Austin, Texas, was that the first Willie Nelson Fourth of July Picnic was held twelve years ago!

Twelve years ago! The thought boggles the mind. When the first one was held, the 1972 First Annual Dripping Springs Reunion, the smell of Woodstock was still in the air, and white kids with ponytails called each other "brother." The kids came to Dripping Springs to get high and see folks like Kris Kristofferson and that no-good looking Waylon Jennings and his mean guitar. They came with a gut feeling that the 1960s, the Psychedelic Sixties, were finally dying, and that the next decade, the one that had been trying to lurch to start for two years, would bring something different. The older folks came to the concert to see their heroes from the 1950s and even the 1940s; to see Roy Acuff and Loretta Lynn; to hear Tex Ritter tell one more time the story of a brave man torn between love and honor:

Although you're grieving I won't be leaving
Until I shoot Frank Miller dead . . .

Like the young people, the older fans knew in their hearts that the times they were a-changin', and after a decade of change, they looked at a hazy future with more than a little fear and not too much in the way of hope.

In these business-like 1980s it is perhaps unfashionable to talk about miracles. Suffice to say that over a cold, dreary, wet couple of days twelve years ago a whole lot of kids discovered that their parents weren't nearly as *hopeless* as they'd previously believed, and a whole lot of parents discovered that their kids weren't nearly so weird as they'd thought. Jointly—an apt word—both groups discovered an old truth: that no generation has an exclusive on emotions, and that music—the best music—speaks to emotions held in common by all people. Willie Nelson had known that truth, *lived* by that truth, his entire life.

Twelve years later, they still come, the not-so-young and the just-a-bit-older, to reaffirm the old coalition, to remember the way it was. Like the Crazy Old Soldier of the Troy Seals song, they just don't know when to quit. Instead, they gather once a year in somebody's meadow or somebody's stadium, in Texas or Oklahoma or even New Jersey, to wear the old hats and chant the old chants and hear the old music, Crazy Old Soldiers rubbing a cherished medal until the surface is smooth and shiny, the inscription lost.

First thing about Willie's Picnics you've got to learn is that you're not talking about Woodstock here, folks. There are 12 levels of backstage passes, for guests, performers, press and a whole bunch of people nobody knows. Many of the passes expire at a certain time, and most of the genteel stage security people look like a cross between your normal backstage people and your average, run-of-the-mill motorcycle gang. So the easiest way to find out where you are and aren't allowed to be is to go there and see if somebody resembling the Incredible Hulk comes along and throws you out.

Also, although it's a Picnic, forget the food. In fact, forget the following items:

- food
- beverages
- coolers
- containers of any kind
- signs and banners
- umbrellas
- movie cameras
- tape recorders
- pets
- weapons of any sort, including pocket knives
- fireworks
- anything that can be thrown, including Frisbees and what-have-you.

To prove the concert promoters weren't kidding, most of the 18,000 people who showed up were required to submit to body searches before they were allowed to enter the picnic ground. The "contraband"—sandwiches, pocket knives, fried chicken, potato chips, beer, ice chests, thermos bottles and other "deadly weapons"—was heaved into one of the waiting dumpsters.

David Allan Coe's daughter wore a t-shirt that read, "Willie, Waylon and Daddy." Willie's t-shirt read, "Life is a bitch. And then you die. Have a nice day." Some of the women backstage wore t-shirts with gaping holes cut for the arms, the necks and backs dished out, and the whole shirt cut short. They sprayed themselves with spray bottles of water. As the day wore on, their noses sunburned a bright red.

Johnny Rodriguez played poker and refused to leave for his next gig until the game was over. David Allan Coe posed at the back of the stage for photographs. Waylon and Jessi visited Willie, who popped out on stage during just about every act to sing a duet with the artist. Faron Young, looking exactly as if he were playing a late-night lounge show on Printers' Alley, talked Willie into a duet on "Ain't It Funny (How Time Slips Away)."

"Here's another song Willie wrote for me when I was just a little boy," said the Singing Sheriff, and Willie just laughed, then joined in on "Hello Walls." Even after all these years, that song and Faron Young's voice remain a perfect match. For a second, watching Willie's intense harmonizing, it was possible to imagine a much younger Faron Young in the cool, dark confines of Tootsie's Orchid Lounge, listening to a much younger (and unknown) Willie Nelson pitch him the song.

To be sure, music is what the Picnics are all about. This year, the line-up featured Waylon and Willie, Jessi Colter, David Allan Coe, Johnny Rodriguez, Moe Bandy, Faron Young, Kris Kristofferson, jazzman Jackie King, Floyd Tillman, Leon Russell, Townes Van Zandt, Billy Joe Shaver, Delbert McClinton, Jerry Jeff Walker and Joe Ely. The sets were either 30 or 45 minutes, and this year the Picnic ran like a well-lubricated clock. Willie and Kris closed it with songs from the upcoming film *The Songwriter*. As befits a Crazy Old Soldiers' convention, most of the music wasn't new. It was, rather, the music of the Outlaws, country music circa 1975–1980, when the whole world was discovering Willie and Waylon and Billy Joe and David Allan and all the rest. "Good-Hearted Woman," "Mamas, Don't Let Your Babies Grow Up To Be Cowboys," "Up Against the Wall, Redneck Mother," "Willie the Wandering Gypsy and Me," "Honky Tonk Heroes"—they sang 'em all, and the crowd drank 'em up like cold Coors in big plastic cups.

Kris came on at sunset, when the sky shaded all different colors and the fiery red sun tinted the white dust the color of fresh blood. He sang about lonely nights and Sunday mornings, and the crowd moved with him in a special way. Although Willie and Waylon became the greatest,

Kris was the first. "They're not following me," said his character in the movie *Convoy*, "I'm just in front." For many of the people in this audience, the music of Kris Kristofferson helped define their generation—the Baby Boom kids, the outlaws, the outsiders, the rebels, the protesters. Now, so many years and miles later, the music echoed across a hot Texas meadow, and the crowd seemed caught up not in nostalgia, but remembering. The hot wind moved the years aside, and Kris Kristofferson sang all the words. And when he finished singing, after the applause and the cheering, everyone in the crowd—even the security guards—seemed to be smiling. Maybe, they all seemed to be thinking, the going up *was* worth the coming down.

CATCHING UP WITH OLE WILLIE

Patrick Carr | January/February 1987 | *Country Music*

Due to an economic crisis during the 1980s, many farmers were forced out of business and had to sell their farms. In reaction, Willie Nelson cofounded the annual benefit concert Farm Aid, the first of which took place on September 22, 1985. His concept was to combine a country music festival with rock music. Consequently, over fifty performing acts congregated in Champaign, Illinois, with an audience exceeding seventy-five thousand people. The first Farm Aid was a success, raising millions of dollars. To date, it has raised nearly $80 million for America's famers. –Ed.

It's always nice to have a little chat with Willie. The man may be mellow, and these days there may not be any personal explosions of his present or recent past to investigate, but he's never dull. Usually, he's funny and honest in a crafty kind of way, down to earth and only ever so slightly slippery. Willie doesn't have one of those special-for-publication raps he can turn on and off whenever a reporter penetrates his environs, and he's not secretive; he's just sort of sharp, light on his feet, and it's part of his personality to enjoy a good game of thrust and parry and evasion and wit. Basically, he has the writer's instinct to edit or embellish himself in conversation: he likes to be succinct, and he loves to put a little spin on things.

Willie's always been that way; was before his wonderful one-in-fifty-million hippie/outlaw/redneck/party-host/groovy-guru image secured his living, secular sainthood in the old and new country circles of the 1970's, still is now that he's acquired exclusive blessing rights to a worldwide fan mass just as loyal and almost as large and certainly as diverse as those which commune in the grace of Saints Springsteen and Jackson.

In other words, Willie's circumstances have changed in the last ten years—changed a *lot*—but he hasn't. Sure, he plays an awful lot more golf than anyone could ever have dreamed he would, and his output of new songs has shrunk to the dribble anyone with half a brain figured it very probably would once the gravy train really started rolling, and the mantles of corporate sponsorship and national-affairs involvement have settled about his shoulders as comfortably as both cynics and optimists expected they might, but otherwise ol' Smilin' Willie just keeps smilin' along his own sweet path at his own serene speed, being the good-guy concerned-but-comfortable gypsy con man his life has taught him to be and loving every minute of it.

His story, and his achievements, are of course well known at this point in media time, so there's no percentage in re-hashing it all in any detail here. Suffice it to say that he saved country music from its suburban self in the 1970's, got the kids and cranks and dopers and Yankees interested like they'd never been before, and then slowly evolved into the globetrotting, movie-starring mellow minstrel he is today, meanwhile acquiring an image somewhere in the schizophrenic spaces between Mahatma Ghandi, Pancho Villa, Andy Williams, and the very slickest of your friendly local pool sharks: Willie your brother in peace and music, vaguely heavy. A lovely, crafty, interesting man.

Willie and I haven't encountered each other in five or six years, maybe even seven, but when I walk up to his bus in Florida and hand my card to the hairy feller in the tee-shirt who answers the door and summons the man himself, it's the same as it ever was; we could have been golfing just yesterday, excepting that I don't golf.

The road digs are great. This is Willie's personal bus, *Honeysuckle Rose*, the pride of the five-bus fleet, and it's done up in the style of the most discreet, respectable Mexican whore-house you ever saw; the textured gray leather lining the roof and upper parts of the walls is especially nice, sort of like the insides of a very rich, satisfied, and substantial megasnake.

Willie's in his informal state (his hair's not braided), and he's working; going over pictures of himself and sister Bobbie standing outside a country church. The church is the same one they sang in together when they were kids in Abbott, Texas, and the job at hand is how best to fit both church and brother and sister on to the cover of their new joint gospel album, a Christmas mail-order special. The man in the tee-shirt, David Anderson, is in charge of implementing decisions arrived at in the process; he's Willie's right-hand man on the spot, and like most of Willie's crew his appearance suggests that his employment by the well-known entertainer and philanthropist might just be saving him from a life of overt crime.

The fact that these two scruffs, one filthy rich and the other merely very well paid, are hard at work on a *gospel* album could seem strange if you let it, but really, little contradictions like that are unremarkable in Willie World these days; we've all gotten used to them. I mean, here's a man who digs Webb Pierce and Julio Iglesias and Kris Kristofferson and Frank Zappa with equal pleasure; why *not* sit around in a mobile bordello, right next to the radio phone and the computer golf game, figuring out a good, conventional, straight-down-the-main-beam gospel album cover in a spirit of perfectly serious sincerity? That's the kind of thing a lot of people, myself included, love Willie for: his bold, calm strokes of complex real-life color splashed in there among the blacks and whites of convention.

The gospel project attended to and little personal curiosities satisfied, we activate the recording unit and turn to another matter a lot of people love Willie for: his crusade on behalf of the nation's family farmers focused in his leadership of the FarmAid project.

FarmAid is going well. Benefit concerts numbers One and Two have so far rendered some fourteen million dollars, and the recent Farming Rights Congress has brought a lot of disparate and often quarrelling factions together behind some specific recommendations for a new Farm Bill, and as we speak (late in 1986) the recent elections have returned a healthy number of new or newly pro-farm senators to Washington.

This is all very good, and Willie is pleased. He has worked and is working hard on the cause; it is he who signs every FarmAid check personally, and it is his personal organization which identifies appropriate recipients, distributes the funds, and does everything else a non-partisan charity has to do—including watching everyone's tail for things like political endorsements guaranteed to bring the Feds down on them like ten tons of paper pulp.

We talk a lot of detail about this stuff, and Willie comes across pretty sharp as usual, but since this isn't *Progressive Farmer Magazine* I'll spare you the ins and outs of it all. The point is that Willie really is active on this front (he's not just a figurehead, it ain't no publicity stunt), and *his* main point is simple: American farmers must get a fair price for their product; everything else follows from that. In the meantime he'll do what he can to help farmers in trouble, and help them make as much noise as possible. "The wheel that does the squeakin' gets the grease," he quips quite rightly.

There remains the question of why, when it comes right down to it, he is involved in the farmers' cause. Well, to cut a long story short, it began as something which just seemed like a good idea at the right time in the right place—the first FarmAid benefit in Champaign, Illinois—and mushroomed out from there. But then there must have been some basic receptivity to the idea on Willie's part to begin with. There was.

"I wasn't a farm kid, but I did grow up in a farm town," he says. "I made my money to send myself to school by working the farms. Picked cotton, pulled corn, baled hay, worked in the cotton gin and the corn silos, was a Future Farmer. I still have livestock, still have horses and cattle, and I'd still be losing money if I depended on farming and ranching to make a living. Nowadays, see, people have farms and ranches as a tax write-off, 'cause it's almost a given that they're not going to make any money out of them. And that's crazy."

We start talking about the new tax laws and what they'll do to such ventures—basically, it's bye, bye, the good ol' profit-gobbling Black Angus herd, farewell to yet another bizarre modern-American institution—but then, thankfully, we get reminded of music by the hearty arrival of Jody Payne, one of Willie's two travelling guitar players—the other's the mature and legendary Grady Martin. Jody's blown in from Austin after a few days off the road, and he's dying for a little picking.

We quit talking. Jody picks up a guitar and sings Willie a love song he's been trying to get right for years. It's pretty nice. Then he gives Willie the guitar, and Willie sings one he put together from scratch just the other night.

It's nicer. He still has the touch.

So really, how *is* Willie's Muse? I mean, there are plenty of Willie Nelson albums—seems like there's a new one—or *two*—every time you stop by the record store to see what new old fashion the teenagers have glommed onto this week—but Willie Nelson *songs* are getting to be a seriously endangered species. Though maybe not; the vinyl output is so staggering that it's kinda hard to get a bearing on the question.

But Willie knows. "Well, I did write that song a couple of days ago," he laughs, "and that makes one in a row. Maybe it's a trend.

"I dunno. I guess probably I'd like to do more of it. I think it's really just a matter of giving myself time to do it; I always seem to write when I get still somewhere for long enough. But I have a tendency to keep myself going so much that I don't give myself that time. I don't know if that's intentional, or what—but that's what happens."

Yeah, say I. Generally, you find that people who were born to write will fill their lives with anything—*anything*—which prevents them from doing so. And then the only question is, how well they can handle the guilt such stratagems cost them.

"Right," laughs Willie. "How long can you go without giving in? That's me."

He's lucky, though. He has plenty of stuff to keep him away from his guitar and notebook. Two hundred–plus road days a year, for instance.

"I've been working a lot," he says. "Probably too much, really. I could probably take off all next year without worrying about it too much. Still, though, after I'm off a few days, I get restless. This time last year I was saying what I just said, and I *still* wound up working over two hundred days."

He loves the roaming life, is what it is; being in that bus, away from whatever stays in one place and bothers him. When he gets off the bus, he heads for whichever of his homes is closest—Colorado, Maui, or the main enclave outside Austin where Connie and the girls live and the private golf course beckons—until the wanderlust strikes and off he goes again. He does it even though the road is far from being his major bread-winner. "By the time you pay for five buses, thirty people, thirty hotel rooms, and all that stuff, it's hard to make money on the road no matter *who* you are," he says. "I make my money from my songs and my record sales; there have been quite a few years when I've had to dip into my songwriting money to finance the road tours."

Then of course there's his movie career, which right now centers around *The Red Headed Stranger*, apple of his eye and the jewel in his crown. As we speak it is headed for release after many, many trials and tribulations but a final conclusion of breathtaking rightness. It was wrapped up one day under schedule, and $100,000 under its amazingly low budget of two million dollars, and furthermore all the investors—Willie's friends, ranging all the way from Coach Darrell Royal to writer Bud Shrake to Frank Tyson of supermarket chicken fame—got every penny of their money back, and then some, out of the distribution deal with Alive Enterprises, an empire built by the very savvy Mr. Shep Gordon on proceeds from his management of the immortal Alice Cooper. In other words, they were in the gravy before the first paying customer walked in a movie theater door. The only one still sweating before release was Shep, and he wasn't sweating that hard.

Willie is proud of *The Red Headed Stranger*, and happy about it. "It came out like I first saw it in my mind, only better," he says. "The actors really added to it; they were *great*. They were wonderful to work with, and we really enjoyed doing it. I mean, raising the money was a giant hassle, and it took forever—we had three or four false starts, you know, days when we had to send actors home—but we made it. It got pretty bad at times, even after we got started. The first week of shooting we had a falling-out with one of our finance people, so there we were with the money gone and the cameras rolling and me writing about $300,000 worth of hot checks, but then word got back to this wealthy girl in Boston, Caroline Mugar—she was a real fan, she'd been coming to the shows for years—and she came down with a check for half a million dollars and said, 'Finish your movie.'"

Caroline saved *The Red Headed Stranger* and has since become a moving force in the FarmAid project, and everybody is living happily ever after.

Next up in the movie biz, Willie figures, is either an as-yet-unformed film about American Indians or another *Barbarosa* flick, this one dealing with the bandit's early life as a Texas Ranger. Willie has a particular affection for Barbarosa, in part because the ol' feller gets to ride horses a lot—and therefore, of course, so does Willie, so maybe he'll finance the project himself again, and maybe he'll get to zip around the mesas on "the best little horse in the whole world" again. And like zipping around the country in his mobile bordello, that "ain't like work at all."

Interviewing can get to be, though, so we hang it up for a while again, and Willie teaches me how to play the computer golf game which fills his road life with joy and frustration—as in real golf, sometimes he's "pretty good" and other times he's "just terrible." Just a touch of it is enough to convince me forever that the stuff is more addictive than Twinkies. Better stay the hell away from it.

As we play, we chat idly about this and that, and then the subject of Willie's appearance as a retired Texas Ranger on *Miami Vice* comes up. All I really want to know about it is the answer to the burning question of the late Twentieth Century: *Does Don Johnson sweat?*

"No, he doesn't," says Willie. "Not at all." His voice becomes appropriately reverent now as he adds, "And yes, he's a beautiful person. We actually touched, spoke, and spent time together. Quality time. Some of it even in his mobile unit."

Well, that does it, doesn't it? In 1986, quite apart from every other accomplishment and accolade—getting voted Man of the Year by the United Jewish Appeal, for instance—our little man from Abbott, Texas, had a whole *Miami Vice* episode written around him and got to glow live-and-in-person with the Don. Nothing else matters now. He is There; he has Arrived. He has earned the right to Golf in Peace.

Which right he is exercising, after a fashion. As another audience begins to filter into the hall behind his bus and little groups of oglers gather around his all-steel gypsy caravan, Willie's little electronic ball describes graceful and impressively lofty parabolas through the computer-generated graphic sky. He's playing well today.

Activity is mounting, and it's getting hard to concentrate on the job at hand. Members of the band and crew keep popping in and out for decisions or chit-chat, spreading good cheer around the place. One of them shares the message of his favorite bumper sticker with Willie—*S--t Happens*—and Willie cracks up, then remembers that that very bumper sticker used to adorn this very bus. Does it still? Nobody knows, and I forget to look. Another functionary reminisces about little difficulties at the Canadian border, which leads me to ask Willie if there are any countries he's not allowed into these days. No, he says, none—though there are a few where it would have to be just him and his guitar; seems that some of the crew aren't quite so unblemished in the legal department. Then Sister Bobbie arrives in the nick of time, a slightly flustered but still very matronly, down-home-correct gypsy lady. Then Gina, a young thing whose home base is Manhattan's ultra-exclusive Park Avenue, arrives more calmly, changes into a skintight black leather outfit, and sits quietly and adoringly as the fun rolls on around her. During a lull she pulls out a large notebook and commences writing with great intensity. "Songs?" I ask on one of those think-I've-been-*here*-before hunches. Her eyes glow. "Always," she says.

But time's wasting, so on goes the tape recorder and up come some fast essential questions.

The fabled jogging, for instance. Once upon a time the notion of Willie Nelson out there pounding the pavements seemed about as likely as the Pope out there spearfishing for barracuda, but yes, we got used to it. Willie's not jogging right now, though. When he broke his thumb last year he also hurt his back—which he didn't know about for a while because the pain pills were so wonderful—so jogging is out. He'll get back to it, though. "It's addictive, you know," he says. "It can really get to feel good, out there running around like a deer."

And the other hobbies? Well, there's the golf of course, and there's the horsemanship he loves so much. Any shooting these days? I ask, mainly because I've become such a gun freak myself lately. Nah, not any more, says Willie, and that pleases the horses. "Of course, you can always put cotton wool in their ears, but then they can't hear *you*, either." He sighs. "It's just one big problem after another we cowboys run into, you know."

Moving right along, I'm wondering about corporate sponsorship. Willie of course is signed up with the Wrangler clothing company, which helps promote his shows and pays him an annual fee in exchange for the loan of his image. Specifically, I'm wondering how comfortable such a publicly vulnerable concern feels about certain well-known components of the Nelson lifestyle.

"Well, they're great people," says the man. "They're a lot of fun. We had a party a while back at one of their people's houses, and a couple of us got pretty friendly around a bottle of Cuervo Gold. We came to a mental agreement somewhere along the line. But no, they didn't ask me about any of my other habits. I'm sure they knew what they were before we even started talking about the deal." Willie adds that these days he's not drinking like he used to, by the way. Right now he's just sipping beer; the traditional Jack Daniels bottle is absent from the crook of his arm.

A couple more questions. First, the book. At long last, after years of invitations and many, many memos and lunches, the publishing industry has finally persuaded our man to construct an autobiography. As we speak, the deal is not finalized, but the terms have been agreed upon. Simon & Schuster has offered Mr. Nelson and his golf-buddy ghostwriter Mr. Bud Shrake 1.25 million dollars for said work. "That got my attention," says Willie.

It's not likely to hurt too bad, Willie figures. Bud can roll tape as they ride the links together, and it will all be about as hard as falling off a log backwards. As to the nature of the final work, well . . . as the autobiographer puts it, "I'm gonna tell as little as I can get by with. You think I'm gonna go out there and tell everything I know about everybody I know—like you, for instance? There ain't enough money to get either one of us out of jail."

I venture the thought that Simon & Schuster's definition of "as little as I can get by with" might be a tad broader than Willie's, and appraise him of the reputation of Michael Korda, the brilliant Hun who runs the show up there and makes a tidy penny on the side by writing books with titles like *Winning Through Intimidation*. This doesn't faze Willie one bit. "*Winning Through Intimidation*, eh?" he muses. "I sorta like the sound of that; he sounds like he might be okay."

Which leaves us, somehow or other, with The Big One. God, the afterlife, the world of the spirit. Where these days does Willie stand on this ultimate turf?

"About the same as ever," he says. "I personally believe in reincarnation. I don't have any awareness of any other incarnation, though, and I'm really not that interested or concerned about what I was or what I'll be next time. I'm too busy working on this one, trying to figure this one out. All I really know is that I'm right here; that's all I'm sure of. me and Patrick Carr are right here on this bus, and I'm sure of that—almost."

And since we are after all talking to our guru here and the crowd in the hall is growing impatient, we just have to wrap this up with any thoughts he might have about the condition of the human race, the progress of man. How about it, Dr. Nelson?

"Well," quoth he, "mankind is plodding along. Grazing occasionally and running for cover now and again, but mainly just plodding along. Moves when it has to; just follows the good grazing, like the rest of the herds."

Thanks, Willie.

WILLIE NELSON

Alanna Nash | 1979–1985 | from *Behind Closed Doors*

American journalist and biographer Alanna Nash interviewed Willie Nelson in person several times between 1979 and 1985 in Lexington and Louisville, Kentucky. She published them in collection in *Behind Closed Doors: Talking with the Legends of Country Music* in 1988. This then is a composite of those years of interviews, which contributes to its lengthy duration. Nash's deft frankness and Willie's amiable personality are engaging and refreshing. –Ed.

At the mere sight of it, a tourist in Nashville would probably become so unglued as to drop his Instamatic. There, jogging up and down Music Row, was none other than Willie Nelson, clad in running shoes and jogging shorts, the likes of which are sold along with T-shirts at his concerts. A bandana tied above his red-orange pigtails held the sweat off his face, a dusty road map of the places he's been and played in his thirty-year rise from obscurity to superstardom, every mile and every day of his fifty-five years etched there in testament. "I run five or six miles a day. Sometimes I'll run twice a day," he was to say later in his soft Texas drawl. But this morning's run is only for show—a local television personality wants Nelson on the six o'clock news.

Willie Nelson has always jogged to his own pace. In late 1970, after his house burned down, Willie left Nashville, where he'd come in 1959, for his native Texas. Despite the 1962 hit "Touch Me," his eighteen or so albums hardly ever passed the cash register. No thanks, he says, to the record company executives, who had little faith in him as a vocalist, feeling his strange, haunting baritone clashed sharply with the prevalent smooth and sweet Nashville Sound. For a long time, he stuck it out in Music City, playing bass—at twenty-five dollars a day—for Ray Price, and watching the songs he wrote for himself—"Crazy," "Night Life," "Hello, Walls," "Funny (How Time Slips Away)"—become major hits for other people. The songwriting money started rolling in, but finally it came down to either compromising or cutting out for Texas. There, even if he didn't get rich, he was his own man, making his own kind of music, a curious and personal blend of country, blues, gospel, honky-tonk, western, and Texas swing. Nelson opted for Texas, where not even he knew there was an audience waiting for him, an audience made up of folk, country, and rock, of hippies and rednecks, oldsters and youngsters, liberals and conservatives, bound together by an undeniable energy and appreciation of plain good music.

A year after leaving Nashville, Nelson recorded *Yesterday's Wine*, a concept album he still considers his best work. RCA, however, didn't see it that way, and his last two singles went nowhere. In 1973, then, Nelson hightailed it to New York and Atlantic Records, becoming the first country artist to sign with the label. There, he recorded *Shotgun Willie* and the critically acclaimed *Phases and Stages*, another concept LP, about the breakup of a marriage, told from both the male and female. viewpoints. The album sold an astounding 400,000 copies. With that, Columbia Records offered him a contract that gave him just what he wanted: total artistic control.

The result was 1975's *Red Headed Stranger*, the brilliant, if flawed, theme album of love and murder. Produced by Nelson in three days on a budget of $20,000, the album used such sparse instrumentation that at first, Billy Sherrill, then the top executive in the Nashville office (as well as a producer well known for his intemperate use of orchestral overdubs), argued against its release. But Nelson reminded the label of his creative-control clause, and pledged that if the album bombed, he would relinquish his autonomy on future projects. The LP became a best seller on both country and pop charts, yielded the crossover hits "Blue Eyes Crying in the Rain" and "Remember Me," and would eventually sell two million copies. Suddenly, the hottest things in country music were

Willie Nelson, the "new breed" of singer-songwriter, and what someone quickly termed the "Austin Sound." The attendance at his annual Fourth of July picnic—which started out at 50,000 paying customers—swelled to twice that number.

If *Red Headed Stranger* was Nelson's breakthrough album, the one that secured his superstar status was RCA's *Wanted: The Outlaws*, released in 1976. Essentially a sampler of "Nashville rebel" music, the album featured Nelson, Waylon Jennings—who got top billing, for contractual reasons—Jessi Colter (Jennings' wife), and Tompall Glaser. Although the company hoped it would do well, nobody foresaw what was to happen: *Wanted: The Outlaws* sold like Gatorade at a chili cook-off, becoming the first country album ever to "go platinum," selling more than a million copies. The irony of the project is that the LP was made up of mostly old material that had appeared elsewhere, often in better versions. But the mission was accomplished. "Outlaw" was now the operative buzzword, and Nelson and Jennings took on a stature of semi-mythic proportions—that of hairy, hell-raising, nomadic loners who broke all the rules and got away with it.

In the next few years, not only Nashville bowed at Nelson's nylon-sneakered feet but seemingly the whole country, including President Jimmy Carter, who asked Nelson to sing the national anthem at the 1980 Democratic National Convention, and went on to become a genuinely close friend. By that time, Hollywood had also beckoned, and Nelson received critical praise for his first acting role as Robert Redford's manager in *The Electric Horseman*. If most of Nelson's subsequent films—*Honeysuckle Rose* and *The Songwriter*, in particular—seem to be just more rehashing of the well-known Nelson saga, enough people still find him fascinating that four biographers—Bob Allen, Michael Bane, Lola Scobey, and Willie's daughter, Lana—have written accounts of his life and career. He is, in the words of musicologist Bill C. Malone, "the hottest commercial property that country music has ever had, as well as one of the most visible figures in American popular culture."

Certainly that is true, but in recent years Nelson has scattershot his musical energies in a variety of projects that teamed him with literally dozens of big names in music, from Julio Iglesias to Neil Young. While there has been no solo LP to rival *Red Headed Stranger*—another theme album, *Tougher Than Leather*, which explores the idea of reincarnation and was released after Nelson suffered a collapsed lung in 1981, paled in comparison—Nelson has continued to turn out albums of quality, a feat for an artist so prolific. So far, his most valuable contribution to the '80s has been spearheading Farm Aid, the concert marathon that raised money for the plight of America's farmers. But he has maintained an excellent showing on the charts for more than a decade, long after most careers have seen their peak.

"I thought I'd peaked several times," Nelson said in this interview, conducted in person, in Louisville and Lexington, Ky., and on the telephone over a five-year span, from 1979 to 1984. "Now I don't think I have peaked," he continued. "Everything just seems to be getting a little bit better every day."

Q As a performer, you've managed, at various stages, to win the youth market, with your duets with Waylon Jennings, the Middle America market, with your collection of standards such as "Stardust," and even the easy-listening market, with a big hit such as "Always on My Mind." Obviously, the response you get in Nashville now is a little different from the one you got when you first went there.

A Yeah! Considerably. I like it better this way.

Q In 1979, you became the Country Music Association's Entertainer of the Year. But your most triumphant return to Nashville must have occurred in 1976, when you performed on the CMA awards show, and you and Waylon Jennings went on to rake in most of the honors. What did that feel like?

A Oh, I enjoyed it. That was a big evening. They threw a big party for us. I sang all night long. At two or three different places. Yeah, I reveled in it.

Q Are you bitter about those early days?

A Well, no. Not really. Not now.

Q How often are you back in Nashville now?

A Every chance I get. When I'm out on the road and I've got a couple of days off and I'm close, I'll fly in there. I still have a farm and a house out there north of town [in Ridgetop, Tennessee], where I used to live, and my nephew lives out there. It's [my sister] Bobbie's son, Freddie. And my son is building a place out there, too. So Nashville is still kinda home.

Q You once tried being a pig farmer in Nashville.

A Yes, I really did. I lost a fortune on pigs. I had the fattest pigs in town, or in the country. I paid twenty-five cents a pound for 'em and fattened 'em up for six months. When I sold 'em, I got seventeen cents a pound for 'em. Lost my ass and all its fixtures. (Laughter)

Q How did you let that happen?

A Oh, I had nothin' to do with it. It was just that I got into the hog business at a bad time. I found out from the old-timers that you can't just get in it one year and expect to make a killin' and get out. You've got to stay with it and raise hogs every year.

Q Had you been a farmer before?

A Oh, yeah. I was raised in a small farmin' town [Abbott, Texas], so I farmed all my life, really. Usually for somebody else, because my grandparents [who raised me] were too poor to own their own farm. So we were working for the *other* farmer. But I raised for the FFA [Future Farmers of America] back in school. I used to raise one pig at a time, to show. But I'd never raised that many before, and I never will again.

Q There are some funny photographs of you taken during that time. You looked like the straightest guy in the world.

A I looked like a young baby boy in some of those pictures. Yeah, that was just about the time that I started raising hogs, and growing my beard back and wearing my overalls again.

Q Do you ever run into anybody in Nashville who gave you a particularly hard time when you first went there?

A I don't really know the answer to that question, because I probably couldn't name the people who gave me a hard time. They were always nameless. They were always in New York, or somewhere. There was a computer somewhere that hated me, I think. But as far as enemies in Nashville, I don't have any. Everybody I know there has always been real good, real nice. I haven't seen any bad guys in Nashville. I've seen some people who were uninformed. But it was out of ignorance; it wasn't intentional. No, Nashville hasn't treated me any worse than any other town.

Q So nobody ever treated you badly—they just weren't anxious to have you do your music your own way?

A Well, sure. In other words, these people had things goin' their own way and they were successful doin' it the way they were doin' it. Some upstart from Texas come running up there, runnin' around sayin', "Well, this is the way I want to do it"—I'd probably have reacted the way they did. Because they didn't have any idea that I knew what I was talkin' about.

Q Was there ever a time when you were tempted to compromise to get ahead?

A No. I honestly can't say there was, because I got mad somewhere along the way, and decided I would not do it, and it got to be fun, not doin' it. I mean. not compromising really got to be a thing, maybe to the point where we went overboard in the other direction. Of course, we were doin' okay, the way we were goin'. We weren't getting' rich, but we were eatin'.

Q Why did it finally take off in such a big way after all those years?

A The energy, I think, from the young people. When that much energy gets behind any project, it's got to skyrocket. You know, when they got behind the Beatles and rock and roll—and there's millions of those kids out there that buy records. And that audience all of a sudden became a country music audience.

Q But why did they focus on you?

A I don't know the answer to that one. I really don't know.

Q And now kids wear T-shirts that say. "Matthew. Mark, Luke, and Willie."

A Well, that may be carrying it too far. It's a nice thought, though.

Q You give the impression that it wouldn't bother you if the crowds didn't keep coming, as long as you could still play music.

A That's true. We just enjoy playin' for whoever's there. I enjoy playin' in a motel room, just sittin' around pickin'.

Q When did you realize you'd made it?

A I think probably the first time was when I went out—I'd been makin' two dollars a day choppin' cotton, and I went out one night and made eight dollars playin' music. I think I was about eleven years old then. From that day on, I had it made. That was the turning point. That was it. No more cotton choppin' for me.

Q What sort of kid were you?

A Well, when I was a kid, "long hair" meant a long-haired musician. And that was long-haired music, long-haired musician. Of course, I wasn't then. I played country music, but I had fairly long hair, and long side-burns. And my hair was always in my eyes for as long as I remember, except a couple of times when I got a burr haircut. I usually went from one extreme to another.

Q Were you outgoing, active in sports?

A I was very active in all kinds of sports. Played basketball, baseball, football, ran track, was a pole vaulter. I just did anything that I could do.

Q Were you mischievous?

A Oh, yeah. That, too. There wasn't a lot to do in Abbott, so you had to be real creative to come up with something to do on a Sunday afternoon. Which we were.

Q Did you think all this was waiting for you?

A No, I didn't. I didn't really know about any of this. I did know what I wanted to do. I wanted to be a guitar player and a singer. And guys like Ernest Tubb, Bob Wills were my heroes, so I wanted to be just like them. And I wanted to have their life style. And now I do.

Q Did you have a feeling of being special?

A Well, I thought I was better than I was doing. I didn't know whether I was special or not. I wasn't that knocked out over my singing voice back then because I had a real high singing voice, before my voice changed. And when my voice started changing, I sounded like a frog croaking for a few years there. So, no, my singing really didn't knock me out, and it doesn't today. You know. I don't think I'm a bad singer, but I don't think I'm that great, either. But I love to play the guitar, and I thought I could write songs.

Q Does your fame keep you fairly isolated? Can you go out in public and mix with people?

A Sure, I went out and played golf all day yesterday at a country club. I get out all the time. I would hate to think that I couldn't, you know. There are people who come up and want autographs. But that's nice, too. It's a lot better than sitting around in your room all the time.

Q You don't have people tearing your clothes off.

A No, fortunately. I've heard all these things about the Beatles and Elvis. But nobody's even, well, tore a button.

Q What have been the major disappointments of your career?

A Well, I've had some major setbacks, that's for sure. There's lot of years where it was touch and go financially. Trying to keep a band together when you're not making all that much money is a difficult thing to do, as any bandleader can tell you. So we had some lean years there. With a lot of disappointments. A lot of albums that didn't sell. But as far as any one specific thing. I can't think of anything particular.

Q RCA's handling of your first concept album. *Yesterday's Wine,* which is one of your finest LPs, must have been a disappointment.

A Yeah, I thought that was my best one. Well, all those albums that I did back then when they didn't sell, they were all major disappointments. Because each one of those albums had ten or twelve songs, pieces of my life in them, you know. And I felt very strongly about all those songs, and still do. I think a lot of those songs never had a chance to be accepted.

Q Did you always feel secure about your talent back then?

A Well, that's two different things there. I was never doubtful of my talent, but the odds on anything happening—I mean, there was a time or two that I had a lot of negative thoughts about what my future would be. I wasn't sure whether I might be back pumping gas or picking cotton for a living. Which could have happened. Or really, I think the worst that could have happened was I would go back to playing in small nightclubs around the country again. But that's not too bad, and not a bad way to make a living, either. You can only spend so much money, as long as you're making enough to buy groceries and pay rent and buy a few clothes, and buy a car. That's about all you can expect, anyway. I don't think I would ever have had to go back to picking cotton, but the thought did cross my mind when things weren't going that well. I wasn't going up, but I wasn't going down, either. I was just kind of hanging in space there for years.

Q Where are you now?

A I really don't know. I thought I'd peaked several times. Now I'm not sure. I don't think I have. Everything just seems to be getting a little bit better every day.

Q Do people still call you an "outlaw"?

A I don't know whether they do or not.

Q That term was misunderstood, wasn't it? Originally it meant that your music didn't conform to the Nashville standard, but then some people thought it meant that you beat up people and took a lot of dope.

A Well, some people misunderstood it, I think, or maybe they didn't. (Chuckling)

Q Did you mind that label?

A No, I don't care. It was funny then, and well, I still think it's funny every time I read something where it says, "Willie Nelson, the outlaw." But I guess it makes good reading for somebody.

Q How did that get started?

A Oh, I don't know. Somewhere between Tompall [Glaser] and [Jerry] Bradley [formerly in charge of all operations of RCA Nashville], I guess. They thought it might be a good idea, and evidently it was. It caught on.

Q You seem to always be full of surprises. The music industry, for example, thought you were out of your mind when you said you were going to do the *Stardust* album, made up of old pop standards. Did you ever have any doubts about it?

A No, I never did, because those were songs that I've been doin' for people every night nearly all of my life, and I knew that people liked 'em, and I knew I could do "Stardust" and turn around and do "Fraulein" or any kind of music. Those people didn't know whether they were country or pop. Somebody had to tell them later on. They just knew they liked music. They'll sit out there and drink a beer, and they'll dance to "Stardust," and they'll dance to "You Are My Sunshine." They just like music. And I just like music. And those were just songs. They didn't have labels back then. The more I got into the record end of the business, I found out they had music sliced up into a bunch of different categories. And that was very confusing to me. Then I had to start slicin' up what I knew. "Well, you can't play this one, 'cause it's not country," or "You can't play that one, 'cause it's not commercial." So there's a lot of people that still live under the illusion that music is sliced up, but it's not. A G is a G. A quarter note is a quarter note. Whoever's doing it makes it different.

Q Some people think you're largely responsible for bridging country and pop. Would you agree?

A Well, that's a nice thought. Whether it's true or not, I don't know. I may have been partly responsible for exposing both kinds of music to both audiences. *Maybe*. But, of course, I wasn't the only one. There's guys been doin' it all along. I just sneaked some stuff in and caught 'em not lookin', and they liked it before they knew it.

Q But if you didn't look the way you do, with the beard and the long hair, would the kids listen to you sing "Stardust" and some of the older songs?

A Yeah, I think the kids would accept those albums. They're not buying a look, they're buying music. I think the fact that I had long hair and an earring probably got their attention a little bit, and the older people, too. Made some of them pretty mad, I think. But, I mean, there's nothing not to like about those songs. I would question someone's sanity a little bit if they didn't like "Moonlight in Vermont" or "Sunny Side of the Street." A good song doesn't get old. It doesn't die out. A good song just stays and stays forever. There are hundreds of thousands of songs that are still laying there waiting for someone to come along and pick them up again. They were hits twenty, thirty, forty years ago, and they'll be hits in the next twenty to thirty to forty years also.

Q Probably no one else in country music is capable of pulling off these things the way you do. Any idea why?

A Not really, no. I'm not that great a singer. I know the songs and I sing the melody. I don't try to get tricky with them. I think a lot of the singers who know these songs are the pop singers who have such good voices that they usually wind up oversinging those songs. And I think the melody and lyric of those particular songs is so special that it doesn't need anything other than just saying the words and following the melody, really.

Q So you never consciously thought about crossing over?

A That's a term I wasn't familiar with until I got to Nashville. Then I started hearing words like "commercial" and "crossover." Because music had always crossed over. There had never been any divisions in Texas, where I came from.

Q Is music really any different, or played any differently, in Texas, say, as opposed to Nashville? Can there really be a "sound" that's confined to a certain city?

A Oh, no. I don't believe that. I don't believe the Nashville myth or the New York myth. I think they're all musicians travelin' around all over the world makin' music. If they stop in Nashville, they're not gonna sound any different than if they stop in Austin. It just doesn't make sense. Now, there might be some towns where good musicians gather more than they do in other towns. Austin is that place, for sure. There's probably more good bands playing live music in Austin than in any other city in the country.

Q Why is that?

A The climate is good, the attitude of the people is good, the attitude toward strangers is good, and then it's just a nice place to go.

Q Has it changed much through the years?

A No, there's more people down there. It's like Nashville and every place else—it's grown.

Q But did you develop this Austin music scene, or was it already there and you just became the big symbol for it?

A All the ingredients were there. The audience was there. I just happened to stumble onto an audience, really. I just saw that there was a lot of young people who liked country music, and I may have been one of the first ones to see that. And so I started lookin' for the young crowds because I enjoyed that energy. I like bein' around young people. And I thought it was great that they were beginning to like country music and they were beginning to like what I was doin'. So we started seekin' each other out, I guess. But, say, when Leon Russell came out with that album, *Hank Wilson's Back*, that helped a lot, too. Because there was a lot of Leon's rock-and-roll fans that listened to country music for the first time, And they heard "The Window Up Above," "Rollin' in My Sweet Baby's Arms," and "Goodnight, Irene." Leon laid the groundwork for guys like me, who was comin' along singin' those same songs.

Q You did an album with Leon, *One for the Road*, and then you toured together. How did that pairing come about?

A Actually, Leon and I have been friends for a long time, and I'd been tryin' to figure out a way to make records with him for years. And when he did his *Hank Wilson* album, I thought it was great, and I wanted to see him do some more of those. I finally talked him into doin' one with me.

Q When did you first meet him?

A The first time we knew anything about each other was in a studio on the first album that I cut, on Liberty Records. Leon was a sideman, playin' piano, and he didn't know me, and I didn't know him. But we found out later that we'd been on the session together. He recognized himself on one of my records one time, playin' "Mr. Record Man." He said, "Hey, that sounds like me!" Leon is just a genius, I think. He may be the greatest musician I've ever known, alongside of Booker T. Jones.

Q Actually, *One for the Road* sounds as if it were done almost spur of the moment, and that you settled for the first take on a lot of the songs.

A Yeah, it was one of those deals where I was talkin' to Leon and we had a week off at the same time, and he had his studio, so we just sailed into California and spent the week out at his place there, and recorded every day and every night, and filmed it all. We got, I think, a hundred and three songs in six days. And everything filmed. Course, all those are not keepers. *Most* of those are one takes, and there's mistakes that had to be fixed. We had a lot of fun doin' it. One night we did eighteen songs, just he and I and the piano—songs like "Tenderly," and "Stormy Weather," and a lot of those old pop standards that we both knew. So it was easy to do it, and then he took those and went into the studio and put all the other parts on there himself. And there's like ten songs on that album where it's just Leon all the way. He played every instrument on there.

Q Most people consider *Red Headed Stranger* to be your masterpiece. How did you come up with that?

A I really had a movie in mind from the beginning. [A film version of the story, starring Nelson, Morgan Fairchild, and Katharine Ross, was finally released in 1987.] Well, I was thinking about a concept album, too. But I felt like I was writing a sound track when I did it. And I wrote it as if I *were* the guy, which is probably the way I write everything.

Q You've done quite a few films now. How much different is acting from your usual work?

A It's really easier. You've got more time to do what you have to do. The only thing is, you never know how good you did until later.

Q Has anybody accused you of having "gone Hollywood"?

A Oh, I don't care what they say about me. It doesn't really matter.

Q Kris Kristofferson has gotten a lot of criticism that he's gone off and done the movies and ignored his music. Have you heard those criticisms about yourself?

A Oh, I'm sure I'll be criticized whatever I do. While they're talkin' about me, they're lettin' somebody else rest.

Q Is the desire to do movies strong, or do you do them because they're fun to do? Do you want to make a statement with them, for example?

A Oh, no. I just want to play cowboys, is all. I've been wantin' to be in the movies ever since I saw Gene Autry up there, singin' and pickin'. Don "Red" Barry, Whip Wilson, Lash LaRue, I guess I'm like every other kid. I wanted to be in the movies.

Q A singing cowboy?

A Sure! Why not?

Q Did you think you were good in *The Electric Horseman*?

A I thought I was *real* good.

Q You really did?

A Yeah, I really did! What I was doin' wasn't that hard, and there wasn't really that much to do.

Q Did you play yourself? Is it basically your personality?

A Yeah, that's the good part about it. They let you be yourself. In fact, they encourage it. They just let you be natural. Sydney Pollack, the guy that directed it, was real good. He helped any way that he could. But you asked me if it was harder. It isn't as hard physically as doing one-nighters. But when you do the shows, you know how well you did, and you get the audience response immediately. You've got to wait a long time on these movies, I found out. The time between the time that you first think of doing a movie and then you actually see it on the screen is a long, long time. But as long as you've got a lot of patience, I think movies are okay.

Q For a while, you were considered to play in *The Best Little Whorehouse in Texas*.

A Well, I was just one of the guys I think that they had considered for the part. They flew me to New York and I saw the play. And I met with Larry King, the writer. And I met the producers, and at the same time I understand they were talking to Burt Reynolds, and I think he had said no one time, and then he said yes. So it wasn't surprising to me that they had chosen Burt Reynolds over me to do that part. In fact, I'm not sure that that part would have been right for me, anyway. I'm not a very good song-and-dance man. which, for that particular role, you had to be.

Q You haven't done much television. Have you intentionally shied away from the small screen?

A Well, you're always a little afraid of overexposing, you know, if you do too much TV. So that's why.

Q Do you have any specific plans for TV?

A Well, I don't know. I haven't got any plans right now.

Q Surely there are offers every day.

A Well, no, not today . . . (Laughter) Nothing came in today.

Q You apparently aren't afraid of overexposing yourself with records. It seems as if you've got a new one out every time turn around.

A Well, I'm watching it to see what happens. I know I've got a lot of albums out there, and every time I put one of them out, I think. "Well, maybe this one has no chance at all because it's the ninth album this month," you know. But they seem to all be doing very well. So long as they're selling. I'm not going to worry about it.

Q You also have recorded duets with everyone from Julio Iglesias to Bil Monroe.

A Yeah, I'm up to the M's now. (Chuckling)

Q *Poncho and Lefty,* your duet album with Merle Haggard, was one of your most critically acclaimed albums. How did you and Merle decide which songs you were going to do?

A Well, some of them were my old songs, and some were Merle's old songs. And then for the others, we'd just sit around and start thinking up tunes. We'd record one that I thought of, and then it'd be Merle's time to come up with one. And then Chips Moman, who was doing the producing, would come up with one. So we kind of made it a community project.

Q When you sit down to record, is it a spontaneous thing?

A Well, not really for everybody. The musicians could care less what we play. They're just waiting for someone to tell them what to play. And they let us figure out the tunes that we're going to do. But normally, I know what I'm going to do when I get there. But with Merle or Roger Miller or Webb Pierce, it was easier just to sit around and talk about what we wanted to do next.

Q With those albums with Roger Miller and Webb Pierce and some of the others, were you trying to help people in the industry who had fallen on hard times, or were you just wanting to record with people you happened to like?

A Well, mainly it was to record with people that I enjoyed their singing and I knew that we could sing together. I think it's a shame that all the good singers are scattered around on so many different labels that they never get to sing together. Plus, I knew that there was a lot of people that maybe hadn't been familiar with the songs. Maybe they didn't have a chance to listen to them. Maybe they were too young when, for instance, Webb's songs came out. There's a lot of people, I'm sure, who've never heard "In the Jailhouse Now," one of Webb's songs. Same thing with a lot of Merle's early stuff, and Roger's early stuff. And if it turns out to help them in the long run, well, that's great, too. But I had my own selfish reasons. They have very good songs.

Q Are you still touring two hundred nights a year?

A Yeah, probably that or more. Really, we could do 365 days if they were close enough together. And it really wouldn't be that hard. It's not really that much work to me. I enjoy doin' it. If I didn't play music, if I wasn't allowed to play music, I'd probably get physically sick. It's just something I have to do.

Q What does that do to your private life?

A Well, course, I haven't had one of those in years. I've about forgotten what those are.

Q You call your band the Family Band, and you also refer to your entourage as "family." What makes up the family? Just anybody who happens to drop by?

A Well, the family covers a lot of people. Anybody that likes us. It's pretty open. We'll let anybody in.

Q Many of the musicians in your band have been with you for a long time, and have taken on something akin to cult status themselves. You've known Paul English, your drummer, for example, since 1954, and he's been in your band since 1967. You even wrote a song, "Me and Paul," about your friendship. How did you choose the other members of the group?

A Kinda strange. Most of 'em just kinda turned up. Jody Payne, for instance, turned up one day to play with Sammi Smith, who was on the show with me. Bee Spears showed up one day to take over for somebody who went into the Army. So I really haven't had a lot to do with it. Mickey Raphael I met [in 1974] at a party after a football game in Dallas. [Coach] Daryl Royal was givin' an after-the-game party, and we were all settin' around playin' music, and there was this harmonica player who was just playin' fantastic, so we played together that night, and a few days or weeks later, I did a benefit over in Lancaster, Texas, and Mickey showed up with his harmonica. He's been with me ever since.

Q You do basically the same repertoire every night, and you have for years now. How do you keep the songs fresh after literally thousands of performances?

A Well, we do 'em different each night, basically. When we hit the bandstand, everybody's coming from twenty different directions. I'm always amazed that we ever get a show done. But that's the reason. We never do sound checks, and we never rehearse. That way, it's bound to sound different every night.

Q So there's some improvisation to it?

A Sure. Our show is a lot of improvisation. Basically we know the songs, we know the chord progressions, and we've got some head arrangements going. But as far as who's gonna do what, and what notes we're gonna play, we don't really know. I think it makes it more interesting. Everybody looks forward to working that night, because they don't have any idea what they're gonna do.

Q Your guitar has a tone to it unlike any other, How do you mike it? One writer said it sounds like you're playing steel cables.

A (Laughter) Well, that's sort of a bastard setup there. It started out to be a Baldwin guitar with a Baldwin stereo pickup and a Baldwin amplifier. I broke the guitar, and Shot Jackson in Nashville took the pickup from the broken Baldwin and put it in this Martin classical that I've had for years now. I've never been able to get that sound out of any other setup. I don't know what it is. I've tried the same setup with other guitars and other Baldwin amplifiers, and it doesn't work. I guess I just lucked into a real jewel of a guitar. It's like violins. If you happen to get one that's really good, hang on to it, because there's none other like it.

Q You're a strong proponent of positive thinking. How did you get into that?

A Out of necessity, I think. I was so negative and I could see the results of it. And I was very unhappy and I was making myself unhappy, and I'm sure anyone that was around me, I was making *them* unhappy. And I just decided one day that I didn't want to be that way anymore.

Q Did you take a training program?

A No, I read a lot. And I started applying what I'd read, and it worked, so I'm a fanatic about it now. I just can't be around anything or anybody negative. Just refuse to do it. Haven't got time for it. That kind of thing rubs off. There's not a negative-thinking person that I know of on the buses. I don't think he would last long. People would run him off, or he'd have to leave. Because everybody around me knows how I feel, and in keeping those things away from me, consequently they keep them away from themselves. So there are no fights or arguments.

Q Does it keep you from going through periods of depression?

A Yeah, it does. It doesn't keep me from having tendencies—everybody has tendencies to think negative all the time, but it gets easier to turn it around. It's an amazing thing. It snowballs. Just like one negative thought will snowball into a whole big bunch of 'em, a positive thought will do the same thing. And the only thing that'll turn around a negative thought is a positive thought. It helps me continually. Because a negative thought can, and does, produce poisons, releases poisons—actual physical poisons in your body. And they can make you deathly sick. And the first thing you know, you've got stacks and stacks of negative thoughts in your mind. And it gets to a point where nothing is right. You're physically and mentally and spiritually sick. I believe negative thinking causes all kinds of illnesses, including cancer and about any type of ailment you can think of. And it's not easy to turn around in the beginning, because you've spent so many years building those negative thoughts up. And they've been excuses for all your failures. You don't want to start tearing them down, because you don't want to have to admit that you've been that wrong so long. But once you do admit it and start thinking positive thoughts, and replacing the negative ones, then you start having a lot of positive results.

Q Do you sleep easier now?

A I think I could probably sleep the clock around, and do sometimes, but my sleepin' habits are not normal, because I work crazy hours and am not an example of a normal guy. I used to have a lot of bad dreams and nightmares. Maybe fifteen years ago they started fading away and I don't really dream a lot now. Maybe I'm asleep all the time and don't know it

Q Was that during a non-creative period?

A No, I think I was probably more creative back then. I don't know, there were a lot of negative things going on around my life during that period, so I'm sure that had a lot to do with it, too.

Q Did your career start to turn around when you started practicing positive thinking? Was all this happening at the same time?

A Well, it wasn't that great. I was still successful as a songwriter and an entertainer, but I wasn't happy. It wouldn't have mattered how successful I was, I still wouldn't have been happy. Then when I started turning it around, the first thing that I noticed was that things weren't that good.

but they weren't that bad either. They could have been a lot worse. And I started accepting the fact that I wasn't that successful in all the aspects of my career, but I could still make a living and support my family doing what I do. And there's a lot of people who can't do that. So I started looking at how fortunate I was. "Count your blessings," is how the Baptists and Methodists would explain it. But I started doing that and it started turning my whole life around, and I noticed that things didn't bother me as much anymore. Nothing seems to bother me anymore, really. I've learned to roll with the punches. I think.

Q This is interesting, because your personality has been described as "Buddha-like," but you're also supposed to have a nasty temper.

A Contradictory reports, I'd say. Somebody's lyin'. Or else they're both right, I don't know. No, really, I do have a terrible temper I can't think of any specific things that *make* me angry. but it used to make me mad when people would try to tell me what to do. Like a guy would blow a whistle and wave a flashlight and try to direct me places I didn't want to go. There must be some significance to that somewhere back in my past. I don't know.

Q How would you like people to think of you?

A Oh, I think everybody likes to be liked. I like people, and there's no reason for people not to like me, really. I don't give 'em any reason to, or I try not to.

Q I saw a show of yours in Waco once, and backstage people were talking about your legendary healing powers. I kept waiting to see a test of that, but it never came up.

A I guess nobody was sick.

Q Do people really believe that?

A I've heard that a couple of times. I'd read that somewhere, but I never did know that I really healed anybody.

Q Isn't there some famous story of some friend of yours sitting in the front row and jumping up and claiming he was healed from a crippling disease?

A I think probably his downer wore off or something.

Q Let's talk some more about your writing. You had a good case of writer's block for a while. How did you get over that?

A I go for a long time when I think, "Well. I'll never write nothin' else. This is it. I've written my last song." And then another idea will come along. Just about the time I give up, I write somethin' else. Oh, I don't give up. I was just kiddin' you, really. I don't worry about it when I don't write. Practically every time that I make myself sit down and rest for a few days, well, I'll start writing. As soon as my mind gets still. That's hard to do these days. I go for months when I can't write my name.

Q Do you go through spells where you'll write one sort of song a lot?

A Yeah, I'd go on house songs for a long time. Every song I'd write would be about a house. "Hello, Walls" was one of them. Probably the rest of 'em you're not familiar with: "Hello, Roof." (Laughter) "Hello, Car" . . .

Q The first project that really got you writing again was *Tougher Than Leather,* right?

A Yeah, that was new material, original material, about a gunfighter who killed this young man, and then got away free. And then he died, and then he was reborn again later as a modern-day urban cowboy, and bad karma caught up with him. And he's sent to prison for something that he didn't do and the whole theme of it is "Was it something I did, Lord, a lifetime ago? Am I just now paying a debt that I owe?"

Q Do you believe in reincarnation?

A Yes, I do. There's a recent survey somewhere that says that over forty percent of the people believe in reincarnation in this country. Other countries, there's a higher percentage than that.

Q Where do you think you are in the cycle?

A I don't really know. I'm not really concerned about who I was or who I'm going to be. I don't think that's for me. And I haven't spent any time trying to find out or think about it that much. I'm more concerned about what I am today, and I kind of let other people think about what

I'm going to be or what I used to be. But I do believe that I was here before, and you were, and we all were.

Q What sort of religious teachings did you have as a child?

A I was brought up as a Protestant, a Methodist. And then I went to the Baptist church later on when I was just in my early twenties. And then I started checking out other religions around the world just to see what other people believed. But if you believe that for all actions there is an opposite and equal reaction, then karma and reincarnation are very real. To me, it's the only thing that does make sense. You can see that everyone is not equal. And you will always find someone who is one of the nicest, finest people in the world who's being miserably mistreated. So in order to justify that, this person has to have something in his karmic past. He's paying for something that he did before. Otherwise, it's all injustice.

Q Do you think of music as being spiritual?

A Oh, I think it's definitely spiritual. All music is. I think it's maybe one of the highest forms of spirituality. Every singer who stands up there is responsible to put across his ideas and beliefs, and I think people expect him to do that, whether he's a preacher with a sermon or a singer with a song. I think basically that's what we all do. We're all teachers, rather than preachers, I think. Each individual has his own little bit of teaching to do each day. If there's a key word, it's "communication." An artist communicates with the audience, and the audience communicates with the artist, and there's an exchange of energies that takes place. And so in that respect, everyone who's standing up there is delivering some sort of message.

Q I read that when you first started out, you played in places so rough that the management had to put chicken wire in front of the bandstand so you wouldn't get hit by flying beer bottles. Is that true, or just another country music myth?

A Yeah, there was a place we used to work in Fort Worth, over on the North Side, on Exchange Avenue, where the musicians had gotten together and decided they didn't want to work this joint unless the guy would put this chicken wire around there. It was too dangerous. You're standin' up there playin', and somebody hits you in the back of the head with a beer bottle. Maybe not intendin' to—maybe he's throwin' it at his wife, or somethin'. Throws your timin' of. But, yeah, it does get a little rowdy in Texas. It's always been that way. Their mothers and dads were that way, so they get it naturally.

Q Probably not too many people realize that you took Charley Pride on a package tour throughout the South when he had only one single out. And this was when the civil rights movement was at its height. What was it like when you were trying to introduce Charley to your audiences? The story goes that you'd give him a big buildup, and then when he came out, you kissed him full on the mouth. By the time the audience got over the shock, Charley already had them hooked.

A (Laughter) Well, it was a little scary, back in those days, and it was, I guess, the first time that a black kid had ever crawled up in front of thousands of white people and started singin' country songs. I wasn't exactly sure how Charley was going to be accepted, but they loved him. And it was sort of controversial. I mean, a lot of people didn't think it was a good idea to put Charley on the show. That took a lot of nerve on his part, too. But when they found out how good he was, and how the people accepted him, then they wanted him on all the shows. Some of the motels wouldn't let him in, and some of the clubs didn't want him to be on the stage, even. So it was interesting going through places like Dallas and Shreveport and San Antonio. But everyone was really very nice, and no one ever said one thing. I guess everyone's imagination was running away with them with what possibly could happen. I still see Charley occasionally. Mostly at golf tournaments. That's about the only place we run into each other these days. He's doin' okay.

Q Do you ever long for those old days, when it wasn't quite so crazy?

A Yeah, I really do. You know, not to the point where I want to go back to 'em. but I think about 'em a lot, where the places were smaller and the crowds were smaller. The reaction was smaller. So I think about it a lot, but I don't really want to go *back* to those days. And I think about why I made it and some of the others didn't. But I'm not gonna question it. I'm just gonna enjoy it.

Q Are you really having as good a time as you seem to be?

A Oh, yeah. I'm getting to do what I like to do, which is play music and travel So I'm enjoying myself a lot. I'm having a big time.

Q Do you feel like a legend?

A Well, not really. I'm not sure how I'm supposed to feel.

Q Is it embarrassing to you?

A Not really, because it's kind of an overused word, anyway. It's kind of like "outlaw." It's just another label. I suppose "legend" is supposed to be a positive label. So it doesn't offend me. It's really a compliment in a way. But it sure makes you sound old.

MINDING WILLIE'S BUSINESS

John Morthland | May/June 1990 | *Country Music*

Willie Nelson's nine-hole Pedernales Country Club (a.k.a. Willie's Nelson's Cut-N-Putt) is located near Lake Travis approximately thirty miles west of Austin. Willie purchased the property in a bankruptcy sale for $250,000. The course was constructed in 1969 on the banks of the Pedernales River. After buying the grounds, Willie built a recording studio that was ultimately responsible for the recording and postproduction of his albums *Tougher Than Leather* and *Pancho and Lefty*, a collaboration with Merle Haggard. In 1991, the club was auctioned by order of the IRS after they froze Nelson's assets. Friend Darrell K. Royal won the auction and bought it for safekeeping. However, the IRS refunded Royal upon learning of his scheme to return the property to Willie. Instead, they resold it to an Austin investor. Ultimately, Willie was able to procure the club once again after agreeing to pay more than what the property was valued. Throughout the years, Pedernales Country Club has become a family destination as well as the location where many of Willie Nelson's studio releases were recorded.

This and the next interview detail Willie's IRS woes and his life while living under their tyranny. Journalist John Morthland effectively describes Willie Nelson's multifaceted personal and professional life with deft ease. His portrayal of Willie as a businessman, musician, and family man is engaging and well-rounded. –Ed.

Willie Nelson opened the door to the recording studio at his Pedernales Country Club headquarters outside Austin, and the lobby area filled with the sound of Johnny Gimble, fiddling around . . . sweet as ever. As Willie started to step inside the studio, an aide rushed up and shoved a manila folder in his hand, urging, "Here, Will, you gotta look this over right away." So Willie stood there in the doorway, one foot in the anteroom of the studio, one foot in the office area, an ear cocked to the music and his eyes on the business papers. That's a pretty fair picture of how things are for Willie these days in Texas.

Willie, the musician, recently enjoyed his first Number One single in quite a while, "Nothing I Can Do About It Now," from *A Horse Called Music*. Willie, the businessman, is contesting an IRS claim that he owes Uncle Sam another $25 million or so. Willie, the musician *and* businessman, is in the process of launching his Cowboy Television Network, a 24-hour satellite cable station which, if all goes according to plan, should be on the air sometime during the fall of 1990.

On the personal front, Willie is enjoying being a father again, for the sixth time in his 56 years. His 18-year marriage to Connie is over; and Lucas Nelson was born on Christmas Day 1988 to Willie and his girlfriend, Annie D'Angelo. Asked if he'd recommend being a father at 50, Willie grinned and replied, "It's great. I'd recommend being a father at any age."

On the professional front, though, the big news for Willie is the Cowboy Television Network. The idea came from Mack Long, who goes back to the early 1960's with Willie when Long was editing *Performance*, a concert trade magazine out of Fort Worth, and Willie was working the friendly neighborhood honky tonks in those parts. The two men stayed friends over the years as Mack left journalism and went to California to become that most mysterious of showbiz creatures, the freelance deal maker. Mack booked and managed some rock bands, did management projects for record companies, managed arenas, worked for various promoters. Basically, he put people together to their mutual advantage. A little less than a decade ago, he put Willie together with Wrangler—reportedly to the tune of $9 million, and that is, of course, a very good way to make friends. So when Mack got the idea for the Cowboy Network early in 1989, he knew right where to take it.

"I walked into Willie's office and he was playing checkers," Long had recalled a couple of weeks earlier, standing outside a honky tonk in Bandera, Texas, while Willie prepared to go inside and join Johnny Bush on stage. "I said, 'Will, I've got a heck of an idea,' and he said, 'What is it?' And I told him and he said, 'Well, shoot, let's call so-and-so.' A week later I was sleeping on the floor at one of those condominiums at the country club, working on the project, with my family still a couple thousand miles away in Los Angeles. And we've been working on it ever since, but now my family's out here, too."

Long and Nelson picked up two partners immediately—Bud Shrake, the Austin writer who ghosted Willie's autobiography, and Doug Halloway, whose Pedernales Films made one B-movie and shot a lot of TV commercials and public service announcements in the area. By October, when the network was actually filming shows such as *Johnny Gimble's Music Ranch* and Willie's appearance with Bush, which will be an installment of the *Honky Tonk Concert Series*, they were entertaining offers from other backers, including The Family Channel. They had their place on the satellite and were set to go into some 10 million homes, a drop in the bucket by cable standards, but still a start. They had already sold some $15 million worth of advertising contracts, and all systems were go. A staff of 12 was working out of the country club headquarters, but Long was predicting a payroll that would ultimately grow to 100 or so. The plan was to begin by showing a lot of already existing material they'd purchased, along with some new shows, but to be airing 12 hours of original programming daily within the next two years. There was talk of documentaries and regular series and all the usual things you see on network TV, the difference being that most (but not all) of these dealt with music. So things were definitely heating up out at WillieWorld, as the locals refer to the golf course, offices and condos overlooking Lake Travis that make up the man's Hill Country base of operations.

In the lobby area of WillieWorld headquarters, between the pro shop and the studio, a makeup artist had set up next to the pool table that looks out over the swimming pool and then out over miles and miles of Texas. On the walls are photos of Willie in various incarnations—from child to Nashville slicky to cosmic cowboy to all-around entertainer—plus Farm Aid plaques and a slew of gold and platinum records.

While Gimble taped his show, a pair of women set up a chicken-fried steak lunch buffet for the musicians and crew, grumbling good-naturedly about hangovers as they laid out the food. Kris Kristofferson wandered through looking for directions into town; he was there because he co-stars with Willie in *A Pair of Aces,* a CBS/TV buddy flick written by Shrake and Gary Cartwright (of *Texas Monthly*) that was due to begin shooting in a few days. A doctor arrived to give Willie physical.

Back in his private offices, decorated with Indian headdresses and antique farm implements, Willie sat behind a table, calm and collected as ever after a morning out on the links, dressed in black jeans, a blue tee-shirt under a blue v-neck sweater, red bandana and running shoes. He was going over a list of shows the network has lined up and talking about his idea of a cowboy.

"It's always been a freedom-of-spirit type of thing with me," Willie said. "I never thought the Indians and the cowboys were that much different. The cowboy is a person that has a lot of freedom and a lot of soul, and we think there's a lot of modern-day cowboys out there, not just in Texas but in San Francisco and Miami, Florida, and even New York City. So we'll do things that relate to modern-day cowboys, not just show old westerns and things like that, much as I like those old westerns myself."

They had indeed purchased a package of classic western movies and cowboy series, but they've bought up more than 2300 hours of old music TV shows, too—some 580 editions of the vintage *Porter Wagoner Show* featuring a young Dolly Parton and two or three other guests per installment (including, sometimes, Willie himself), plus about 300 old Wilburn Brothers shows with the young Loretta Lynn, some Billy Walker shows, even a black dance party called *The Beat* that features soul stars like Joe Tex.

But there are also plans afoot for original material like a cowboy cooking show called *Home on the Range*, hosted by Gordon Fowler, from the first family of Texas chili; *The Sammy Allred Show: Radio—Live on TV*, which will take Austin's whacked-out morning radio show full of humor and old and new records and give it visuals; *Noontime in Nacogdoches*, music and chatter with Paul Buskirk, from the oldest city in Texas; some kind of nightly live show out of Nashville; *Austin Nightlife*, live showcases hosted by Ray Benson of Asleep at the Wheel; *Johnny Gimble's Music Ranch*; and the *Honky Tonk Concert Series*. Willie will make frequent appearances on the last two; years ago, after all, he played on Gimble's TV show out of Waco.

All in all, it looks almost as if Willie is attempting to reconsolidate his affairs in Austin, the town that launched him a decade-and-a-half ago when beer-guzzling old cowboys and pot-puffing hippies gathered at places like Armadillo World Headquarters and annual summer picnics to discover that they had a lot more in common with each other than they thought. A lot of faces out at WillieWorld working on the cable network these days look familiar to anyone who was around Austin in the mid-1970's. Some local skeptics have speculated that the network closely resembles many of the other pipe dreams Willie used to have in those days, most of which wafted off with the smoke, as pipe dreams so often do. Whether they're jumping the gun by predicting the same for something as ambitious as the network is a question to consider. But it's hard not to want to ask Willie one, too. Is he, now that his concert fees and record sales are beginning to taper off, looking to rebuild a base in his old stomping grounds, to "get back," as the catch-phrase goes?

"Well, maybe in the back of my mind that's what I'm thinking, but I sure don't think so," he replied. "I dunno, I'm still just sorta taking things as I go. This is just where we are now, and it's time to try to utilize all the talents around here. It's really just like it was when I first came. There's always been plenty of talent here. It's an amazing place for talent."

And in many cases, it's the same talent as ever. Willie is not one to forget the old friends, the people he met on the way up and no matter how many times he goes around the world or visits the White House or duets with Julio Iglesias, his idea of a Big Time remains to jam in a Texas juke-joint with a hardwood floor. So what if guys like Johnny Bush or Johnny Gimble aren't exactly everybody else's idea of a star?

"The thing is, in my mind, those guys *are* stars," Willie emphasized. "These are guys who, to me, *did* make it, even if maybe they didn't make it on the scale I supposedly made it. They're great musicians, good showmen and lousy businessmen—just like me and everybody else. I may be making more money than them, but believe me, there's more money going out of here, too. Sometimes it feels like my situation isn't much different than theirs. But these are the people that I've always liked to play with and always will."

Indeed, just a couple of weeks before saying that, Willie had joined Bush at the Cabaret in Bandera, a beautiful western town surrounded by dude ranches a few short hours from Austin that bills itself as the "Cowboy Capital of the World." When Willie first fled Nashville in the early 1970's, he and Paul English and various members of the entourage settled into five houses at the Lost Valley Dude Ranch there and made it their base for the next year. Willie was even in residence at the Cabaret. Now Johnny Bush, who lives an hour away in San Antonio, is in residence there weekends. What better place to shoot a segment of the *Honky Tonk Concert Series*?

The marquee out front billed it as Johnny Bush and The Bandoleros with Special Guests. Billy Joe Shaver, whose next album will be on Willie's revived Lone Star Records label, was one such guest, and the name of the other was one of the worst-kept secrets in the Hill Country that weekend. Once 1100 people had crowded in, the doors were shut so the dancers would still have some room. Up on the stage, Johnny and The Bandoleros, now up to a whopping 13 musicians, all dressed smartly in cavalry shirts, were stomping through an unusually brassy set of Western swing. Johnny, whose throat problems put him out of business for several years, was in especially good voice early on; it took no imagination to recall the days when he was called "the country Caruso."

After a few numbers, he stepped up to the mike and announced, "This next man don't need no introduction, so I'm not gonna give him one. Ladies and gentlemen, here's one of the best entertainers that ever lived, Willie Nelson." And Willie, Johnny and band jumped right into "Time Changes Everything," followed by "Whiskey River," the perennial Willie set-opener that Johnny wrote.

As the band reeled off into "Blue Eyes Crying in the Rain," "I Saw the Light," "On the Road Again" and the like, the evening began more and more to resemble, yes, one of those nights from the early 1970's in Austin when Willie was right on the verge of making it big and everyone in the room knew it and wanted to savor this moment while they could, when people drank maybe a little too much and got a bit crazy without being obnoxious, and the music went on and on into the night. Austin hasn't really seen nights like that for a while. If Willie has his way, Austin will now be seeing them again more regularly and sending them out to the rest of the world as well.

WILLIE NELSON: THE PILGRIM

Michael Bane | March/April 1992 | *Country Music*

Willie Nelson faced one of the most infamous tax battles in music history after his former manager, Neil Reshen, allegedly failed to pay his client's taxes over many years. According to Nelson, Reshen instead filed extension after extension, gradually amassing interest and late fees and entangling Nelson in a catastrophic IRS situation that ultimately resulted in a $32 million debt.

After firing Reshen, Nelson got further involved in risky tax shelters. In a creative effort to repay the debt, he released the album *The IRS Tapes: Who'll Buy My Memories?* Fans helped him reclaim auctioned-off property. This financial saga remains a cautionary tale about trust and oversight in the entertainment industry. However, what could ruin others was just a bump in Willie's long road. –Ed.

"And now, ladies and gentlemen," the unseen Nashville Network announcer says in his perfectly modulated radio voice, "America's favorite outlaw . . . Willie Nelson."

And Willie Nelson strides to center stage, as he has a million times before—and as he probably will a million times more—oblivious to the incongruity of the words "favorite" and "outlaw" being strung together in his introduction; oblivious to the cameras and lights and dancers and producers and directors and general mayhem that accompanies any television production; oblivious, as always, to the storm of controversy that has once again descended on his long-haired head.

Craggy and timeworn, he is as he has always been—unlikely golfer, long-distance runner, famous songwriter, semi-fugitive from justice and, of course, the Lord High Zen Master of the Road.

"Howdy, folks," he says in his perfect Willie Nelson voice. Next he will say, "Good to see you," and damned if he doesn't mean it.

You've probably been reading a lot of news about Willie recently, and none of it has been good news. Depending on which tabloid you happen to be reading at the time, Willie Nelson is broke, destitute, desperate and probably living in some cardboard box under an Interstate overpass. He does, in truth, owe the Internal Revenue Service around, oh, say $16.7 million ("Say it real quick," Willie confides, "and it don't sound so bad."). The federales auctioned off his property to pay the debt, although, other than a few souvenir-hunters, there weren't a lot of takers. It just wouldn't, you know, be right, somehow, profiting from Willie Nelson's distress.

I have caught up with Willie Nelson, whom I have known for the better part of two decades, to ask him two simple questions I already know the answers to. Both are pretty obvious. The last time Willie and I talked, it was in a ritzy club in New York City, Willie and Burt Reynolds, actresses Carol Lynley and Candice Bergen and me. It's sure as heck, I say, not the bad old days.

"No," Willie laughs, "thank God, it's not."

Question One, then, is how did the bad old days come back with such a vengeance?

Question Two dates back to the first time we met, not surprisingly in another older and substantially more decrepit tour bus parked outside a gig in Charlotte, North Carolina, where a younger Willie Nelson told a much younger me, win or lose, that this—the bus, the road, the gig—was his life, and he never wanted it to change.

Question Two, then, is has it changed?

Let's let Willie answer in his own words.

To Question One:

"Ah, Michael," he says, shrugging his shoulders. "You know how it is."

And to Question Two:

"Look around you, Michael," he says, his arms encompassing the Honeysuckle Rose II tour bus, his manager Mark Rothbaum doing business in the back, Kris Kristofferson exchanging "remember when" stories with assorted Family members, all the flotsam and jetsam of a life on the road. "Do you see anything different?"

That's a fair question, but it" not what you can see that gets you. What happened to Willie Nelson was, as Robert Draper in his exhaustively chronicled financial story in *Texas Monthly* said, not "a story of greed that backfired. It's instead a story of generosity to a major fault."

In a story that's suitable for the lyrics of a country song, the single most successful act in the history of country music made it all, then gave it all away—unfortunately, before he had paid any of the taxes due. In the scrambling to salvage his life and lifestyle, Willie Nelson has been forced to make decisions that make the bad old days look like a church picnic. So far, he hasn't had to race back into another burning house to rescue his legendary guitar, but it's been close.

Might as well blame it on the road.

Here's one of my favorite images of Willie on the road. We're out somewhere, Louisiana, I think, ten years or so ago. Outlaw music is riding high, but Willie hasn't yet reached the stature of saint—at least, not nationally.

The show's been over for a while, and the road manager comes onto the bus.

"Well," he says, "guess it's time to get the money."

Everybody laughs, and the road manager goes over to his briefcase, hauls out a battered Colt .45 automatic and racks a round into the chamber, clicking the safety on. This is, for most of the history of country music, business as usual. Pick up the gate money from the show promoter or the club owner, stuff the cash in a briefcase and walk it back to the bus, or whichever beat-up car or truck was carrying the freight. The hardware, of course, was for that long, dark walk back to the bus, but it didn't hurt for your average sleazy promoter to understand that this was serious business. Other money came from song royalties and record company advances—no one ever expected the record company to sell enough records to pay off the advance—but it seemed like magic money, to be spent just about as quickly as a person could lay hands on it. I recall one singer-songwriter from that period who had a genuine million-seller on a song he had written and sung. Because he had a couple of kids and a wife he adored, and because he'd just scraped through a dirt-poor, eat-the-dog period, he took the money from the record and invested it in savings bonds or something equally mundane. Invested it! I happened to be at the recording studio when his pal-around buddies found out that instead of buying a Cadillac, a bus and a 27-year-old waitress from North Carolina, he invested the whole batch in boring stuff! Didn't he understand that this was miracle money, and he didn't need to worry because the money always came? He was a total object of derision. I remember him sitting there, his face beet-red and, later, painfully trying to explain to me why he hadn't pissed it all away, why he'd done something . . . responsible . . . with the bucks.

Business as usual, but then, for people like Willie Nelson, the money got bigger. Unimaginably bigger. Once the Outlaw Train began rolling, around 1976, there was no stopping it.

Everybody, though, did start casting around for a conductor.

For Willie and Waylon Jennings, the conductor came in the form of a hot-shot New York music business wiz named Neil Reshen, who signed on as manager to both Willie and Waylon. Reshen brought a shock of negotiating to small-town Nashville.

"Why are they afraid of him?" Waylon told me when I was working on the Outlaws book back in the 1970's. "'Cause he knows where all the bodies are buried, man! I tell him, 'You're my ole mean dog. I got you on a chain over there, and every once in a while I'm gonna pull it and you just bite."

Unfortunately, the chain proved to be a speck too long, allowing the "ole mean dog" to bite the hand that held it.

"I can't be sure the taxes are paid and records kept and also write songs and play music," Willie says. "At some point you have to trust somebody. And that's always dangerous."

Willie broke with Reshen in 1978 and sued him two years later. One particularly bitter point of contention being that, according to Willie, one of his manager's prime duties was filing Willie's returns and taking care of the taxes, something Reshen disputes.

Even more controversy swirled around the famous Fourth of July Picnics. Willie had been concerned with Reshen's handling of the events, and there were serious questions of where the money went. Willie claimed that was something he'd like to know. So did the IRS.

Willie's troubles continued to escalate. All his financial records for the year 1975 through 1978—the Outlaw years—had been destroyed, and the IRS is asking $2 million for those years, according to Draper. Willie and new manager Mark Rothbaum went to one of the top accounting firms in the world, Price-Waterhouse, for financial help and advice.

What followed there, as evidenced by a 1990 lawsuit by Willie against Price-Waterhouse, was nothing short of falling out of the frying pan and into the fire. A series of disastrous tax-deferred investments left Willie in worse shape than ever. In 1984, the IRS began getting serious, demanding taxes due from the mid-1970's. The tax notices began snowballing while Willie tried to tread water.

In fact, he didn't have the money to pay. To Willie, maybe all money was miracle money, to be touched, but never held. The Family had become a bloated caricature of the Sherwood Forest crazies of the old days. Willie was, as Robert Draper pointed out, supporting an entire community, and like any community, it had its share of lowlifes. Deals, scams and projects seemed to pour off Willie's organization like heat from a forge, and Willie's response was to do what he had always done—play music and put the miles on the bus. He paid his people exorbitantly, and when anyone needed the money, Willie was there.

More and more of the concerts were benefits—some huge media events such as the FarmAid shows for displaced farmers. Others, in typical Willie fashion, were done quietly, with minimum fuss.

In 1990, the man who once sold the classics "Night Life" and "Family Bible" for the grand total of $200, sold his publishing company, Willie Nelson Music, for $2.27 million. After all the debts were paid, Willie lost not only his songs, but $35,000 on the deal.

And now we're in Nashville where "America's favorite outlaw" and Kris Kristofferson, in jeans and ragged T-shirts, are on the set of a television show, performing to the vast chasm of the Opryhouse.

"They wanted us to wear tuxedos," Kristofferson says later. "Ha ha." Some things, I suppose, never change.

There is, I think, a tendency to want to pick through Willie's troubles again and again, feeding those two base feelings—How could he do it? and not me, thank God, not me!

The horror novelist Stephen King, when asked once about the most terrifying thing he could think of, replied not with slimy monsters of the rising undead, but with the simple statement, "Financial ruin."

Predictably, Willie sings his barroom anthem, "Whiskey River," and Kristofferson sings "Me and Bobby McGee." Also, perhaps predictably, when he gets to the refrain of "Freedom's just another word for nothing left to lose," he pauses. "Just ask Willie," he adds. The crowd gives an appreciative laugh.

We are on the bus later, and we are laughing. Kristofferson is telling Kris stories, Rothbaum is doing business and the whole bus has the atmosphere of an old club. Earlier, I'd grabbed Rothbaum and asked how things were really going.

"Willie's Willie," he said, shrugging his shoulders.

I grab Willie and tow him to the back of the bus. We sit on the edge of the bed, Willie with his hands clasped and his uncanny ability to tune out the entire rest of the world.

"How do you survive in all this crap?" I ask.

"I maybe even thrive in all this crap," he says.

"Has it been pretty hard on you?"

"Not on me, Michael. A lot of people worry about me, and it's been hard on them. I haven't noticed any major changes in my life . . . You know, the road is really the only safe haven. Once I get stopped in one place too long, I get in all kinds of trouble."

"You told me once that it was hard to write when things were going too good . . ."

"Well, that's true . . ."(*Laughter.*)

"Where are you living, anyway?"

"Well, I've still got a house in Austin and a house in Abbott, my home town. I move around a bunch on my days off. 'Course, there's not many of those this year."

We talk about running, about doing FarmAid in Russia, about *Who'll Buy My Memories: The IRS Tapes.*

"Somebody asked my bass player, Bee Spears, if I was in trouble. Be says, 'Well, if he owed them $1 million, he'd be in trouble. But he owes them $17 million, so they're in trouble!"

"You still give away everything you get?"

"I try to. It's hard to carry all that shit."

In the front of the bus, Kristofferson has everybody on the floor laughing, and, pretty soon, we join them. Stories are the currency of the road, maybe what we've bought and paid for. I can't help thinking of another Kristofferson song, one I'd heard when I was just starting out on the road . . . "Once he had a future full of money, love and dreams, which he spent like they were going out of style . . ." I had thought "The Pilgrim" was the most romantic song I'd ever heard. Having it, losing it, still knowing that, "The going up was worth the coming down . . ."

Hell, maybe it still is the most romantic song I've ever heard.

20 QUESTIONS WITH WILLIE NELSON

Michael "The Gray Headed Stranger" Bane | March/April 1993 | *Country Music*

The 1990s, for Willie Nelson, was a decade of constant touring and continued film and television work. Not only did he record several solo studio albums, but he also collaborated with many celebrated performers of the time, including Johnny Cash, Toby Keith, and the rock band Phish. By the following decade, the USA television network would be celebrating Willie's seventieth birthday with an all-star bash. Far from winding down his career, Willie continued at a frantic pace well into the new millennium. –Ed.

What can you say about Willie Nelson that hasn't already been said a couple of dozen times? From a confidant to Presidents to the best-known tax outlaw in America, Willie's been there and back. He's got a major new album on the way recorded with lots of guest artists and produced by mega-producer Don Was (Bob Dylan, Bonnie Raitt and The B-52's, among others), he just got back from the desert in California, where he filmed one of those weirded-out Taco Bell commercials. and he's touring like a crazy person. We caught up with the Red Headed Stranger just outside New York City, where he sat patiently for 20 Questions. His tax bill had just been settled to the tune of $9 million.

1. So the Federales have finally agreed to a settlement of back taxes. You can come out of hiding now?

Hey, I never had to go into hiding! It wasn't no big deal. Not a big deal at all.

2. You've got a new record that's already generating a lot of interest . . .

Well, I think it's real good. Some people think it's the best one ever. Some people say it's the best since *Stardust* and *The Red Headed Stranger*. I do think it is one of the better ones.

3. *Are these more songs you picked up on the road?*

All these songs, except the ones I wrote, Don Was brought to the session. These were songs that I never would have recorded if he hadn't suggested them.

4. *Don is one of today's hot producers. Any thoughts on working with him?*

It was great. He's a musician, and he's got a great ear. And he knows how to let an artist do what he does. And he had a hell of a track record. It wasn't as though I took on an unknown.

5. *When's your next FarmAid?*

April 24th. Ames, Iowa. Number Six.

6. *Who's on the schedule?*

Well, you've got me and Neil Young, Mellencamp, John Conley, Waylon, Kris and John R. Cash. We're all easy. We've also got Paul Simon, maybe Bob Dylan, Ricky Van Shelton, Delbert McClinton. The Geezinslaws. Asleep at the Wheel. All my friends.

7. *This sounds like a real familiar cast.*

Well, it is. And there's going to be some different, too. A black gospel group out of Austin called "The Belles of Joy." They've been around a long time—they're all older than I am. Great gospel!

8. I hate to say it, but I didn't know anybody was older than you!

These are the only people on the planet! (*Laughs*)

9. All right, that was mean. But your birthday is coming up soon. And I think it's the big 6-0 . . .

April. Big 6-0.

10. *I believe I asked you what it was like to turn the Big 5-0.*

I believe you also asked me what it was like to turn the Big 4-0 . . . *You* know what it's like to turn the Big 4-0!

11. *Okay, this line of questioning has lost all its appeal. Are you out then running?*

Oh, yeah. I still run. I still exercise. Try to undo what I did the day before.

12. *Sounds like a country song, don't it? What do you think of the new administration—a bunch of Southern boys who don't like country music?*

Oh, I don't know that they don't like country music. Bill Clinton came to see me one time when he was governor. And there was a lot of country running around up there in Washington for the Inauguration. Asleep at the Wheel's country, and they played. Doug Sahm and the Texas Tornados played up there.

13. *They ain't country, they just crazy.*

When you think about it, there's a lot of similarities.

14. *The last time I talked to Waylon, I asked him for his favorite Willie song. How about the same? You want to get even?*

Ohhhhhhh, I don't know. Waylon, he's gotten so *quiet* lately (*laughs*). He hardly does anything offensive these days and he's really boring (*laughs*). Waylon takes a lot of people to lunch these days (*laughs*). That's what he does. Hey, the drugs didn't kill him, but the food will (*laughs*). That's why they called it the Food And Drug Administration.

15.*Got any movies in the works?*

Not anything that I'm going to start tomorrow. There's some talk about a couple of things, but nothing close.

16. *Is that something you want to get back to?*

Not really, I don't go out looking for movies. If one really comes by where I can ride a horse or play a guitar, I'll look at it.

17. *So how much are you on the road?*

Well, I took off for a little while, but last year I toured as much as I've ever toured in my life. I started out first of the year, then we went to Europe—nine countries, 23 cities in the month of April. Then after that, we hit Branson, and I did 144 shows there in six months. Then out and back doing other shows on the weekend. So I had one hell of a year, really. I don't know. I still enjoy it out here. It's still fun. I still enjoy it. Hell, I better!

18. *So I heard that the first time you played Branson you had some trouble, because you weren't used to people who went to bed early.*

(*Laughs.*) Hey, that didn't bother me. I go to bed at 9:30 myself. The people who live in Branson will party on down with you. Most of the fans are not your late-night drinking crowd.

19. *So what do you think of all these new hats in country music?*

Hell, it never did bother me who wore the hats. I guess Waylon and I wore hats once. Ernest Tubb used to wear a white hat all the time, and they didn't call him a hat guy. He would have kicked the shit out of them if they had. Ain't nobody called me a hat guy lately, and I still wear a hat.

20. Remember the article you wrote for Country Music Magazine on Bob Wills back in 1974?

Yeah, that was fun. Any time you want me to write another story, I will. Why don't you pick a subject? *(Laughs.)* More than you ever wanted to know about any subject, by Willie Nelson.

ROAD WARRIOR

Holly George-Warren | Winter 1994 | *Country Guitar*

A constant wish by Willie is to be appreciated for his guitar-picking skills. Here, Willie stakes that claim with veteran music journalist and writer Holly George-Warren, not only with his picking experience but also sharing his warm insight into performance. –Ed.

"Hey, this is for all you farmers and ranchers out there!" hollers an energized Willie Nelson, breaking into a rambunctious "Milk Cow Blues," from the stage of the Colorado State Fair's rodeo arena. Sure enough, along with the dust, appreciative applause rises from the deep brown dirt packed full of Pueblo cowboys and cowgals of all ages, welcoming their favorite outlaw—and the tireless champion of Farm Aid—back to the fold.

It's been a grueling past few years for the veteran singer-songwriter-guitarist. At the same time that he was losing almost everything he owned, including his prized recording studio and Texas home, to cover back-tax penalties and interest he owed the IRS, he was also losing ground commercially to the likes of Garth Brooks and Billy Ray Cyrus. But one five-month stint in Branson, a Taco Bell commercial, and a solo acoustic recording (*The IRS Tapes*) later, Wilie has straightened things out with the Feds and recorded a new album. The result, *Across The Borderline*, produced by Don Was (Bonnie Raitt, Bob Dylan), is a masterpiece. Showcasing Willie's evocative, Spanish-tinged guitar and transcendent, mellifluous tenor, the album also features duets with Raitt, Dylan and Sinead O'Connor. All fourteen tracks, including compositions by Dylan, Lyle Lovett, Willie

Dixon, Paul Simon, Peter Gabriel and the "Red-headed Stranger" himself, radiate with a sense of artistic renewal, matching Willie with expert session players—as well as old pals and his regular Family Band.

Partner-in-crime Waylon Jennings finishes the opening set here on this breezy August Saturday night by imitating his old buddy's vocals on their signature tune "Mama Don't Let Your Babies Grow Up To be Cowboys." For his part of the show, Willie returns to the stage backed by his ace band of 20 years: sister Bobbie Nelson on keyboards, veteran guitarists Grady Martin and Jody Payne, Mickey Raphael on harmonica, percussionist Billy English, bassist Bee Spears and drummer Paul English.

Willie and his band's enthusiastically played material exemplifies the country vet's lifelong musical eclecticism: a mixture of country classics ("If You've Got The Money," "Whiskey River"), his own brilliant songcraft ("Crazy," "Nightlife," "It's Funny How Time Slips Away," "Angel Flying Too Close To The Ground"), pal Kris Kristofferson's tunes ("Help Me Make It Through The Night," "Me and Bobby And McGee," "Loving You Is Easier"), sentimental ballads ("Blue Eyes Crying In The Rain," "Georgia On My Mind"), and some hard-to-categorize numbers from his new album (his mystical "Still Is Still Moving Me," Lovett's "Farther Down The Line," and Dixon's "I Love The Life I Live").

The one constant in Willie's repertoire is his beat-up Martin N-20 nylon string guitar—festooned with scratched-on signatures, dents and a jagged gash—upon which he improvises astonishing leads hinting at a wealth of influences. Elements of country, jazz, blues, and flamenco can be heard in Nelson's unmistakable guitar technique, which sometimes sounds deceptively simple, other times surprisingly baroque.

Under a nearly full moon, Willie treats the Coloradans to some lively picking and singing and seems sorry to leave the stage after a compelling nonstop 90-minute set. Afterwards, relaxing over a cup of black coffee in the Honeysuckle Rose, his cozy, wood-panelled touring bus, the 60-year-old maverick seems in a celebratory mood as he chats with Country Guitar. Perhaps it's because he knows that in a few hours time, when Sunday morning starts comin' down, he and his entourage will be hitting the highway for a 24-hour drive to their next stop—happily on the road again.

COUNTRY GUITAR: [*Music critic and author*] Chet Flippo once described your guitar style "as a starting mixture of Charlie Christian and Mexican blues picking." Would you agree with that categorization?

***WILLIE NELSON*:** [*chuckling*] That's quite a compliment, quite a compliment.

***CG*:** What kind of music inspired you early on?

***NELSON*:** I had a lot of Mexican friends in school in Abbott [*Texas*], and so I grew up listening to Spanish Mexican music. I've been listening to Mexican and Tex-Mex music all my life, and I love to play it. I've always said that in my last lifetime I was Mexican or in the next lifetime I'm gonna be Mexican, because I just love the music too much. There's a lot of Spanish in my blood somewhere."

And [*jazz great*] Django Reinhardt is a hero of mine—he had the Gypsy touch, which is also very close to the Spanish flavor. Naturally every guitar player loves Django's guitar playing.

***CG*:** How did you learn to play guitar?

***NELSON*:** My grandfather and grandmother raised me from the time I was six months old, and my grandfather started teaching me when I was five. He showed me the basic open chords. I was writing a few poems then—why, I don't know. But all of a sudden I was putting some of the chords I'd learned to the words of the poems that I had written. My grandmother, who played piano and organ a little bit, taught my sister [*Bobbie, two years Willie's senior*] how to read music. And when she learned a song, she'd teach it to me.

***CG*:** Did you start performing together when you were kids?

***NELSON*:** Yeah, we did at school, and there were always people coming by the house and wanting us to play a song for them—and we always did. And we played at school, at study hall or for special programs. Back then I thought we'd always be together and always be playing.

***CG*:** What kind of music did you listen to back then, besides the Mexican stuff?

NELSON: I listened to the radio a lot and I listened to a lot of country music—Bob Wills, Hank Williams, Roy Acuff, as well as the "The Grand Ole Opry" [*on the radio*]. I also listened to the blues that came out of New Orleans, along with the Johnny Mercers and Hoagy Carmichaels—we learned whatever was being played on the radio and the jukeboxes, because we played a lot of the clubs and when you take requests you play what's current. We'd play "Stardust" or "Fraulein," "San Antonio Rose."

CG: I've heard that you played with Bob Wills. How did that come about?

NELSON: I was playing with a band called Bud Fletcher and the Texans. Me and my brother-in-law booked Bob Wills over in a little club in Whitney, Texas, called Shady Grove. While he was there, I got up and sang with him. Later on I got to sing with him again. And I wrote the liner notes for one of his albums. He and I got to be buddies.

CG: Before we discuss your technique for a bit, can you tell me a little about your guitar's history? It looks like it's been down quite a few roads.

NELSON: That's Trigger Junior, named after Roy Rogers's horse. The Baldwin guitar people gave me one of their acoustic guitars many years ago, in the late Sixties, and I accidently busted it. It was a great guitar. So I called my friend Shot Jackson in Nashville and told him the problem, and sent the whole thing up there to him. He took the guts of the Baldwin and put it in this Martin N-20 guitar he'd found. I bought it, sight unseen—and wound up with a fantastic guitar, through no fault of my own. It's the combination of a Martin guitar and a Baldwin pickup, which is a stereo pickup, and you can't play it through any other amplifier but a Baldwin. So every time I find a Baldwin amp I hang on to it, latch onto it, and people who know I use the Baldwin amps are always bringing me any they find in their garages. I'm still using the original one.

CG: What are some of the other guitars you've played?

NELSON: The first guitar I ever owned was a Stella, a Sears Roebuck guitar; it cost six dollars. After that, when I was about 12 or 15, I got a Gibson electric guitar and an amp. When I started moving around, I picked up a nice Epiphone and played it for a long time. But then I lost it in a pawn shop in San Antonio.

CG: Maybe the person who bought it will read this article.

NELSON: And maybe they'll give it back . . . When I recorded my first album—it was a live album of a show I did in Panther Hall in Ft. Worth, Texas—I used a Fender Stratocaster. But since I was always doing a lot of after-hours partying and playing in the motel room or whatever, I wanted an acoustic guitar that I could do both with: play on stage electrically and then unplug and go play in the room. I used to travel around with a lot of writers, and Jimmy Day and Kris [*Kristofferson*] and all of us would pass the guitar around a lot. So I wanted one I could hear without having to plug in. So that's how I got on the acoustics.

***CG*:** So you gradually played the acoustic more and more and started using it on stage?

***NELSON*:** Yes, and I got this Martin that I dearly love. The sound is . . . I can't duplicate it anywhere. I've tried.

***CG*:** You record with it too?

***NELSON*:** Yes, and the Baldwin amp too, unless I play it unamplified. It sounds good unplugged too.

***CG*:** What kind of strings did you use?

***NELSON*:** Gut.

***CG*:** How did your guitar get that large hole in it?

***NELSON*:** If you're gonna use a pick, your guitar should have a pickguard. But I never use a pickguard on there—since it's a classical guitar, it didn't come with one. So after banging "Whiskey River" on it all these years [*laughs*], it just got worn through along with my fingernails. But I would never consider replacing it. There's no way to replace it if something happened to it. The insides have been rebuilt several times; the wood is rotted in there and has been reinforced. It looks real strange when you look at it from the inside.

***CG*:** The guitar's body is covered with autographs. What's the story behind those?

***NELSON*:** Just signatures from people I know. [*Rock singer/songwriter and pianist*] Leon Russell got me started doing that. He had his guitar and wanted me to sign it, and I said, "Why, man?" and he said, "It will make it more valuable." And I said, "Well, thank you very much," and I had him sign mine and that's how it got started.

CG**:** Is it signed mostly by people you've played with?

NELSON**:** Yes, friends too, people I've known through the years—Kris and Rita [*Coolidge*], back when they were together, both of their signatures are on there. And my lawyer buddy Joe Jamel, Roger Miller, just a lot of people.

CG**:** Let's jump here from the guitar to the guitarist. Do you fingerpick or flatpick?

NELSON**:** I like to mix it up; some things I do one way one time and one way another. It can depend on the room, the night, the feel—I don't know. Sometimes I play hard; sometimes I play soft. Sometimes I'll use a pick, sometimes I won't.

CG**:** Your solos are improvised?

NELSON**:** Everything.

CG**:** During a concert, do you prefer to not play when you're singing?

NELSON**:** I don't plan anything. When I don't need to hear me play I won't play. If I need something to accentuate a spot, I'll play. I don't know, it's just things that happen during the course of a show—where you need to put an emphasis here or something there, or a turnaround here. Or a fill that you won't have any idea you're going to play until you get there.

CG**:** Do you still like to sit around and play guitar?

NELSON**:** Honestly, when we're doing two hour performances every night, touring a lot of weeks in a row, I don't really feel like sitting around and playing after a show. I want to get away from music for awhile, so that when the show starts tomorrow night, I'll be ready for it. I won't be too tired of music.

CG**:** Are there any guitarists, country or otherwise, whose playing particularly impresses you these days?

NELSON**:** Clapton. Eric's great. There are a lot of guitar players that are real good; Eric just stands out. Grady Martin, who plays guitar with me, is one of the best all-around guitar players I know. Ever since I've known him he's been great and I think he gets better every night.

CG: When did he start playing with you?

NELSON: He came to me when I did the movie *Honeysuckle Rose* [released in 1980]. I brought him in to help me do the soundtrack and play in that movie, and he's been here ever since.

CG: How do you approach your songwriting?

NELSON: Melodies are a lot easier for me to write than lyrics. If you play a musical instrument, and you play lead, it's not that difficult to come up with melodies. It's easier to be creative melody-wise than lyric-wise for me. Usually I never play the same melody twice, but if I get a good lyric that requires a melody to be played more than once, then I'll find a melody that goes with that thought, or lyric, and it builds from there.

CG: How do you choose other writers' songs to record?

NELSON: [*chuckles*] The songs that I do are those that I wish I had written. And they're easy for me to do most of them. I would have never done a lot of the songs on my new album [*Across The Borderline*] had it been up to me to find them—because I would have never found them. [*Producer*] Don Was picked out a lot of obscure things to bring to me. Some songs, like "Don't Give Up," by Peter Gabriel, and Bob Dylan's "What Was It You Wanted," I thought were great the first time I heard them. Still, if I'd been choosing for myself, I wouldn't have selected them. Don sent me a tape of songs and I lived with them for several weeks. Don could hear me doing them, so I gave them a try.

CG: Didn't Paul Simon try to get you to record "Graceland" several years ago?

NELSON: Yeah. He called me and wanted me to do that song back before he had it out. But I listened to it and though I thought it was a great song, I just didn't hear it for me. Then he called me back again, after he'd sold about a hundred million copies, and said, "Now what do you think?" I said, "I think it's a great song, I think you did a great job on it." And he said, "I want you to record it—still." And I said, "Okay, he must be on a mission from God, so I'm gonna do that song." Mine is very much like his [*version*]. He produced it and plays on it, and he's got the African musicians that played on his version.

***CG*:** It looks like you're still a man of the road. How frequently do you perform?

***NELSON*:** We do 150, 200 nights a year.

***CG*:** Do you like going on the road better than doing Branson for five months straight?

***NELSON*:** Yeah, that was a little too confining. I rented a theater there for a year. Branson is quite a phenomenon; there's a lot of people going there. I think eventually there's going to be a lot of little Bransons springing up around the country because it's such a good idea. Branson's pretty full; there's not much room for any more theatres up there.

***CG*:** Any film projects in the near future?

***NELSON*:** Not that I know of. There's been talk—two or three scripts laying around that they're talking about. I'm supposed to maybe do a part in a new television series called "Ned Blessing." The show's writer is Bill Wittliff, who wrote [*the Nelson vehicles*] *Barbarosa, Red Headed Stranger* and the television mini-series "Lonesome Dove." A lot of Ned Blessing is being shot near Austin at this Western town that I built to do *Red Headed Stranger*, so it's real close to the house.

***CG*:** One final question: What do you think of the latest crop of country stars?

***NELSON*:** Every generation has its heroes, and this is the time period for Garth, Billy Ray and them boys. That's fine—they're good and they deserve everything. I think our audiences grow only when someone like a Garth comes out—he draws a lot of the younger people in again. And that's what we have to keep getting in country music. Some of the first guys who started blending country music and rock and roll were Johnny Cash and Bob Dylan. And then Ray Charles did a country album. There's been a lot of things that have happened over the years that enlarges the audience—I think it's good for everybody. And no one really ever leaves country music, once they become fans. It just keeps building.

WILLIE NELSON'S FAMILY AND FRIENDS

Russ Barnard | November/December 1994 | *Country Music*

Country Music magazine founder and chief editor Russell Barnard interviewed Willie Nelson on several occasions. Here, Barnard extends his hospitality to Willie's inner circle, the Family Band. This piece explores Willie Nelson's life on the road, highlighting how he connects with family, friends, and fans through his music. Willie often tours with his family members, including his sister, Bobbie Nelson, who played piano in his band until her passing in 2022. His sons, Lukas and Micah, also join him on stage, making his tours a family affair. –Ed.

He steps briskly to the microphone and lets it fly, "Whiskey River don't run dry!" Just as he has at the beginning and at the end of each show, about 200 nights a year, for the last 22 years. That's about 8,800 trips down "Whiskey River." This one is seemingly attacked with the same joyful , adolescent enthusiasm as all those past.

Willie Nelson is happy on stage. It's how he has fun.

How does this come to pass? A 61-year-old grown up man with a two-foot-long hair braid voluntarily riding around all day and playing music all night with a bunch of other grownups. That's the question I've been chewing on for the last 24 hours. The question is partly about Willie, but I'm beginning to think it's mainly about me. Why am I voluntarily going to see Willie Nelson do what I've seen him do dozens of times over the last 22 years since we started this magazine?

These were my thoughts as I crawled into the red Mustang this afternoon, heading for my umpteenth Willie Nelson Show. It's the kind of car I would have loved to have had growing up in West Texas in the late 50's. I bet Willie would have, too! Maybe I'll ask him that.

As I pulled onto the Interstate and kicked the ponies up to a steady 80, I popped my advance cassette of the soon-to-be-released Brand New Willie Nelson Album into the slot. The idea for me to write this piece only came up yesterday, so I needed to hear this new album quick. The nearest copy was at Willie's manager Mark Rothbaum's house just a 15-mile drive from mine. So after work last night my wife Helen and I drove over to Mark's. We'd been working on a book, *The Illustrated History of Country Music*, which features some nostalgic pictures from Willie's early Fourth of July Picnics, so we took a few along to play "Remember This?" with Mark.

On our arrival, we found that Willie's longtime sidekick and drummer Paul English, and harmonica player, Mickey Raphael, were at Mark's for supper. Mark's wife Carol asked us to stay for what was a very pleasant evening of reminiscing.

Now, here's the deal with Paul English. When I first saw Paul English 20 years ago, he was the scariest, most evil-looking man alive: wearing a shiny black beard (trimmed just like, uh, could it be, uh . . . *Satan*?), crowned with a flat-brimmed black hat, perched like some bird of prey behind his drums. Sometimes he even wore a cape! Women and children—and tough men, too—would have crossed the street to avoid Paul English. Now, with the beard a softened gray and without the hat, he looks like what he is: a soft-spoken, gentle man who has been Willie's closest friend for nearly 30 years.

Here's what Mark Rothbaum says about Paul English: "He's honest. He'll tell you where it's at, and he tells the truth. He gets the show from place to place, keeps the band happy, is everyone's sounding board. I would rather die than hurt Paul. He deserves nothing but good things. He's with Willie because they love each other." Paul English, however, will tell you there was a young Paul English who, before hooking up with Willie, was more adept at picking locks than playing drums.

Mickey and Mark, even though grownups, are considerably younger. They treat Paul with the fondness some nephews would have for a favorite uncle and it's mutual. It's a nice feeling to see these guys so close after all those trips down the river together.

This family feeling glues the whole band together onstage. Willie's sister Bobbie on keyboards has been making music with her brother for more than 50 years! In addition to Paul on drums and Mickey, whose harmonica coupled with Willie's guitar anchors the trademark sound, there is Bee (Daniel Spears) on bass and Billy English, Paul's brother, who beats on a variety of odd items with sticks.

Off the Interstate toward the town of Patterson, the big Ford V8 pulls strong in third gear, doing a nice dance down the twisty country two-lane. The throaty exhaust rumble provides a nice harmony to the album. I'm now on my third time through:

They'll lead me safely through the night,
And I'll follow as though blind,
My future tightly clutched within
. . . those healing hands of time.

"The Healing Hands of Time" is the title song of the new album, the first on Willie's new record deal with Liberty/EMI. It's one of those songs that is so breathtakingly beautiful it could make you weep. Willie wrote it many years ago but never recorded it. That's testament to the songwriter: to write so many great songs that you can afford to leave one like that on the shelf.

But hold on, folks. This album ain't country. It actually opens with an oboe solo—hey, Willie, there was no oboe in Ray Price's Cherokee Cowboys—and an ocean of violins. At first I thought Mark had handed me a Mantovani album by mistake! This is sort of Willie Nelson and Nelson Riddle's Orchestra, produced by Jimmy Bowen. Well, don't forget, Bowen did produce Frank Sinatra and Dean Martin records before he landed in Nashville.

Don't get me wrong. I'm not reviewing this album. That's too dangerous for me. I'll leave that to a critic in our next issue. But, I'll say this: if country radio programmers don't make "The Healing Hands of Time" a hit, they'll be guilty of what we frequently suspect. Stupidity!

This album reminds me of Willie's *Stardust*, a bunch of pop, definitely-not-country tunes released in 1978 on Columbia. Our review at the time said Willie was crazy to record "Stardust," "Moonlight in Vermont," "Sunny Side of the Street," stuff like that. Stick to "Luckenbach, Texas." Considering that the album sold several zillion albums and landed Willie the CMA Entertainer of the Year award, I was always a little embarrassed by that review, until I read in Willie's book that my friend Rick Blackburn, Columbia's boss at the time, had said, "Willie, you're crazy to record 'Stardust' and stuff like that. Stick to 'Luckenbach, Texas.'" Maybe I won't ask Willie about that.

Passing dairy farms with dilapidated barns and rusting equipment, boarded up farm equipment repair shops, out-of-business stores, I can see that this very rural community, like many throughout the country, has been in a recession a long time with no signs of coming out. It's beautiful: rolling hills, woods, corn fields, some alfalfa. It could be Middle Tennessee. But it's not. It's Putnam County, New York. Head straight south for an hour, and you'll be in Times Square, The Great White Way. The Big Apple. But here you'll find farmers, mechanics, carpenters and Willie Nelson's show.

As I pull in the backstage parking area after a nice one-hour run from my house, I realize that part of the answer to why I'm doing this is because the trip is so much fun. It's an hour and a half till show time. Willie won't arrive for another hour. Three tour buses glisten in the late afternoon sun along with a couple of eighteen-wheelers. They carry the band, the crew, instruments, amplifiers, lights, sound control consoles and lots of other "stuff." When Willie shows up in about an hour in his personal bus, Honeysuckle Rose II, there will be well over a couple of million bucks worth of rolling stock parked backstage, not counting my Mustang. There's a lot of money tied up, but that's what it takes to keep an operation like Willie's on the road.

The crew has been here for hours, setting up the equipment, getting everything ready. There's last-minute details being tended, lots of activity. Paul English is responsible for knowing that all is done right. He is calm and relaxed, gossiping with me and several other visitors. He seems to have nothing to do, but his eyes are alert. In fact, everyone is calm, very busy, but calm. After all, most of them have been doing this for 20 years. They should have it figured out by now. Once in a while a crew member says something quiet to Paul. He nods. I guess it's all getting done.

What I'm watching is no doubt a part of why Willie still does this. Many of the crew are wearing black t-shirts or satin baseball jackets that say "Willie Nelson and Family" on the back.

According to Poodie it wasn't always so smooth and calm. Poodie is Randy Locke (I had to call Dandelion—who writes Willie's fan club newsletter and has her own late night show on a country music station in Hershey, Pennsylvania—to find out how to spell Poodie. There's no doubt a story behind that nickname, but I don't know what it is. Maybe I'll ask Willie that.) In the early days, Poodle says they would do a show, drink all night, chase women, get up at noon, drive for six hours and barely make it on time to the next show. "Here would come 13 Texas yahoos, piling out of buses and trucks at the last minute. We do things a lot different now. We're organized, calmer, saner, use tons more equipment, try to arrive at the gig with plenty of time to set up. But the spirit is the same. We're still a bunch of Texas yahoos."

Like a band of gypsies
We go down the highway
We're the best of friends
Insisting that the world keep turnin' our way . . .

There's still an hour to kill, so I check the crowd. The site in colder weather is a ski slope. Now it is set up with a large stage, seating for maybe 4,000, all covered by a canvas tent to keep off rain, but with all sides open to the unseasonable chilly evening air. It's like a giant revival setup.

Pickup trucks are heavily represented in the parking lot. There's a guy with a John Deere cap and another with a Harley Davidson t-shirt. The crowd is enthusiastic. You can feel their eagerness in the chatter. The age ranges from kids to grandparents, but it is generally an older, calmer, better-behaved crowd than you would have seen 20 years ago, but so are Willie and his crew. There is a sprinkling of people who look like they were outfitted at J. Crew. The area is a place where high-paid Wall St. and Madison Ave. execs bought up farms cheap years ago for weekend places to escape the tensions of New York City. That was in the days when the government helped people with high income tax bills buy up land that farm families couldn't afford to own anymore. But mainly these are working men and women and their families and friends, the kind of folks Willie and his band and his crew and I grew up with.

The distinctive note of a Detroit Diesel announces the arrival of the Honeysuckle Rose II. The backstage crowd stirs into motion. Kris. Kristofferson, who will do a set before Willie goes on, arrived a few minutes ago with Mark Rothbaum and now heads for the bus to greet his mentor and road buddy. The plan is for me to say hello to Willie on the bus before the show and then "interview" him afterwards. I'm a little skeptical about that last part, for two reasons. First, if I know Willie, there will be gobs of fans lined up for autographs and pictures after the show, and he'll accommodate them. Then the bus will be jammed with people he knows well and will want to speak to. I'll be one of many. And I know there's a 10 or 12-hour drive ahead of them to get to tomorrow's show somewhere in Ohio. Second, I'm not going to "interview" Willie Nelson. What would I ask him that you and I don't already know? Where did you grow up? We already know: Abbot, Texas. What's Waylon like? We know what Waylon's like, and we know Willie loves him. We know he had a whole successful life as a songwriter, writing songs like "Four Walls" for Faron Young and "Crazy" for Patsy Cline, before he became a star. We know the IRS is happy, finally.

We know that if his Nashville house hadn't burned to the ground in 1970, he might never have moved to Austin and helped spawn the Austin sound. He might never have stirred together beer-soaked rednecks and dope-addled hippies into the same audience without serious bloodshed. And then there wouldn't have been any Outlaw movement.

And we know the story about how when he passed out drunk one night, his first wife, Martha, sewed him up in a bedsheet and beat him with a broom stick. We even know that story isn't even true. As Martha says, "The truth is, I tied him up with the kids' jump ropes before I beat hell out of him."

No, I don't have any interest in interviewing him. I want to *talk* to him, just like you would if you had the chance. And *that* I'll be able to do. But that may leave me a little short when it comes to writing a magazine cover story. But I'll enjoy it just the same. Meanwhile, Natalie Coté, a French Canadian singer, from White River Junction, Vermont, has started the show, and it sounds like the crowd likes her.

Mark motions me to join him on the bus. Willie greets me, asks about the magazine and asks to be remembered to our editors, Michael Bane and Patrick Carr. As always, his eyes sparkle, he listens close to what I say and looks me right in the eye, as he does with anyone he's talking to. Kristofferson heads out to do his part of the show.

An hour later I'm standing in the wings with Rothbaum and Kristofferson watching Willie do his stuff. It's the middle of the show. Kristofferson, who hoots and whistles after every tune, is as genuinely excited as any fan in a paying seat. He's heard this man sing these songs a thousand times and he still loves it. It can only be because he loves the man like a brother.

After the closing "Whiskey River," L.G. (Larry Gorham, head of security and former Hell's Angel) whisks Willie to the bus where he is ushered in by Ben Dorsey. Ben was once John Wayne's valet and chauffeur and is sort of the butler on Honeysuckle Rose II, keeping the rolling home shipshape and maintaining a constant supply of Power Coffee. Ben is a man of many actions and few words.

In a flash Willie heads back to the stage and delivers his patented, all-out, half-hour long encore set. You always get your money's worth at Willie's show.

Now at 11 P.M. the show is really over, and the bus becomes the center of Willie's post-show activities, which will run to about 2 A.M.

Opening act Nathalie Coté gets her picture taken with Willie as do superfans Eileen Lange and Joan Fitzpatrick from Bronxville, New York, who attend every East Coast show. A long line of other photo and autograph seekers forms outside the bus. Willie excuses himself and spends close to an hour having fun by making these people happy.

In between these various activities, Willie and I talk with each other and with others who come and go. Willie is friendly, laid back, quick-witted, funny, interesting and interested. I love this, but it's no setting for an "interview." But it, and the rest of the evening *are* a good setting for a story.

It's the story of why two grownups from Texas, Willie and me, did what we did today. For Willie, it's another day with family and friends: band, crew, colleagues in "the business" and the audience. What more could anybody want? For me, it reconnects my youth with my present, because the people in the audience and the crew and the band are all like the family and friends I grew up with, the people I work with and the people (like you) who are *my* audience. I expect that, without realizing it, the same is true for most people there. Maybe that's why a Willie Nelson show seems so satisfying. It's not just the music.

The band and crew buses and the trucks have been gone for hours. Goodbyes are said and Willie's driver, Gator Moore, heads Honeysuckle Rose II for Ohio and another day with family and friends. As I whip the Mustang back onto the moonlit Interstate and kick the ponies up to a steady 80, I pop the cassette in the slot and reflect, listening to Willie's croon . . .

Ain't it funny . . . how time slips away.

INTERVIEW

Michael Hibblen | May 26, 2005 | *Hibblen Radio*

One of the many causes supported by Willie Nelson is to combat global warming and crude oil dependence on foreign nations. Here he details to reporter Michael Hibblen his choice to use biodiesel fuel and the formation of BioWillie, his own biofuel company. –Ed.

Very rarely in life, if we get the chance to meet people we admire, do they live up to our expectations. Willie Nelson couldn't have been cooler. My opportunity to interview him came when Willie was in South Florida for a concert on May 26, 2005, with Bob Dylan at Fort Lauderdale Stadium. Much of that tour was playing in old minor league baseball parks around the country, which Willie told me was Bob's idea. As I mentioned during the interview, they were also playing later in the tour at Ray Winder Field in my hometown of Little Rock, Arkansas, which would be closed the following year and eventually torn down.

At the time, I was working for Miami NPR station WLRN, which had a partnership with daily newspaper the *Miami Herald*. It was a surprise assignment from morning anchor Rhonda Victor Sibilia, so I have to say THANK YOU! I already had tickets to attend that night's concert, but she noticed while going through the newspaper's planning for the day that the business section was preparing a story about Willie Nelson's push for more use of biodiesel fuel.

So I joined print reporter Patrick Danner and photographer Candace West to produce a radio version of the story. We met Willie as he was refueling one of his tour buses that ran on biodiesel. Nelson owned a truck stop in Texas selling what he called BioWillie and promoted the fuel, which is made from products like soybean oil. As he explained in the interview, it's a source of revenue for farmers, is better for the environment, and can help reduce the U.S. dependence on foreign oil.

As Willie tours the country, he has to find people along the way to refuel his buses. In this case it was Jim Robertson of Fort Lauderdale's Bio-Fuels America. Jim drove a pickup truck with a large tank in the back to the hotel where Nelson and his entourage were staying in Plantation, Florida. He filled the three leased buses with about 200 gallons of biodiesel fuel.

I had always heard that Willie was a nice guy, but I was amazed just how cool he was. Many times when you meet people you admire, it can be a let down when they're in a hurry or just don't live up to your expectations. But after meeting Willie and spending about a half-hour talking with him, I became an even bigger fan. After finishing the interview and turning off my recorder, I figured he would leave. But instead he just dug his hands deeper into his pockets and starting talking about how nice the weather was and that he was looking forward to playing golf that afternoon. I thought to myself, wow, I'm here making polite conversation with Willie Nelson about the weather.

As a kid, I remember during family trips that my mom would break out her Willie Nelson 8-track tapes. At that age I didn't really appreciate his music, but albums like *Red Headed Stranger* and *Stardust* would later become favorites of mine.

Michael Hibblen: Describe what we're doing here.

Willie Nelson: Well, we are seeing a tour bus being filled with biodiesel, and that's all we burn in our tour buses is 100 percent whatever blend we can acquire in biodiesel.

MH: And why is this important for you?

WN: For a lot of reasons. First of all it's fuel that can be grown by farmers, and I've been involved with the farmers for a long time. I see it as a way for those guys to have a better life—and at the same time it's good for the environment. It also reduces our dependency on energy from around the world where we could become more self-sufficient.

MH: You've got kind of a business interest in this as well. Describe that.

WN: I have a company called "BioWillie" which so far we have one pump (*laughs*) in Texas somewhere, and we hope to have two or three before it's over. But what we're trying to do is mainly draw attention to biodiesel, whether it's mine or yours or anybody's, because right now the only difference between yours and mine would be the quality, and we'd have somebody checking on that to make sure it's the best quality.

MH: Is there any challenge in getting fuel everywhere you go?

WN: Well it is, because it's not everywhere, and the demand is growing and so the supply will pick up, I'm sure. There are more and more people thinking about it. I was talking to the Travel Centers of America and they have several areas, several truck stops, and we talked to them several months ago, and they've been trying to put it all together and now it looks like they're going to be doing some things. Love's truck stops are going to be doing some biodiesel. It's going to pick up, and more and more people are going to learn about it.

MH: Can this run in regular diesel engines?

WN: The original diesel engine was designed to run on peanut oil. So, for all these years, yeah, a diesel engine will run on peanut oil, soybeans . . .

Miami Herald business reporter Patrick Danner: Do you own the tour buses?

WN: No, these are leased from here in Florida. Florida Coach Company. That's from the Calhoun Brothers, and they're also interested in putting some biodiesel tanks around on their properties and also interested in placing them around the country where they can be able to find biodiesel.

PD: These are your full-time buses, I presume?

WN: Yeah.

PD: OK, so you use those all around the country?

WN: Yeah.

PD: OK, all right. The gas station that you own, I say "gas station," but the biofuel station that you own, where in Texas is that?

WN: It's Carl's Corner. It's Exit 374 off of I-35 East. [Now called Petro Carl's Corner —Ed.] south of Dallas, between Dallas and Hillsboro. Waco, down in that area. It's a truck stop that's been there for a long time. My friend Carl Cornelius—the joke is that I won it in a poker game, and now I'm trying to lose it back. But it's a great spot to promote biodiesel because we have a pump there, and we got some BioWillie there, and a big sign, and we're doing a lot of business with XM radio. And [WBAP radio truck program host] Bill Mack talks to the truckers, and [country music producer] Eddie Kilroy and all those different guys talk about biodiesel. So we're getting a lot of good free publicity from people around the country. We're in the process of putting entertainment in the back, and broadcasting live from XM radio there, and putting studios. We have a grand opening on the third of July. First, second, and third of July there's a chili cook-off, and a barbecue, and a truck-pullin' and all kinda things goin' on.

MH: How's your tour with Bob Dylan going?

WN: Well, last night was the first night this year and, of course, last year we did several days and it's always good.

MH: You're playing a minor league ballpark mostly. How did that happen?

WN: I think it's a great idea. I'm not sure. I've been telling everyone it was Bob's idea. (*Laughs*) But it's a good one, and people enjoy coming to these facilities. The price is right, and children under twelve are free. It's a community gathering–type thing.

MH: Is it any different than playing regular venues? Are the acoustics a little different?

WN: Well, maybe a little different, but with good sound, you can play large areas.

MH: A lot of these places are pretty old. Some of them, I know the place in Little Rock, Arkansas—my hometown—where they just announced that you're going to be playing, it's probably going to be torn down by the end of the year. So, these are a lot of funky old eclectic ballparks.

WN: Well, you know, hopefully, some of them will hang around for next year.

MH: Is it entirely ballparks you're going to be playing in?

WN: Not really. On the Fourth of July, for instance, we're gonna' be playin' in Fort Worth, Texas, in downtown North Side Fort Worth. But most of them are.

MH: How often are you playing these days?

WN: Every day. It seems like I've been busy every day. We've had days off from the tour, but I've been doing other things. I did a day in the studio with Booker T. I did a video with Jessica [perhaps Jessica Simpson, whose video for her 2005 rendition of "These Boots Are Made for Walkin'" featured an appearance by Nelson —Ed.]. A coupla three days shootin' a movie, then went to Jamaica and did two videos down there, and then flew in last night to Fort Myers. So I've been workin' every day. Even though I'm not singin' every day, I've been doin' something.

MH: I heard you weren't able to play guitar for a little bit last year.

WN: I had a four-month period there where I couldn't play. That was interesting. (*Laughs*)

MH: How are you doing now?

WN: Doing fine, yeah. Playin' too much now.

MH: You just needed a little rest time?

WN: Well, I had to have a carpal tunnel operation, and that took a while to get over it. They first said six weeks, but they didn't mean guitar players. It took a little longer.

MH: So how's Dylan to perform with? You've played with him plenty of times before.

WN: He's great. He's a lot of talent. A great writer. A lot of fans.

MH: You're both people that a lot of people thought wouldn't be around this long.

WN: I thought the same thing. (*Laughs*) I'm a little surprised that any of us has been around this long. But here we are, you know, and we still wake up on the right side of the ground and everything's good.

RESCUING WILD HORSES

The Barbi Twins | 2013 | *Origin Magazine*

Willie Nelson has always been an advocate for the humane treatment of horses. For his part, he campaigned for the passage of the American Horse Slaughter Prevention Act as well as for the Animal Welfare Institute. He personally rescued seventy horses destined for the slaughterhouse and permitted them, possibly for the first time in their lives, to roam free over the five hundred acres of Luck Ranch, his wonderland. –Ed.

Barbi Twins: Why have you and your family become so active specifically in anti-horse slaughter?

Willie Nelson: I'm a little prejudiced when it comes to horses. I have always loved them. I currently have about 68; 25–30 were rescued directly from slaughter. I got involved 8 years ago when Animal Welfare Institute (AWI) first made me aware that American horses are being slaughtered and shipped overseas for human consumption. It's a shame that horses—or any animal—be treated this way when horses are the foundation of America. Horses were a way to travel to get to where we are today, and it is our job to protect them.

BT: The wild horses have been in the news, but most people don't understand that horse slaughter is legal. Can you explain what the government does?

WN: The Bureau of Land Management (BLM), the agency in charge of protecting wild horses, has been rounding them up at an alarming rate, supposedly for their own good. Sadly, there are more wild horses in holding pens than in the wild. Something is wrong with that, so we must act now before the BLM has managed these magnificent animals into extinction.

BT: Why should Americans be worried about horse slaughter still being legal?

WN: Americans don't eat horses. They are not raised as food animals and they are treated with chemicals that render them unsafe for consumption. The regulations needed to change their status to "food animals" would cripple every aspect of the horse industry as we know it. Plus, it would be wrong.

BT: What benefit does horse slaughter have if most people are against horse slaughter?

WN: America's horses and horse industry are under attack by a small group of folks out to line their pockets at the expense of our wild and domestic horses, American taxpayers, and those restaurant patrons who are ingesting toxic horse meat. However, we can pass the Safeguard American Food Exports (SAFE) Act, which will ban the slaughter of all American horses for the purpose of human consumption, while also ensuring they aren't sent abroad to suffer the same fate. My family has been working closely with our friend Chris Heyde at AWI on the SAFE Act and other important horse welfare issues for years. I encourage everyone to join with us by visiting www.awionline.org, taking action, and signing up for eAlerts today. Together we can make a difference.

BT: What can you tell people about how they can help stop horse slaughter of domestic and wild horses?

WN: Folks, please join my family and friends at the Animal Welfare Institute to see how you can help with this important American cause.

WILLIE NELSON: THE OUTLAW COUNTRY LEGEND REFLECTS ON HIS PERSONAL CANNABIS HISTORY

Ricardo Baca | March 21, 2018 | *Cannabist*

Willie Nelson has been a longtime activist and crusader for the legalization and responsible use of marijuana. Following his 2010 arrest for marijuana possession, Nelson founded the TeaPot Party, promoting the motto "Tax it, regulate it, and legalize it!" Nelson also serves as cochair of the advisory board for the National Organization for the Reform of Marijuana Laws (NORML), actively working to change cannabis legislation. Beyond activism, he has also ventured into the cannabis industry. In 2015, he launched Willie's Reserve, a marijuana brand that partners with local growers to offer various related products. He aims to support small farmers and ensure that quality products flourish. Though he mentions he'd smoke with Donald Trump in this interview, by the 2024 election, Nelson had publicly joined the opposing campaign, appearing at a rally for presidential candidate Kamala Harris, an advocate for the recreational and medical use of marijuana. —Ed.

Willie Nelson's relationship with cannabis is the stuff of legend.

Nelson is a legalization activist, a social warrior and now a ganjapreneur via his own Willie's Reserve pot brand, and he still gets high regularly at age 83. But he's also not the most discerning of cannabis consumers. Does Nelson prefer energetic sativa marijuana strains to the more calming indicas? "They're both good," he tells me. Does he prefer smoking weed to vaporizing cannabis oil? "I enjoy smoking both ways," he says with an affable smile.

Nelson becomes more passionate when addressing how this plant is often grown, especially in unregulated environments: "I don't like it when they put chemicals and pesticides in it; that makes it not much better than a regular old cigarette."

Sitting across the table from an eagle-eyed Nelson in his tour bus, I ask the country music legend if he considers himself to be a connoisseur of cannabis.

"I guess if anybody is, *I would be*," he says, letting out a grizzled laugh that virtually self-italicizes the last part of the sentence.

It's mid-October T-shirt weather here in southern California as a capacity crowd of 1,400 fans assembles inside the seaside Humphreys Concerts by the Bay venue—and also as more than 71 million viewers tune in to the third and final presidential debate between Hillary Clinton and Donald Trump.

Right as the San Diego venue's doors open and as the candidates begin their sparring match more than 300 miles away in Las Vegas, my producer and I are ushered into Nelson's tour bus—the fifth to roam roads under the Honeysuckle Rose banner, Nelson's wife Annie kindly tells us. A few minutes later I'm sitting across a crowded table from the man, the myth, the legendary stoner.

When I mention that evening's debate and the unprecedentedly bizarre presidential campaign leading up to it, Nelson grins.

"I just wrote a song called 'Delete and Fast-Forward.' I'm in the process of writing it. It's 'Delete and fast-forward, my son. The wars are all over, and nobody won. But don't worry too much about it. You'll just go crazy again. So just delete and fast-forward, my friend.'"

I ask him if he's applying his metaphor real-time, given that he's talking to a journalist instead of watching the debate before his concert. He looks around his silent second home and laughs.

"Notice we're not watching (the debate)," he says. "That's a good sign. Delete and fast-forward—we're moving on."

**

It's not every day you get to chat up an original Outlaw. As an ex-music critic of a dozen-plus years, I have so many songwriting questions for Nelson—some of which had been contributed by readers and friends on social media earlier that day. But as a cannabis journalist, I'm now more interested in understanding Nelson's longstanding, complex relationship with pot, especially given his unofficial role as Weed Ambassador to the World.

Still, I can't help but start with the music. Do any of the songs he plays still make him misty-eyed?

"I could name a hundred. 'Today I Started Loving You Again' is a great song," Nelson says of the oft-covered Merle Haggard tune. "I'm So Lonesome I Could Cry,' Hank Williams. A fantastic song. I still love hearing those songs, and I still get emotional for some of those songs."

Was he speaking literally when he wrote the hit "Roll Me Up and Smoke Me When I Die"?

"Literally," Nelson says, pausing for effect, "I don't give a damn. It was just a funny thing to say."

Does weed help with his creative process?

"It has a lot to do with calming the nerves," he says, "which makes the creative juices flow a little easier."

Eventually I give in to my impulses and ask Nelson about his personal cannabis history, including his first time smoking marijuana.

"I think I was probably 19 or 20 years old playing in bars in Fort Worth, and I ran into a guy who smoked pot and I'd never smoked it before," he says. "I smoked (weed) for a long time without getting high—for months I would smoke and smoke and I wasn't getting high, and I couldn't figure out why. And then one day I did and I said, 'Oh OK, that's what it's all about.' But I guess I'd smoked so much other stuff, cigarettes and things, that my lungs weren't in great shape."

When Nelson gets stoned, it's not recreational use, he says: "It's medicine, and it's already been proven to be medicine. End of story." Cannabis cures what ails him, Nelson tells me, and it also keeps him from getting into the trouble he used to get into with beer and whiskey and cigarettes.

"I had emphysema, had all kinds of different health problems caused by drinking and smoking," he says. "So I decided I wasn't getting high from smoking cigarettes, and I had a pack of Chesterfields, so I took them all out, threw them away, rolled up 20 big, fat numbers, stuck them into the Chesterfield pack and I haven't smoked a cigarette since. And that's been 30, 40 years ago."

While Nelson will occasionally have a sip of wine, he's mostly given up drinking: "I'm not afraid to take a drink of anything, but I just don't get a thrill from it. I don't need it." And even though he still enjoys the act of combustion, putting fire to flower, he also considers himself "my own voice doctor" and says vaporizing is healthier than smoking.

"I'm sure lighting up a joint is not that easy on your lungs," Nelson says. "A singer has to think about stuff like that. Smoking a joint in paper is not as good for your lungs as it is doing it in a vaporizer. It's a no-brainer, really."

Nelson calls cannabis-infused edibles "different—it's more of a body stone, I guess. It took me a while to acclimate to it. I wasn't sure of it to begin with, but now it depends on what you want to do. If you wanna go to sleep, eat a piece of candy and you'll doze off."

As you'd imagine, the singer-songwriter seems to have an endless supply of compelling stories that revolve around this still-controversial plant. The only time he's grown pot from seed to harvest was decades ago when he lived in Nashville writing songs between tours. He smiles when he talk about cutting "It's All Going to Pot" with his pal Haggard. And on one of his many early-career tours he recalls being broke down on the side of a road in Kansas and coming across a towering patch of what he thought was cannabis growing down by the railroad tracks.

"We cut down a tree of it and put it in the back, and we thought we were really gonna have some fun," Nelson says. "But we got back to the hotel and cut it up and started smoking that damn stuff, and there wasn't nothin' to it. It was nothing but hemp, which is a different deal there. You don't get high smoking hemp, you just get sore lungs. So we had a big laugh on ourselves."

Nelson, who lives in 420-unfriendly Texas, doesn't remember the first time he was arrested on weed-related charges: "I've been pulled over many times and busted many times, but I don't really remember the first one, it was so long ago."

He does remember being lied to about marijuana, a substance that is scientifically less addictive than unscheduled drugs nicotine and alcohol. He remembers finding out for himself that weed is safer than alcohol—a fact research now backs up. And he won't forget being demonized for his embrace of cannabis.

"It's not the only thing we've been lied to about, if you stop and think about it," he says. "I think we knew more than what most people gave us credit for knowing. We knew we're supposed to be bad people because we smoked marijuana, but we knew we weren't bad people. So we know somewhere in there was a discrepancy that people had to realize that, 'Wait a minute: It don't make him a bad guy just 'cause he smokes weed.'"

But what surprises him the most about the world's recent shift toward decriminalization and legalization?

"I'm still surprised it took this long for educated people to get a little sense," Nelson says. "We've had so many negative things thrown at us about what it does to you and the bad things that marijuana can do to you. And 'Reefer Madness,' I don't know if you remember that movie or not, but it was horrible and it made people really scared. And fear is a hard thing to overcome, so all that had to be overcome. Now when people smoke or eat a piece of candy they realize that, 'Wait a minute. What's the big deal?'"

When talking more about the War on Drugs' negative consequences, Nelson unknowingly echoes the data in a Gallup poll released earlier that day showing that 60 percent of Americans want cannabis to be legal—an all-time high in nearly 50 years of polling on the question.

"Most of us have (overcome the fear)," he says. "Not everybody. I don't think we ever will be 100 percent for it. We're not really 100 percent for anything. There are always a few stragglers over there who can't really understand it."

The conversation steers toward the presence of dry counties in the American South that still disallow alcohol sales, and I take the opportunity to get Nelson's take on the legalization movement in Arkansas, where the Bible Belt state will vote on two potentially history medical marijuana initiatives on Election Day (although one of the measures was disqualified in a court ruling Oct. 27).

"Well, it's in the Bible," Nelson says flatly. "Ezekiel 34:29, where Jesus is talking about seeds and he said, 'I bring you a seed of renown for the miseries of humanity.'"

My time with Nelson is almost up. We've covered a lot of ground, and the election talk leads again to national politics when he offers up an anecdote that perfectly encapsulates Nelson's open-armed philosophy to weed, to music, to life.

"Somebody asked me the other day if I'd smoke a joint with Donald Trump," Nelson said, almost as if he was setting up a punchline—only he wasn't. "I said, 'I'll smoke a joint with anybody.'

"I would. I don't care."

A CONVERSATION WITH WILLIE NELSON

Peter Blackstock | March 12, 2021 | *Austin American-Statesman*

By March 2021, COVID-19 protocols had relaxed long enough for Nelson, who had been forced off the road for a year, to resume his hectic touring schedule of live performances. He wasted no time announcing the Outlaw Music Festival Tour, to kick off in summer 2021 with a lineup of notable musicians including Lucinda Williams and Chris Stapleton. This return to touring marked a significant moment for Nelson, who, at eighty-seven years old, remained committed to live performances and connecting with audiences. Nelson also extended the reach of his 4th of July Picnic in 2020 through live-stream technology. –Ed.

"It's been exactly a year that I haven't done anything, been anywhere."

It's almost impossible to fathom this quote coming from Willie Nelson, who's done everything and been everywhere for the better part of his nine decades on the planet. But pandemics have no exceptions for living legends, which means the man who wrote "On the Road Again" has been off the road since March 4, 2020.

"We played the Houston Rodeo," Willie says, bittersweetly recalling the last full gig he played with his band before the coronavirus pandemic took over the world. "We had 80,000 people there. It was one of the best shows of the year. I remember it well."

Speaking by phone from Luck, Texas, the sprawling horse ranch about an hour west of Austin that has been his home base for decades,

Willie is in good spirits on a late February afternoon. (It's about an hour past 4:20, for what that's worth.)

We have lots to discuss in our 15-minute window: a new album of songs that Frank Sinatra made famous, his first-ever South by Southwest keynote address, possible plans for an in-person Fourth of July Picnic this year, a new book written with his pal Turk Pipkin, and more.

But first, we talk a little bit about the pandemic, and the toll it has taken. Willie wants to make it clear that he knows it's been hard on everyone.

"I'm not the only musician who's hating this," he says. "There's a lot of them out there, not only musicians, but everybody. Promoters, audience—everybody associated with music is really tired of this, and ready for it to go away."

As for when that might be, your guess is as good as Willie's. Check his website, and you'll find four shows scheduled for April and May that seem questionable. But other dates in August—plus two October shows at Whitewater Amphitheater in New Braunfels—feel more in reach.

"Well, you've got to be optimistic," he says of the April dates, not giving up hope yet, even as he acknowledges the odds. "Personally, I'm thinking more about August-September.

"I know we set up Farm Aid for September 26, I think up in Raleigh, North Carolina. I think for sure by then we'll be able to go out. Between now and then, I don't know; we'll have to look at it and see. I'd love to do them all, you know."

Farm Aid became a virtual event in 2020, following the lead of both Willie's iconic Fourth of July Picnic and the Luck Reunion mini-festival, a newer tradition that's taken place during the week of SXSW over the past decade. The Luck Reunion livestream was a ramshackle but remarkably enjoyable affair, especially given that it was thrown together in a matter of days after SXSW got shut down in early March.

Willie's hard-working Luck Productions crew spent the spring honing their livestream skills with a series of large and small events before an ambitious Fourth of July Picnic that blended live performances at Luck with recorded submissions from luminaries including Lyle Lovett, Ziggy Marley and Margo Price.

The Picnic, which began in the Austin area in the early 1970s and then hopscotched across the state and country for several decades, returned home in 2015 for a five-year run at Circuit of the Americas. Nelson says he has no plans to move it out of the area in the future. He fully expects to bring it back as an in-person event, perhaps by this summer if the dominoes line up right.

"We might have it here in Luck," he says, intriguingly. When the pandemic hit last March, a 2020 Picnic site had not yet been announced, so it's unclear as to whether Circuit of the Americas may still be in the cards.

"Last year I threatened to not do the Fourth of July Picnic until December, but I was just kidding," he says with a chuckle. "But we'll see. We'll take it a little at a time and see what happens. Hopefully we can do the Fourth of July Picnic (this summer), and then everything around that."

In the meantime, there's the matter of the SXSW keynote, which is set for 1 p.m. on Wednesday and is open to official registrants only. It's been 29 years since Willie was scheduled to deliver the event's keynote in 1992, only to miss it when he was late getting back to Texas after an out-of-state gig. He did arrive in time to perform a hastily arranged free show at Auditorium Shores that evening as a make-good of sorts.

What does he remember about that day? "Not much," Willie confesses. "I kind of remember that I was supposed to get there, and we couldn't make it."

South by Southwest director Roland Swenson recalled the day's downs-and-ups more vividly in "SXSW Scrapbook," published in 2011 (I was one of three editors on the book). When he got an 8 a.m. call that Willie wouldn't make the 11 a. m. keynote, "I was too stunned to say much, except to ask if there was a chance he would appear later in the day," he said.

Later, Swenson's contact for Nelson invited him to visit Nelson's bus at Auditorium Shores before the show there, "Climbing aboard, I immediately had a serious contact high," Swenson wrote.

Willie was seated at a small table and reached out to shake Swenson's hand. "I had no idea what to say, except to tell him, 'We have the same birthday, April 20.' Willie replied, 'Then you must be a very stubborn man.' . . . He smiled beatifically as we exited the bus. A few minutes later, Willie went out by himself and did a short, great set of songs as the sun was setting."

The 2021 keynote will be in a different format than the solo speeches that were de rigeur back then. Willie convened remotely with local media personality Andy Langer for a conversation that was recorded ahead of time.

When I spoke with Willie, he wasn't sure what he and Langer would talk about—or whether they might already have taped it. "I've got so many interviews," he explains. "I may have already done it. Or it may be coming up in 10 minutes!"

I checked in with Langer a few days later, who confirmed that by early March, the keynote had been completed. "He was in storyteller mode—talkative, loose and funny," Langer recalls via text.

Langer decided "to go a little broader that I usually do, specifically because it's his first keynote and there's an international audience that's probably not read every Willie Nelson interview ever and wouldn't know or care if it's stuff Willie's talked about before," he says. "I felt like scope, instead of digging hard for new takes, was more important for this one, though we do talk about COVID, the upcoming book and what post-pandemic life looks like."

Having the conversation virtually was not really a problem, Langer says. "I was worried going in that it was remote, but I think at this point in the pandemic, Willie and I have both done enough Zoom interviews that a lot of what makes those things feel so weird at first, we'd already worked out on our own."

Zoom interviews have indeed become commonplace for Willie, who did one for NBC's "Today" show just before last month's storms. (He says he didn't lose power or water at his ranch but had a couple of pipes freeze.) Nelson joked with NBC interviewer Willie Geist about possibly taking up skydiving, but his wife Annie was in the room, just out of camera range. "She just said no," Nelson relayed with a laugh.

When asked by Geist if he had any regrets about his career, he turned philosophical. "If I changed anything in the back, it would change where

I am now,' he said. "And I really like where I am now. So I wouldn't change a thing."

Skydiving lessons may be on hold, but Willie says he hasn't had much difficulty keeping busy during the pandemic. "I've been lucky enough to be able to kind of do what I want to do—travel if I want to, but not if I don't want to," he says.

He's not been to his residence in Maui, where he typically has spend the holidays in recent years. But he traveled to Los Angeles, where sons Lukas and Micah Nelson have been based as their careers with the bands Promise of the Real and Particle Kid took off during the last decade (along with their roles in Neil Young's band).

And, Willie adds, "I've gotten into the studio a lot." He and producer Buddy Cannon have been writing, gathering songs and recording tracks for a follow-up to last year's "First Rose of Spring," the latest of more than a dozen records Nelson and Cannon have made together since 2007.

The pandemic has meant relying on remote procedures, but that's largely how Nelson and Cannon, who lives in Nashville, already had been operating for several years.

"The way Buddy and I work, he records in Nashville, with the Nashville musicians," Willie explains. "He puts his vocals on there, a scratch vocal. He sends them to me down here at my studio, and I go in and I put my voice on there. It's really easy to do that way."

The way they write follows a similar model. Cannon told me in a 2017 interview that it's "the strangest way of songwriting I've ever heard of: We write the whole lyric via text, and then we'll figure out the melody later.

"We've never sat down and held a guitar and written a song. We've talked about trying that, but neither one of us want to mess up what we've got going."

Cannon also joined Willie and co-producer Matt Rollings for a second tribute set of Sinatra songs that came out last month. "That's Life" follows 2018's "My Way," which won a Grammy in the traditional pop vocal album category.

The two albums came from two different sessions. I asked Willie if he knew when they were making the first one that they'd do another so soon.

"Naw, we didn't," he says. "We were just glad to get one out there, and thought it was sounding pretty good. And then it sold real good and got a Grammy.

"I'm a huge Sinatra fan, and it wasn't that hard to come up with more songs to do for a second record. The record company wanted one, so we said, 'Why not?'"

He might not be done with the Sinatra songbook. "Oh, there's several hundred (songs) I haven't done, and I loved everything he did," Willie says. "It wasn't hard to pick out the first album, it wasn't hard for the second, it wouldn't be for the third, either."

Sinatra has such a strong identity as a singer that doing albums of songs he sang almost necessarily requires a distinctive voice. Willie certainly fits the bill. When the two shared a bill in Las Vegas in the 1980s, Sinatra reportedly said that Nelson "can sing my stuff, but I don't know if I can sign his."

Willie's greatest claim to fame is as a songwriter of American standards such as "Crazy" and "Night Life," and he's also widely respected for his inventive, jazz-informed guitar style. I asked him if he's always felt his voice also was part of his identity as an artist.

"I think I realized pretty soon that some people liked my singing," he says. "And maybe some people don't, but that's cool. Enough of them seem to like it that it's kept us pretty busy."

Also keeping Willie busy during the pandemic was a book project with Austin entertainer and entrepreneur Turk Pipkin, with whom he collaborated on the 2006 book "The Tao of Willie: A Guide to Happiness in Your Heart." Their new "Letters to America" is due in June from Harper Horizon.

"Turk an I are old buddies and we've done a couple of things together," Willie says. "I always have a lot of fun doing it. Somebody wanted a book, and I said, 'Well, let's see if we can give them one.' And I thought Turk did a good job."

"Letters to American" is different from last year's "Me and Sister Bobbie," a biography of his lifelong ties to his older sister and longtime pianist Bobbie Nelson, and 2015's memoir "It's a Long Story: My Life," both of which he wrote with author David Ritz.

Via email, Pipkin reports that this one "is more a personal book and is essentially pure Willie. We wrote the book during the pandemic, by text, email and phone. The long text exchanges gave me lots of opportunity to ask questions about his life, and for Willie to tell me great stories that had never come up in 40 years of friendship.

"Working remotely presented some challenges. It would have been fun to be playing chess and dominoes while we were working, but I think the book was made stronger by both of us having so much time to devote to getting it right.

"I've been fortunate to work with Willie at concerts, on television, film, fundraisers, magazines and books—and with every project I've been more and more astounded by his talent as a great writer, an incredible musician and a wonderful human being who always manages to carry love in his heart."

ABOUT THE CONTRIBUTORS

Bob Allen is a longtime country music journalist, historian, and critic. He is the former Nashville editor of and a contributor to *Country Music.* His writings have appeared in *Esquire*, *Rolling Stone*, and numerous books. He is the author of *George Jones: The Life and Times of a Honky Tonk Legend* (2014).

Nelson Allen was an award-winning journalist who was proud of his coverage of the outlaw country music scene. He was a regular contributor for *Picking Up the Tempo* and *Country Music* magazines.

Ricardo Baca was the first full-time marijuana rights editor for a major American newspaper, the *Denver Post*. He wrote for the *Cannabist* for three years and is now founder and CEO of the Grasslands PR and marketing firm.

Michael Bane is the author of T*rail Safe: How to Avoid Danger in the Backcountry* (2009) and a host of the Outdoor Channel show *Shooting Gallery*.

Modeling duo **the Barbi Twins** are animal rights advocates. Sia Barbi is the author of *Dying to Be Healthy: A Breakthrough Diet, Nutrition and Self-Help Guide* (2001). Sia and Shane Barbi were producers for the film *Your Mommy Kills Animals!* (2007) and contributors to *Up All Night* (1989) and *Saving America's Horses: A Nation Betrayed* (2012).

Russell Barnard was cofounder of *Country Music* magazine. He was also editor of *The Complete U.S. Country Music Encyclopedia* (1995). Barnard was principal owner of Silver Eagle Publishers, the parent company of *Country Music* magazine.

Austin native **Peter Blackstock** began writing for the *Austin American-Stateman* at seventeen and launched *No Depression* in 1995. He now covers the music scene in San Diego.

Country singer **Debbie Brimer** of Dallas, Texas, was roundly admired for her rendition of Slim Willet's "Don't Let the Stars Get in Your Eyes" on the now-defunct Blackbird label. She occasionally wrote for various country music magazines, including the *Country Music Reporter*.

Patrick Carr is a music journalist and was a frequent contributor to *Country Music* magazine. He is the writer/editor of *Willie Nelson Songbook* (1976).

Holly George-Warren is a two-time Grammy nominee and the award-winning author of sixteen books, including *The Road to Woodstock* (with Michael Lang) and the biographies *Janis: Her Life and Music*, *A Man Called Destruction: The Life and Music of Alex Chilton*, and *Public Cowboy No. 1: The Life and Times of Gene Autry*. She has written for a variety of publications, including *Rolling Stone*, *New York Times*, *Village Voice*, and *Entertainment Weekly*. George-Warren teaches at the State University of New York at New Paltz.

Stacy Harris is the publisher/executive editor of *Stacy's Music Row Report*, a veteran Nashville author, a music historian, and a broadcast professional.

Jim Hatlo was an editor, with Roger Siminoff and Rick Gartner, of *Frets* magazine, which ran for just over ten years, from the late 1970s to late 1980s.

Michael Hibblen is the host of *Hibblen Radio*. He has worked for newspapers and radio and TV stations around the country and is director of public affairs at Arkansas PBS.

Grace Mikel, known as "Marvelous Mickey" to her friends and associates, was a Savannah, Georgia, native. She joined the US Navy WAVES in 1954 and left for Brunswick, Maine, for training as a communications operator specializing in Morse code. After four years of service, Grace returned to

Savannah and attended Armstrong College, where she began her career in broadcasting with numerous voiceovers in radio and television.

Bob Millard is a former correspondent for *Variety*. He is a contributor to *The Country Music Book* and the author of *Amy Grant: The Life of a Pop Star* (1996); *The Judds: A Biography* (1988); *Country Music: 70 Years of America's Favorite Music* (1993); and *Country Music What's What: The Fan's Guide to the People, Places and Things of Today's Country Music* (1995).

John Morthland was an associate editor of *Rolling Stone* and contributor to *Texas Monthly* and *Creem*.

Texas native **Judy Myers** was a writer for *Country Song Roundup*.

Alanna Nash is a journalist and biographer. She is the author of several acclaimed books, including *Dolly: The Biography* (2002); *The Colonel: The Extraordinary Story of Colonel Tom Parker and Elvis Presley* (2004); and *Baby, Let's Play House: Elvis Presley and the Women Who Loved Him* (2010). Nash was voted one of the "Heavy 100 of Country Music" by *Esquire* magazine and earned the 2004 CMA Media Achievement Award and the 2004 Belmont Book Award. She has reviewed for *Stereo Review* magazine, *Reader's Digest*, and others.

Bill Oakey is a music aficionado and writer for the *Rag Blog* (https://www.theragblog.com/tag/bill-oakey/). He was a regular contributor to *Country Music* magazine.

Joe Nick Patoski is a freelance music journalist, senior writer for *Texas Highways*, and author of *Austin to ATX: The Hippies, Pickers, Slackers, and Geeks Who Transformed the Capital of Texas* (2019).

Cliff Radel's award-winning work has appeared in the *Cincinnati Enquirer*, *New York Times*, *DownBeat*, *Chicago Tribune*, and *Los Angeles Times*. He bats left and throws left and lives with his wife, Debbie, on Cincinnati's far-flung West Side.

CREDITS

Deepest gratitude to everyone who gave permission for material to appear in this book. Every reasonable effort has been made to contact copyright holders. If an error or omission has been made, please bring it to the attention of the publisher.

"The Willie Nelson Story," by Judy Myers. Published February 1969 in *Country Song Roundup*.

"Willie Nelson First in Nashville Club," by staff writers. Published March 1972 in *Country Music Reporter*.

"An Interview with Willie Nelson," by Debbie Brimer. Published July 1974 in *Country Music Reporter*.

"Willie Nelson: The Emperor of Austin," by Nick Patoski. Published July 18, 1974, in *Zoo World*. Reprinted by permission of Joe Nick Patoski.

"A Tribute to Bob Wills," by Willie Nelson. Published August 1974 in *Country Music*.

"Willie Nelson Talks," by Nelson Allen Jr. Published May 1975 in *Picking Up the Tempo*. Reprinted by permission of Nelson Allen Jr.

"Willie Nelson: The Second Crowned King of Country and Western Music of Texas," by Grace Mikel. Published 1975 in the *Country Hotline*.

"The Man Who Beat the System," by Patrick Carr. Published February 1976 in *Country Music*.

"The Mystic Willie Nelson," by Nelson Allen Jr. Published June 1977 in *Country Music*. Reprinted by permission of Nelson Allen Jr.

"The Nashville People," by Stacy Harris. Published June 1977 in *Countryside*. Reprinted by permission of Stacy Harris.

"On Picnics and Things," by Stacy Harris. Published July 1978 in *Country Song Roundup*. Reprinted by permission of Stacy Harris.

"A Voice Crying Out of the Country . . . ," by Cliff Radel. Published April 19, 1979, in the *Cincinnati Enquirer*. Reprinted by permission of Cliff Radel.

"Willie: The Gypsy Cowboy Goes Hollywood," by Michael Bane. Published May 1979 in *Country Music*. Reprinted by permission.

"Further Adventures of the Gypsy Cowboy," by Nelson Allen Jr. Published May 1979 in *Country Music*. Reprinted by permission of Nelson Allen Jr.

"Bikers and Texas: An Interview with Willie Nelson," by staff writers. Published December 1979 in *Easyriders*. Reprinted by permission of *Easyriders*.

"Willie Goes to the Movies: Honeysuckle Rose," by Bill Oakey. Published March 1980 in *Country Music*.

"Willie Nelson: Being a Movie Star Sure Beats Working," by Bob Allen. Published October 1980 in *Country Music*.

"Willie," by Bob Millard. Published September/October 1983 in *Country Music*.

"Willie Nelson," by Jim Hatlo. Published December 1984 in *Frets*. Reprinted by permission of Roger Siminoff of *Frets*.

"The Picnic," by Michael Bane. Published July/August 1985 in *Country Music*. Reprinted by permission of Michael Bane.

"Catching Up with Ole Willie," by Patrick Carr. Published January/February 1987 in *Country Music*.

"Willie Nelson," by Alanna Nash. Published in *Behind Closed Doors: Talking with the Legends of Country Music* (New York: Knopf, 1988). Reprinted by permission of Alanna Nash.

"Minding Willie's Business," by John Morthland. Published May/June 1990 in *Country Music*.

"Willie Nelson: The Pilgrim," by Michael Bane. Published March/April 1992 in *Country Music*. Reprinted by permission of Michael Bane.

"20 Questions with Willie Nelson," by Michael "The Gray Headed Stranger" Bane. Published March/April 1993 in *Country Music*. Reprinted by permission of Michael Bane.

"Road Warrior," by Holly George-Warren. Published Winter 1994 in *Country Guitar*. Reprinted by permission of Holly George-Warren.

"Willie Nelson's Family and Friends," by Russ Barnard. Published November/December 1994 in *Country Music*.

"Interview," by Michael Hibblen. Published May 26, 2005, in *Hibblen Radio*. Reprinted by permission.

"Rescuing Wild Horses," by the Barbi Twins. Published 2013 in *Origin Magazine*. Reprinted by permission.

"Willie Nelson: The Outlaw Country Legend Reflects on His Personal Cannabis History," by Ricardo Baca. Published March 21, 2018, in the *Cannabist*.

"A Conversation with Willie Nelson," by Peter Blackstock. Published March 12, 2021, in *Austin American-Statesman*.

INDEX

All songs and albums are by Willie Nelson unless otherwise indicated